OLYMPIC EQUESTRIAN

OLYMPIC
EQUESTRIAN

The Sports and the Stories from Stockholm to Sydney

BY JENNIFER O. BRYANT

Foreword by William C. Steinkraus

Library of Congress Card Number 99-68800

ISBN 1-58150-044-0

Printed in Canada
First Edition: May 2000
1 2 3 4 5 6 7 8 9 10

TABLE OF CONTENTS

FOREWORD 6
INTRODUCTION 9

Part One: *Horses and the Games*
CHAPTER ONE
The Olympic Equestrian Disciplines 12

CHAPTER TWO
Behind the Scenes: The Organizations that Govern the Sports . . . 28

CHAPTER THREE
Are the Olympics Good for Horses? 46

Part Two: *The Equestrian Triumvirate*
CHAPTER FOUR
Those Who Went Before Us 70

CHAPTER FIVE
Three-Day Eventing 104

CHAPTER SIX
Show Jumping 148

CHAPTER SEVEN
Dressage 186

Part Three: *Looking Ahead*
CHAPTER EIGHT
The Millennium Games 232

CHAPTER NINE
The 21st Century 250

REFERENCES 258
INDEX 261
PHOTO CREDITS 268
ACKNOWLEDGMENTS 269
ABOUT THE AUTHOR 270

FOREWORD

Equestrian Olympics — what magical memories these words evoke for me! I first became aware of their meaning in 1935, a year before the Berlin Olympic Games. At that point I was ten, and already totally addicted to horses. I thought about horses non-stop when I was awake, dreamed about them when I was asleep, and never passed up even a remote chance of riding. I knew that horses would play a major role in my life, but hadn't yet decided if I would be a cowboy, a steeplechase rider, or a Master of Foxhounds. (I didn't aspire to being an Olympic rider since I was aware, quite early on, that only serving officers could compete internationally.)

In those days the primary outlet for my passion for horses was reading, and I devoured everything horsey I could lay my hands on, periodicals as well as books. My favorite horse magazine was *Horse & Horseman*, edited by Peter Vischer, a brilliant and very internationally minded former journalist, and it was the pages of *H&H* that gave me my first introduction to the equestrian Olympics. Vischer's coverage of the Berlin Olympics was marvelous, from the run-ups through the actual event and to the post-mortems the following year, and they inspired in me an interest in Olympic equestrianism that I have never lost. (In the 1930s there were no books in print in English about the equestrian Olympics, but I'm sure that if the present volume had existed then, I would have consumed it in one sitting and then tried to memorize all the winners!)

Only a dozen years intervened between the Berlin Games and the London revival in 1948, but the fact that these years witnessed the Second World War made them seem like an eternity. By the time the 1948 Olympics came along I was back from the war (having succeeded in getting my basic training mounted, even though we finally went into combat on foot), and was halfway through my senior year in college. I spent that last summer vacation on a trip to Europe, the high points of which were a visit to England to see the Games and a side trip to Dublin for the horse show, in which our military show-jumping team took part. The whole thing dazzled me, and I returned home drunk with excitement and enthusiasm for Europe, the Olympics, and our team.

I was somewhat surprised, in London's Games, to find an occasional scarlet coat among all the uniforms. Indeed, the French show-jumping team included one of the civilians, Chevalier Jean d'Orgeix, who distinguished himself by edging out our own Col. F. F. Wing, Jr. and Democrat for the individual bronze medal. However, since our Olympic representation was then and had always been exclusively military, it was not in my wildest dreams that four years later I would be riding in the Helsinki Olympics myself, and then later riding the same Democrat on the North American circuit, competing against both the 1948 and 1952 Olympic champions!

London and Helsinki were to be the first two of a string of thirteen Olympics that I would either witness or participate in, in one role or another. Six times I was a competitor (though a training injury to Sinjon relegated me to the sidelines in Tokyo); four times a television commentator, once a judge, and twice just a plain spectator.

(Perhaps I shouldn't include Rotterdam's 1980 "Alternate Olympics," though all the strong teams were actually there instead of at the "real" Olympics in Moscow, which President Carter's boycott had obliged us to ignore.)

I've often been asked to pick a favorite from all these different Games, and usually demurred. For in truth, each of the Games was so entirely extraordinary in its own way, by reflecting so richly and so variously the culture of the city and the country that staged it, that comparisons are truly invidious. I can't deny, however, how satisfying it was to break, myself, the long U.S. jinx of never having won an individual Olympic equestrian gold medal; or to have been present at Atlanta in 1984 when Joe Fargis did it again, as well as helping to break our jinx of never having won the team gold in show jumping, after so many near misses. (On top of that, in Los Angeles we also won the team three-day gold and an individual silver. Just think of it: superb setting, huge audiences and marvelous weather in our own country, and five medals, three of them gold!)

These days, as I get a bit too long in the tooth to gallivant all over the world, the chances are that I'll experience the first of the new millennium's Olympics, in Sydney, the way most horse lovers have always had to do so — via the media. I surely hope the TV coverage will be more comprehensive than it has often been in the past, and know that I will long for the immediacy that can only come from being on the spot. Nonetheless, I'm sure that Sydney's Games, like all the others, will have their full share of dazzling performances and high drama, and even if I have to experience them more vicariously than in the past, I'm sure that I'll be enthralled all over again.

What happens next? As you will note in Chapter 9 of this book, I am one of those who has expressed some concern about the future of the Olympic movement unless truly meaningful reforms are introduced. The Games have surely grown bigger and more successful financially, but perhaps at a price; somehow much of the ideal-

William Steinkraus has had a role in thirteen Olympics, six times as a competitor.

ism that characterized de Coubertin's original concept seems to have eroded. But even if the Olympic leadership should suggest, by its actions, that it has lost its way, and become more interested in competing head-to-head with the professional sports establishment for "big bucks," then we shall simply have to reinvent the Games once again. We have to look no further than to de Coubertin's original emphasis on the pursuit of excellence for its own sake, and the value of participation in the furtherance of peace and the brotherhood of man. For surely, these lofty aims have never been more valid or more meaningful.

The story of the modern equestrian Olympics is not only absorbingly interesting, but also very complicated to present, and Jennifer Bryant has done the English-speaking equestrian community a great service by researching it so thoroughly and telling it so well in *Olympic Equestrian*. Yet since the equestrian Olympics are still very much a "work in progress," to use the current catch phrase, let us hope that the very finest Olympic revivals still lie ahead of us, and that the future achievements of the world's best horses and riders will surpass even the marvelous accomplishments that are recorded in the following pages!

William C. Steinkraus
Chairman Emeritus of the U.S. Equestrian Team

INTRODUCTION

Let the Games Begin

When Eclipse Press approached me about writing a history of the Olympic equestrian events, I was both thrilled and terrified. Thrilled, because the subject matter is fascinating and often the stuff of horse-world legend; terrified, because I didn't know if I could do justice to the enormity and significance of the subject.

I decided to give it my best shot, and you hold the results in your hands. What I've tried to do is to give you a sense of the evolution of Olympic equestrian competition, from its formal introduction at the 1912 Stockholm Games to the fast-approaching inaugural Games of the new millennium, and beyond. In a way, Olympic equestrian history is the evolution of the sports of three-day eventing, show jumping, and dressage in a nutshell: They're not the entire picture, but they're a darn good snapshot.

Before I go further, a confession: I hated history in school and found it deadly dull. Recitations of facts, dates, and names do not intrigue me, nor do they give me any sense of what the events of the day were really like. With that in mind, and in the hopes that I'm not the only non-history-scholar out there, I've tried to bring Olympic equestrian history to life by — as much as possible — letting the people who lived it talk about it in their own words.

I had three main goals for this book. First, I wanted to set down in one place some of the important stories and happenings that have shaped the horse world and equestrian competition as we know it today. I've been riding,

writing, and editing for a long time, and I was amazed at how much equestrian history I didn't know. (I also found that equestrian history, by virtue of its subject matter, is automatically much more interesting than the stuff taught in school.)

Second, I wanted to learn and share how the Olympic equestrian events work — who's responsible for what, and how teams of riders and horses from all over the globe are screened, selected, and transported to a patch of land in some far-flung place to vie for the honor and the glory of an Olympic championship. At the same time, the exact same thing is happening in twenty-seven other sports, and this mega-sporting extravaganza known as the Olympic Games gets underway yet again.

Third, and most important, I wanted to capture a little of that Olympic magic: the power of this sporting competition, equaled by no other athletic event, to enthrall and move us.

Time and space constraints prevented me from including all the horses and riders who have reached for Olympic glory. Please realize that the selections herein are just some of the many deserving competitors and contributors; I wish I could have told all of their stories.

For those of you who told me your stories, I hope I have done your achievements justice. I feel honored and privileged to have had this opportunity.

Jennifer O. Bryant
February 2000

CHAPTER ONE

The Olympic Equestrian Disciplines

The Olympic Games — so named for their original location in Olympia, Greece — initiated around 884 B.C. and were held every four years (or "Olympiad") for more than 1,000 years until the Roman emperor Theodosius ordered them abolished two years after the Games of 393 A.D. But modern horse sports are actually quite recent additions to Olympic competition. The ancient Games featured forms of athletic competition that did not include horses: Foot races were the sole events through the eighteenth Olympiad; wrestling and the

Swedish organizers for the 1912 Games. Second from left: Count Clarence von Rosen, who spearheaded efforts to include the equestrian disciplines. Opposite: 1920 individual dressage gold medalists, Janne Lundblad and Uno of Sweden.

pentathlon (running, jumping, wrestling, and discus and javelin throws) later were added. Chariot racing became an Olympic sport as of the twenty-fifth Olympiad, in 680 B.C., and continued in various incarnations — first with four grown horses, and later also with four mules, two adult horses, four colts, and two colts — until the ancient Games ended. [1]

Horse Sports Join the Modern Games

Baron Pierre de Coubertin of France founded the International Olympic Committee (IOC) in 1894 with the goal of reviving the Olympic Games as a modern international sporting competition, and the first modern Olympiad took place in — appropriately enough — Athens, Greece, in 1896. The summer Olympic Games have been held every four years to this day, with

Sweden dominated early Olympic Games. Axel Nordlander and Lady Artist won team and individual gold medals in eventing in 1912.

a few notable exceptions: The 1916 Berlin Games were canceled because of World War I; the second World War forced the cancellation of the 1940 Games, originally scheduled for Tokyo and then rescheduled for Helsinki; and World War II raged on in 1944, forcing the cancellation of that year's London Games. [2] (The 1980 Moscow Games went on as scheduled, despite a boycott by sixty-two countries — the United States included — in protest against the Soviet Union's invasion of Afghanistan.)

The three modern equestrian disciplines made their debut at the 1912 Stockholm Games, thanks to the efforts of Count Clarence von Rosen, Master of the Horse to the king of Sweden. (The 1900 Olympics in Paris included a smattering of one-time equestrian competitions, as would the 1920 Antwerp Games. For details, see "Little-Known Olympic Equestrian Sports" later in this chapter.) Wishing to stimulate interest in horse sports among the non-cavalry-member general public, von Rosen made a pitch for the inclusion of jumping, three-day-eventing, and dressage competition at the 1906 IOC Congress in Athens. De Coubertin, the IOC's president, asked von Rosen for a detailed proposal, which the Count's newly formed International Horse Show Committee submitted the following year.

The IOC approved von Rosen's proposed events, rules, and regulations; and eight countries entered the inaugural equestrian Olympic competition, which was scheduled to be held as part of the 1908 London Games. But the International Horse Show Committee backed out at the last minute, forcing horse sports into a hiatus that lasted until the 1912 Stockholm Games. A three-day event for military personnel, an individual dressage test, and individual and team (*Prix des Nations*) show-jumping competition took place at Stockholm, and these three core events have remained part of Olympic competition to this day, with relatively few changes. [3]

The Olympic Equestrian Trio

The scope of equestrian sport has broadened considerably since the time of the 1912 Stockholm Games. Formed in 1921, the Fédération Equestre Internationale (FEI) or International Equestrian Federation now functions as the international horse-sports governing body. More recent forms of competition, such as endurance riding and vaulting, have become formalized and FEI-recognized in recent years; and that all-American creation, Western riding, encompasses many distinct sports and enjoys continued growth and expanded popularity worldwide. But, given the modern Games' European roots and military connections, it's no surprise that the equestrian events chosen for inclusion were English-riding disciplines with roots in classical horsemanship, fox hunting, and tests of cavalry skills. Some horse enthusiasts would like to see additional sports achieve Olympic status. Reining, for example, became a U.S. Equestrian Team-affiliated sport in 1998 — a move that enthusiasts hope is the first step toward the Olympic nod. (For more on what the future holds, see chapter 9, "The 21st Century.")

The Three-Day Event

The equestrian equivalent of the triathlon, eventing is a direct descendant of the challenges faced by cavalry mounts. Military horses had to be all-around performers: swift, agile, "cat-like" (high praise for an event horse) over obstacles and all kinds of terrain, highly trained, sensitive, and obedient. It's easy to imagine how a cavalry mount who was lacking in any of these attributes would be a liability to his rider, who depended on his horse for escape and survival as well as for attack. Small wonder, then, that the three-day event originally was known as the "Military" and included an endurance test (roads and tracks), a speed test (the individual steeplechase), a cross-country jumping course, a stadium-jumping course, and a dressage test. The Military originally was open only to active-duty military officers, and their mounts had to belong to the competitors themselves or to their respective branch of the service. Military-owned school horses were ineligible for competition. [4] In the first equestrian Olympics in 1912, the Military was held over four days: endurance and cross-country on day one, the speed test on day two, stadium jumping on day three, and dressage on day four. [5]

Today, the "phases" or elements of the FEI-level three-day event are held in the following order: dressage, speed and endurance, and stadium jumping. Olympic three-day events are at the four-star (****) level, the highest level of difficulty in modern eventing competition. Here's what's required of today's Olympic eventers:

Day 1: Dressage. Dressage is the ultimate obedience test for marathon-fit equine athletes, who are carefully conditioned to "peak" for the competition and who may be practically bursting out of their skins in anticipation of cross-country day. They have to try to keep their enthusiasm in

The 1948 three-day-event individual winners, Bernard Chevallier of France and Aiglonne.

check long enough to put in an expressive yet obedient and correct dressage test.

Most Olympic dressage horses are warmbloods or other hybrid sport-horse types, which tend to be stocky in stature with great muscle mass. In contrast, the Thoroughbred and part-Thoroughbred dominates the event scene, and his training regimen of running and jumping hones his naturally leaner, more sinewy muscles

to give him the look of the long-distance runner. His musculature is generally less suited to producing such Grand Prix-level movements as the piaffe and the passage, and so the "eventing dressage" tests are appropriately scaled back in their demands. The FEI Three-Day Event Four-Star Dressage Test equates to about Third Level dressage and includes the following movements: shoulder-in, half-pass in trot, reinback, extended gaits, and single flying changes. Top-hatted and tail-coated riders and their elegantly braided horses perform the dressage test in a standard (twenty meters x sixty meters) arena, which is enclosed by low fencing. A panel of three judges scores each movement on a scale of 0 (not performed) to ten (excellent). The judges want to see a test that bespeaks the horse's balance, lateral and longitudinal suppleness, gymnastic development, obedience, harmony with his rider, and enjoyment of his work.

Because FEI rules stipulate that an international-level three-day event ground jury must judge no more than thirty-five dressage tests a day, the dressage competition at many four-star events, including the 2000 Sydney Olympic Games, is spread over two days of competition. Each horse-rider combination performs just once, the day and time slot determined by draw. (In Sydney, the team three-day-event competition features two days of dressage; the individual three-day competition, which is a separate competition from the team event,

Opposite: American Kerry Millikin and Out and About, individual bronze-medal winners at the 1996 Atlanta Olympics.

will require just one day of dressage.)

Day 2: Speed and endurance. "Cross-country day" is the heart and soul of three-day eventing. The best event horses (and riders) live to run fast

Earl "Tommy" Thomson, the U.S. Army's most successful Olympian, and Reno Rhythm, on course in 1948.

over rolling terrain and jump boldly over natural-type obstacles that feature such elements as hefty logs, water, ditches, banks ("stair-step" type jumps from one level to another), and intimidating-looking drops. Speed-and-endurance day

comprises the following four phases:

Phase A: Roads and tracks. This is the warm-up phase, ridden at a speed of 220 meters per minute (approximately 722 feet per minute) — roughly the speed of a ground-covering trot — over approximately four kilometers on the flat (without jumps).

Phase B: Steeplechase. Much as in a steeplechase race, horse and rider gallop at speed (690 mpm) over a three-kilometer course of eight fences. Galloping horses jump flatter and lower than those who are collected onto their hindquarters before the jumping effort; in accordance, the brush-topped steeplechase obstacles allow horses to go "through" the uppermost portions and thereby lose little speed or momentum.

Phase C: Roads and tracks. The horse cools down and recovers from his steeplechase effort on a second roads-and-tracks course of eight to ten kilometers.

Phase D: Cross-country. This is what the spectators come to watch: the six-kilometer course of thirty-two to thirty-four imposingly solid obstacles (maximum height: 1.20 meters, or approximately 3.9 feet), ridden at the brisk galloping pace of 570 mpm (1,870 feet, or approximately one-third of a mile per minute). But before starting out on cross-country, horses rest in the "vet box" for ten minutes, during which grooms sponge them off and their temperature, pulse, respiration, and soundness are monitored by an official panel of judges and veterinarians. Horses deemed unsound or insufficiently recovered from the exertions of phases A, B, and C are ordered withdrawn ("spun" in eventing-speak) from the competition before the start of phase D.

A good cross-country course challenges both horse and rider yet does not overface them. A course may open with one or two relatively straightforward obstacles, to encourage competitors to ride forward and with confidence. Then it's on to a series of fences that incorporate the features of the terrain and ask various "questions" of horse and rider, such as: Can you make multiple jumping efforts before and after tight, trappy turns? Do you trust your rider enough to jump into a seemingly bottomless pool of water? Are you bold enough to jump from bright daylight into shadowy woods? Can you keep your balance while galloping downhill and "whoa" enough to negotiate an obstacle at the very bottom?

Cross-country obstacles are "flagged" to indicate which way they must be negotiated. Most Olympic-level obstacles are built with two "options": a straighter, faster route (which usually is the more difficult jump); and a longer, slower (but usually less challenging) route. Competitors and their coaches walk every inch of the course beforehand, weighing the obstacles' difficulty against the specter of time penalties and mapping out exactly which option they will take at each fence. When phase D gets under way, plans may change as early riders report back how the course rode and any problem fences show themselves on videotape.

It takes a highly skilled, experienced horse and rider (and perhaps a little luck) to navigate an Olympic cross-country course successfully. The rider must be able to prevent his or her keen mount from using up too much precious energy in early eager galloping. The rider must be able to "rate" his or her mount between fences and, with an excellent sense of pace and timing, to go only as fast as necessary to finish the course without time penalties, thereby conserving as much of the horse's energy as possible for the next day's stadium-jumping competition. The rider must have superior strength, stamina, and balance to help the horse when he needs it and also to stay out of his way when to interfere might mean a loss of balance or impulsion at a critical moment. The horse must be able to maintain speed over a distance while conserving enough strength and energy to rebalance himself before and after jumps and to launch himself over high jumps

and broad spreads. He must be sufficiently clever and agile to get himself and his rider out of sticky situations and to negotiate a host of obstacles that he's never seen before.

Day 3: Stadium jumping. The final element of the three-day event is a stadium-jumping (show-jumping) course over twelve brightly colored, easily displaced obstacles in an arena. Moderate in size and scope as compared to the obstacles in Olympic show jumping, the stadium-jumping event is designed as a final test of the horse's fitness, willingness, and agility. A tired horse is more likely to knock down a rail — which, as he knows, is not solid like the preceding day's obstacles — and so it is not uncommon for the top few placings to shift up or down in the eleventh hour of the competition, depending on how the rails fall. As in show jumping, competitors are penalized for knockdowns, refusals, going off course, or failing to complete the course in the time allowed. Although the stadium phase lacks some of the heart-pounding excitement of the cross-country, the possibility of competitive upset in the final moments keeps spectators in suspense until the very end.

Show Jumping

Show jumping today enjoys the greatest popularity, media coverage, and sponsorship of the three Olympic equestrian sports. It tests a horse's speed, agility, jumping ability, and boldness over an arena course of (usually) brightly painted, non-solid obstacles, the rails of which rest in shallow cups and thus topple easily if they're

The 1992 show jumping individual gold medalists, Ludger Beerbaum of Germany and Classic Touch.

knocked by an errant hoof. Horse and rider race against the clock to complete the course in the time allotted; a knockdown of a rail, a refusal, or a fall incurs "jumping faults," or penalties, while exceeding the time allowed incurs "time faults." In the event that more than one rider has an initial clean round, the top placings are decided by a "jump-off" against the clock.

Olympic show-jumping competition was designed as a stiffer test than its three-day-eventing counterpart, the stadium-jumping phase. Early Olympic eligibility rules were less stringent for show jumping than for the Military event in that non-military horses and riders also could take part; only military school horses were not permitted to compete. [6]

Show jumping's rules governing permitted tack and equipment are somewhat looser than those for three-day eventing and dressage, the result being that a wide variety of bits and bridles — not to mention riding styles and breeds of horses — come through the in-gate. Although most top jumper riders are well-versed in basic dressage and are outstanding horsemen and women, the sport of show jumping seems to engender flamboyance on the part of the competitors and to encourage individualism among both riders and horses — two of the reasons it dominates its fellow Olympic equestrian sports in terms of both ticket sales and television coverage.

Dressage

Today's dressage enthusiasts might be surprised to learn that Olympic dressage competition once included a jumping test! At the 1912 Stockholm Games, dressage competitors had to jump four obstacles — up to 1.1 meters in height as well as one spread jump of 3 meters in width — in addition to executing a test not to exceed ten minutes in length that included a "free and easy" walk, a "slow trot" and an extended trot, a "slow canter" and an extended canter, "ordinary turns," turns on the haunches, small circles, figures-of-eight at the canter with and without flying changes of leg, reinback, and at least four flying changes of leg on a straight line. [7]

The test appears to have been at a level of difficulty approximate to today's Fourth Level — which is to say, not even at the lowest international (FEI) level, Prix St. Georges. Double bridles were mandated, and *haute école* (high school) movements such as the piaffe, the passage, and the Spanish walk were prohibited.

The most formal of equestrian competitions,

dressage is all in the details. At the Olympic level, horses and riders perform an exacting and demanding "test" — the Grand Prix de Dressage — a specified pattern of movements executed in a standard enclosed arena. Around the perimeter of the arena are lettered pylons or markers — no one knows the exact origins of the letters, the placement and order of which defies logic and generally requires mnemonic devices to commit to memory — and each movement must begin or end precisely as the horse's shoulder reaches the designated letter. At the Grand Prix level, the most difficult of the international (FEI) levels of competition, horses are required to perform the piaffe, a trot "on the spot"; the passage, a cadenced, elevated trot of majestic appearance; pirouettes at the canter, in which the horse's hindquarters remain almost in place as his legs continue the canter rhythm; and flying changes of lead at the canter at every stride ("one-tempi changes"), which make him look as if he were skipping along the ground.

At the 1996 Atlanta Games, the results of the Grand Prix decided the team dressage medals; and the top twenty-five horse-rider combinations pro-

The 1932 dressage team and individual gold medalists, Xavier Lesage of France and Taine (far left); and '36 U.S. three-day competitor Captain John Willems on Slippery Slim. Opposite: Anky van Grunsven of the Netherlands and Olympic Bonfire, the 1996 team and individual silver medalists.

LITTLE-KNOWN EQUESTRIAN SPORTS

Eventing, show jumping, and dressage are considered the traditional Olympic equestrian disciplines, but did you know that polo, vaulting, and two now-defunct types of jumping contests were once Olympic sports as well?

The 1900 Paris Games, which were held as part of the Paris Exposition, featured polo competition among four "mixed teams" comprising American, English, Spanish, French, and Mexican players. A team calling itself the Foxhunters — of which ten-goal U.S. player Foxhall Keene (owner of the famed Thoroughbred racehorse Domino) was a member — won the gold medal.

Polo made its second appearance eight years later, at the London Olympics. Only the English and the Irish competed, and the English won the gold. The U.S. didn't compete in Olympic polo again until the 1920 Antwerp Games, at which an all-American team competed against teams from England, Belgium, and Spain, with the English prevailing.

The U.S. polo team's final Olympic appearance would be four years later, when the Games returned to

Polo once was part of the Olympic Games, but had its final rounds in 1936. Inset: Ten-goal Olympic polo player Foxhall Keene (right) with Mike Dwyer (seated) and an unidentified friend.

Paris. The strong U.S. team boasted the talents of the legendary Tommy Hitchcock, but the Americans faced defeat against the Argentineans, who made their first Olympic polo appearance in 1924 and who have since remained a dominant international force in the sport. Argentina captured gold once again — and for what would prove to be the last time — at the 1936 Berlin Games, marking polo's final appearance in the Olympics. [8]

The sport of vaulting, in which athletes perform acrobatic moves on and off moving horses, was included in the 1920 Antwerp Olympics — the first and only time to date that vaulting has appeared on the Olympic roster. Competitors executed vaults at the halt and at the canter, bareback as well as with saddles. Only Army officers were permitted to compete, and three nations sent entrants. The Belgians won the team competition over France and Sweden. In the individual competition, M. Bouckaert of Belgium won over M. Field of France and fellow Frenchman M. Finet. [9] More than sixty years later, in 1982, the FEI recognized vaulting as an international equestrian sport — but it has yet to find its way back into the Olympic program.

The 1900 Paris Games also included three types of jumping competition: one similar to modern show jumping, and two that are no longer practiced. The Grand Prix event was similar to today's individual show-jumping competition and consisted of six rounds, held over three days. Belgium, France, and Italy sent a total of eighty-six starters. Five Frenchmen and seven Italians made it to the sixth and final round, a timed jump-off; and Lieutenant Haentjens of France was the victor. [10]

High-jump and long-jump events — no longer part of Olympic jumping competition — also were part of the 1900 program. France's Dominique Gardère on Canela and Italy's Gian Giorgio Trissino on Oreste each cleared 1.85 meters to tie for first place in the high jump; Belgian rider Georges van de Poele on Ludlow was third with a 1.70-meter effort. In the long jump, Belgium's Constant van Langendonck on Extra Dry made the winning leap of 6.10 meters; Trissino and Oreste were second (5.70 meters), and France's M. de Bellegarde and Tolla were third (5.30 meters). [11]

gressed to the Grand Prix Special, a test of the same movements but shorter and of greater intensity, with more emphasis placed on the piaffe and the passage and the transitions between the two. Then, for the first time in Olympic dressage history, the top thirteen finishers in the Special went on to vie for the individual medals in the Grand Prix Freestyle (or Kür, as it is known in Europe), which is similar to the free skate in figure skating competition in that competitors choreograph their own routines to music while adhering to rules governing required and prohibited movements and time allowed.

In Olympic dressage competition, a panel of five judges awards marks for each movement on the same zero to ten scale used in the dressage phase of the three-day event. The judges sit behind the letters E, H, C, M, and B; the judge at C, whose position is directly across from the arena entrance at A, is the president of the ground jury. Each judge sits next to a scribe, a volunteer who records the numerical scores and comments and who notes any competitor errors, such as going off course. As in figure skating, judges award two sets of marks in the freestyle: technical and artistic-impression.

Unique Among Olympic Sports

The Olympic equestrian events are the only ones in which an animal is part of the competition. The horse is as least as important as — if not more important than — the rider in terms of the outcome, and most riders are quick to credit their mounts for successes and to blame themselves for mistakes. Most Olympic-caliber riders have the talent and skill to make their aids (cues) nearly invisible, which gives spectators the impression that the horses are performing of their own volition but which also prompts the unwitting observation, heard by most riders, that "the horse is doing all the work while the rider just sits there." It is perhaps a combination of this impression and the fact that woolen jackets and stock ties appear less than athletic wear that

The 1928 individual medalists in show jumping, from left: Frantisek Ventura of Czechoslovakia; Pierre Bertran de Balanda, France; and Charley Kuhn, Switzerland.

spurs accusations that riding is not truly a human athletic endeavor and ranks with table tennis and archery in the list of silly non-sports that have somehow gained Olympic recognition. Such perceptions have become more common in modern times; in the early 1900s, around the time that equestrian sports were introduced into the Games, riding's military connections were evident, and riding was regarded as just as much of an activity as other sports.

Olympic equestrian sports were all-male (the riders, that is, not the horses) until the 1952 Helsinki Games, but since that time women have competed in all three events with great success. In fact, the horse sports are among the only ones in the Games in which men and women regularly compete against one another and on equal terms.

FEI rules specify a minimum age for both horse (seven) and rider (eighteen) for eligibility in Olympic competition, but the rules specify no maximum age. Although elite equine athletes generally have fairly short-lived "windows" of peak performance — it's rare to encounter an Olympic jumper or event horse older than the early teens or an Olympic dressage horse older than eighteen or so — many top riders enjoy careers of far greater longevity. Germany's Nicole Uphoff was just twenty-one when she won double gold medals in dressage at the 1988 Seoul Games, but many Olympic-level riders are in their thirties, forties, or even fifties. In an age in which gymnasts and figure skaters are considered over the hill after their teens, it's refreshing to find a sport in which one can participate and excel for life. Plus, as many riders would point out, some equestrian sports are so difficult that it can take decades to get to the top — and even then, the learning never stops!

Germany's Nicole Uphoff and Rembrandt (pictured here in Barcelona) won back-to-back individual and team titles in 1988 and 1992.

CHAPTER TWO

Behind the Scenes: The Organizations that Govern the Sports

To orchestrate, govern, and administrate a sporting competition as huge and comprehensive as a modern Olympic Games — the Sydney Organizing Committee for the Olympic Games (SOCOG) expects more than 10,000 athletes and 5,000 officials from 200 countries to participate in twenty-eight sports at the 2000 Sydney Games — requires the efforts of numerous national and international organizations. The International Olympic Committee (IOC) oversees the Games as a whole and approves competition rules and regulations, but the actual work of governing the sports falls to each sport's international governing body, and successively to that sport's national governing body in each participating nation.

Here's how the organizational hierarchy works for Olympic horse sports.

The International Olympic Committee

Founded in 1894 by the Baron Pierre de Coubertin of France, the IOC is headquartered in Lausanne, Switzerland — coincidentally, the same city the International Equestrian Federation (FEI) calls home today.

De Coubertin is rightfully known as the "Father of the Modern Olympics," for he single-handedly revived the Olympic Games in both event and spirit. A military-school dropout, the titled young man went on to study and write prolifically on the subject of education — an important part of which, he believed, was physical activity. At just twenty-six years of age, in 1888, de Coubertin helped create the physical-education-advocacy organization L'Union des Sports Athlétiques; a year later, he founded the monthly publication *La Revue Athlétique* to further interest in sports.

Think dismay over the commercialization of sports is a late-1900s sentiment? Think again. Circa-1890s sports were bad enough, apparently, to incite de Coubertin to dream of a possible antidote: a revival of the Olympic Games extinct for more than 1,500 years at that point in time — as an international sporting event in which athletic excellence and sportsmanship, not commercialism, would be paramount. He invited representatives from around the globe to attend a L'Union des Sports Athlétiques international athletic congress. It took a considerable amount of convincing, but delegates from France, the United States, England, Sweden, Spain, Italy, Belgium, Russia, and Greece traveled to the Sorbonne in Paris in June of 1894 for the event. There de Coubertin presented them with his vision, the delegates voted unanimously to revive the Olympic Games, and the International Olympic Committee was born.

De Coubertin's original target date was 1900 —

Prince Philip presents the three-day team gold to Mike Plumb, Karen Stives, Torrance Watkins Fleischmann, and Bruce Davidson in 1984.

he wanted the Games to be part of the Paris International Exposition — but the delegates, mindful of the Games' Greek heritage, argued successfully for the first modern Olympics to be held two years later, in 1896, in Athens. [1]

In 1915, de Coubertin moved the IOC's headquarters from France to Lausanne, Switzerland — a wise move, considering that World War I was already under way with France being at the center of the conflict and Switzerland being a neutral country. The IOC's headquarters were established at the Villa Mon-Repos in Lausanne in 1922. The offices were relocated to the Chateau de Vidy, also in Lausanne, in 1968, where they remain to this day. (Lausanne is also home to the Olympic Museum, another de Coubertin brainchild,

By 1924, the equestrian sports were an accepted part of the Olympic Games. Below: Axel Stahle and Zephyr, members of Swedish show-jumping team.

which houses the Olympic archives and which is open to the public.)

The IOC itself is an international not-for-profit organization that is not part of any nation's government. Its main purpose is to supervise the organization and execution of the summer and winter Olympic Games in accordance with its bible, the Olympic Charter. According to its Web site (www.olympic.org), the IOC "exists to serve as an umbrella organization of the Olympic Movement," which "consists of the IOC, the International Sports Federations (IFs), the National Olympic Committees (NOCs), the Organizing Committees for the Olympic Games (OCOGs), national sports associations, clubs and the persons belonging to them, and, not to forget — the athletes."

The IOC's role in staging an Olympic Games is both great and small. The IOC literally owns the Olympics — the name, the trademark intertwined

colored rings, the flag, the anthem, and more. Its president (currently, Juan Antonio Samaranch of Spain, who has held the office since 1980 and whose term ends in September 2001) and its 102 members and twenty honorary members approve the selection of host cities and all changes to the Olympic Charter. Its primary source of revenue is the sale of television rights for the broadcast of the Olympic Games (in the United States, the NBC network had the rights to the 1996 Atlanta Games and will be broadcasting the 2000 Sydney Games as well); additional revenue comes from IOC sponsors and the licensing of IOC-trademarked names and logos.

The IOC selects the sports to be included in the summer and winter Games. Three of the current slate of twenty-eight summer sports are "equestrian," as horse sports are known to Olympic organizers: show jumping, three-day eventing, and dressage. To help prevent the already jam-packed summer Games from becoming impossibly unwieldy to the organizing committee and to the host city, the IOC sets athlete quotas for each sport.

The Olympic Charter contains strict regulations against "doping," as the IOC calls it: the use of prohibited substances to enhance athletic performance. The Charter also governs such considerations as athlete eligibility and qualification; protocol for opening, closing, and medal ceremonies; and the accreditation of members of the media.

What the IOC does not do, however, is govern the sports themselves — that task is left to the international and national federations of each sport. Nor does it organize and administrate the Games themselves; that's the job of the Organizing Committee for the Olympic Games (OCOG) of the host city. (You may recall the acronym ACOG — the Atlanta Organizing Committee for the Olympic Games — from the 1996 Atlanta Games. Sydney's committee is known as SOCOG; for more on SOCOG and its plans, see chapter 8, "The Millennium Games.")

Still, the IOC plays a crucial and high-profile role in the Olympic Games. In 1999, the public learned that a number of IOC officials had strayed far from Baron de Coubertin's sportsmanlike ideals by allegedly accepting bribes from would-be host cities, which vie for the opportunity to showcase themselves to a worldwide audience and to make lavish profits in the process. Several IOC members eventually resigned, and reform measures were enacted to help restore the tarnished Olympic Movement.

On a day-to-day basis, though, athletes and their respective federations are less concerned with the host-city scandals and intrigue than they are with following the rules and making an Olympic team. That's where Gilbert Felli comes in. Felli, a former member of the Swiss national ski team, has held the position of IOC sports director since 1990. Aided by ten staffers, he oversees the IOC's relations with the international federations (IFs) of each Olympic sport and also supervises the process by which cities bid to host the summer and winter Games.

Rule Compliance

The IF's rules for athlete eligibility for Olympic Games must mirror those of the IOC. It is Felli's job to ensure that each IF understands the Olympic Charter and is informed of all rule changes.

One aspect of the rules that is subject to continual change is doping. As performance-enhanc-

31

ing substances are invented or popularized, the IOC must revise its rules and screening procedures. As with athlete eligibility, part of Felli's job as sports director is to ensure that each IF complies with the IOC's policies on doping.

Quotas

Felli and his staff have the at-times unpleasant task of informing the IFs of the IOC's decisions regarding athlete quotas — a practice instituted as of the 1996 Atlanta Olympics — for each Games. For Sydney, the IOC settled on a quota of 225 horse-rider combinations for the three equestrian disciplines, said Felli: seventy-nine for show jumping, sixty for the team three-day event, thirty-six for the individual three-day, and fifty for dressage; plus one reserve horse and rider per four-member discipline team. Modern pentathlon will have the smallest representation, with just forty-eight athletes; track and field is by far the biggest Olympic sport of the summer Games, with a quota of 2,000.

"Track and field is a special case because we believe it's the most universal sport," Felli explained. "We try to afford the countries the opportunity to participate in the Olympic Games, and (track and field) is the only sport that can be open to every nation."

Fans of any sport know that certain nations typically dominate that sport's standings and take home the lion's share of Olympic medals and World Championships honors. Some factors, such as climate, are beyond a nation's control; it stands to reason, for instance, that winter sports such as skiing will enjoy greater participation and support in parts of the world where the snow flies hard and often. But some sports are simply too

expensive, particularly at the elite level of the Olympics, for most denizens of some countries. Traditionally the pastime of the landed gentry, the Olympic horse sports are no exception; and so riders from well-to-do nations such as the United States, the United Kingdom, the western European countries, Australia, and New Zealand have occupied the medal podiums in most Olympics and World Championships. And participation by nations, as well as the overall number of athletes who compete in each sport, have "a significant effect" on IOC quotas, said Felli.

Qualification

After Felli informs a sport's IF of its quota, he works with its representatives to help ensure that the IF's qualifying procedures result in the best athletes being chosen for the Olympic teams. It's up to the IF to develop the qualification system, but the IOC has final approval.

On-site Needs

Felli and his staff discuss with each IF its needs at the Games site: facilities, accommodations, and any special or unique needs. Equestrian sports, of course, present a unique set of issues, including quarantine of horses, stabling, and lodging for grooms and horse owners — all concerns that the other Olympic sports don't have to address. Felli is quick to point out, however, that the horse sports are not more difficult to deal with than some of the other sports on the Olympic summer roster. "At the end of the day, {equestrian} is not more complicated than dealing with some other sports," he said matter-of-factly in his French-accented English. "For example, the sailing, you have problems to carry the boats. {But horse sports are} much more complicated {to organize} than swimming or track and field.

"The complexity is that you have three disciplines," Felli continued. "The three disciplines, the people are very different. It's very difficult to have a united view of the three disciplines; they're very autonomous." He speaks highly of the IOC's "very close" working relationship with the FEI, though, and adds that the FEI's expansion and addition of staff members in recent years has made interacting with the global equestrian body "certainly easier."

Fédération Equestre Internationale (FEI)

No international governing body for horse sports existed before discussions of adding equestrian sports to the Olympics commenced in 1906, spearheaded by Sweden's Count Clarence von Rosen. Indeed, international equestrian competition itself was sparse before that time. Paris had hosted the inaugural International Concours Hippique in 1900, and France was the site of the first-ever three-day event at the Championnat du Cheval in 1902. That same year saw the International Army Horse Show in Turin, and Brussels hosted the International Three-Day Event in 1905. A large international event was held at the Italian Army riding center at Tor di Quinto in 1908; the following year saw the creation of Nations' Cup competitions in San Sebastian and London and three international horse shows, including the famed National Horse Show in New York City.

Early Olympic equestrian competition was run under rules set forth by von Rosen and his committee, but it quickly became apparent that an international governing body was needed to over-

see the chosen disciplines of dressage, show jumping, and three-day eventing. Von Rosen assembled leading horse people from ten nations for a meeting in Lausanne in May 1921, chaired by IOC president de Coubertin. Commandant Georges Hector of France drew up the organization's statutes, which were approved by representatives of France, Japan, Sweden, and the United States. That November, the FEI held its first Congress in Paris, attended by delegates from Belgium, Denmark, France, Italy, Japan, Norway, Sweden, and the United States. The delegates elected Hector the FEI's first secretary general, with fellow Frenchman Baron du Teil becoming the Federation's first president. The 1924 Paris Olympics were the first Games held under FEI jurisdiction. [2]

Today, the FEI is the international governing body of equestrian sport and is recognized by the IOC as horse sports' international federation (IF). According to the Olympic Charter, an IF is responsible for:

- Establishing and enforcing the rules of its sport(s) in accordance with Olympic principles,
- Promoting its sport(s) throughout the world,
- Helping to realize the goals as stated in the Olympic Charter,
- Establishing athlete-eligibility requirements for Olympic Games and submitting those requirements to the IOC for approval, and
- Taking responsibility for the technical control and direction of its sport(s) at the Olympic Games under the IOC umbrella.

As the international governing body of the only Olympic sports in which animals participate, the FEI also creates and enforces strict regulations to ensure humane treatment of horses entered in FEI-sanctioned competitions. Calling the horse "an outstanding ambassador of nature and the animal world," and realizing that unspoiled land and water are essential for both equestrian sports and horse health and management, the FEI's Ethics Committee met with riders, competition organizers, officials, and a member of the IOC's Environment Commission during the 1996 Atlanta Olympics to draft one of the first IF environmental codes of conduct. Adopted at the FEI's General Assembly session in April 1997, the FEI Code of Conduct Toward the Environment re-emphasizes the importance of the code of conduct toward the horse and urges the FEI and its affiliated national federations to foster horse sports "as a means of maintaining the presence of the horse and its natural environment in their countries" and to practice environmentally sound stable and competition management.

When the FEI was formed, it governed the three Olympic disciplines of show jumping, three-day eventing, and dressage. It has since doubled the number of disciplines that it oversees. Combined driving, a wheeled version of three-day eventing, became an FEI-recognized discipline in 1970. Vaulting and endurance riding joined the FEI roster in 1982. A seventh discipline, reining (sometimes described as "Western dressage"), has been sanctioned by several nations; the FEI Bureau has agreed to hear and vote on a formal proposal at the 2000 General Assembly for the adoption of reining as an international discipline.

If Sports Director Gilbert Felli is the key contact at the IOC, then his counterpart at the FEI is Catrin Norinder, who manages the Federation's Olympic department. The soft-spoken Swede is the official IOC liaison and is responsible for keeping the national equestrian federations informed of IOC doings.

Norinder, who evented at the national level for her adopted homeland of Switzerland, joined the FEI in 1987 part-time as manager of the Federation's eventing department. Six months before the 1988 Seoul Games, the already small FEI staff — just ten employees strong at the time Norinder came on board — had dwindled in size even further, and there was no one to handle Olympic preparations. "So I took over the Olympic department at that time, and that is how I got involved in the Olympic Games," she explained. "We just put everything together four months before, and Seoul was a big experience."

Norinder describes her role as Olympic-department manager as "sort of a three-part liaison between the equestrian manager of the organizing committee {of the Games}, the IOC's sports department, and myself." Her primary responsibility is to coordinate the writing of the FEI's rules and procedures for each of the three Olympic disciplines so that they comply with IOC regulations.

"The IOC uses our technical regulations, but adapted to an Olympic situation," she explained. "There are many things that we have to adapt." A prime example of recent years: "Up until {the 1992 Games} in Barcelona, in eventing, we had one competition for both the individual and the team medals. Afterward, the IOC said you cannot win two medals for the same effort. So we had two separate competitions in Atlanta in 1996: one individual and one team competition." (The policy of holding separate competitions stands for the Games in Sydney.)

Norinder also is responsible for preparing and submitting budgets for site and facilities preparation and other equestrian-related expenses for upcoming Games. Her other Olympic-related duties include overseeing the press-accreditation process; handling travel and accommodations arrangements for the many FEI-appointed Games officials, including the judges, the technical delegates, and the veterinary officials; and breaking the news of the IOC-imposed competitor quotas to the various national federations.

Norinder calls handling the quota issue the "most sensitive" of her duties. "We had to set up rules for {working with the quota system}. We had certain qualification rules, and the riders had to come up to minimum standards to participate in the Games. The most challenging {issue} is how that works out — getting the right teams and getting the right information to everybody, so everybody knows where they stand. It's not always fair when you set a quota because you will always miss out on something, some team that actually should have been at the Games, things like that."

In planning and executing an endeavor as enormous in scope as an Olympic competition, there are bound to be challenges and glitches. One such challenge was the mandate to put on two "separate but equal" three-day events in Atlanta. And the biggest glitch in '96? According to Norinder, it was the technological breakdown of the IBM-produced scoring and information systems during the team three-day event. "The TV commentators ended up with no information," she said. "They were actually commenting by guessing who the cap or the number on the rider was." Norinder came to the rescue with her

"little diskette" of horse and rider information, and her computer disk wound up being "the basis of every single information, result, start list, everything, that came out during the Games. I don't think people really saw the breakdown behind the scenes, but it was frightening." To quash the potential of a similar problem in Sydney, the IOC "set up a major committee involving the international federations, together with IBM, to

The FEI's Catrin Norinder oversees many aspects of Olympic Games preparation.

ensure the technology will work out. We have sat down for two years, more or less, to set out a brief that will be a legacy for other Olympic Games."

National-Level Organizations

Each nation that participates in the Olympic Games maintains a national Olympic committee (NOC) as well as a national organization for each sport in which it participates. In the United States, the NOC is the United States Olympic Committee. Two organizations, the United States Equestrian Team and the American Horse Shows Association, share responsibility for representing the Olympic equestrian disciplines in the U.S. — an unusual situation, considering that most other sports have just one national organization. As one might imagine, the power structure and the allocation of duties between these organizations are complex issues — and ones that have been, and will continue to be, debated.

The United States Olympic Committee

One thing's for sure: The U.S. Olympic Committee (USOC) is and will continue to remain America's link to the IOC. Headquartered in Colorado Springs, Colorado, the USOC is responsible for ensuring that America's Olympic-sports organizations adhere to the Olympic Charter. As the IOC-designated NOC for the United States since 1978, the USOC has the following powers and obligations:

- To establish and administer national Olympic training centers and to promote sports education,
- To represent the United States at Olympic Games,
- To designate which U.S. cities will bid to host winter and summer Games (only one city per country may bid on a Games), and
- To strive to uphold the IOC's standards of sportsmanship as well as its policies on doping and drug testing of athletes.

The USOC has its origins in the Amateur Athletic Union, the group that entered American athletes in the inaugural modern Olympic Games in 1896. The organization became a formal entity in 1921 and was called the American Olympic Association. In 1940, it was renamed the United States of America Sports Federation; five years later, that unwieldy moniker was shortened to the United States Olympic Association (USOA). The USOA earned a federal charter and not-for-profit status in 1945; and in 1961, the USOA became known by its current name. In 1978, Congress passed the Amateur Sports Act, which designated the USOC America's coordinating body for Olympic athletic activities and gave the USOC the authority to recognize national governing bodies (including the USET and the AHSA) for the Olympic sports.

The USOC maintains three official training facilities: in Colorado Springs; Lake Placid, New York; and Chula Vista, California. Inasmuch as none of the three is equipped to handle the needs of equestrian training, the USET's headquarters in Gladstone, New Jersey, is an affiliated training center.

Today, the USOC is a large organization, with almost 500 staffers, an executive committee, a board of directors, and numerous sporting committees. (Dressage rider and four-time Olympian Robert Dover is equestrian sport's representative to the USOC.) In addition to its Olympic Games activities, the USOC has similar organizing and administrative responsibilities for the Pan American Games, an Olympic Games-format competition among North and South American nations, held every four years like the Olympics but taking place the previous year. (The most recent Pan Am Games were held in 1999; the next Pan Ams will be in 2003.)

The United States Equestrian Team

The U.S. Equestrian Team (USET) is a relatively young organization — just fifty years of age this year. It succeeds the U.S. Cavalry, which until 1949 furnished and subsidized America's equestrian teams in international competition. But the horse cavalry went the way of, well, the horse and buggy, and suddenly there was no organization to oversee equestrian-team selection and competition. So in 1949, a group of horse-sport supporters — among them Whitney Stone, General Albert Stackpole, General Alfred G. Tuckerman,

Drew Montgomery, Amory Haskell, Alvin Untermyer, Colonel John "Gyp" Wofford, and Spencer Weed — met to draft an application to form a new corporation to "select and obtain for the United States the most competent amateur representation possible in international equestrian competitions." The application was approved the following June, and the USET was born. The members elected Wofford the fledgling organization's first president, with Weed serving as chairman of the board and Stone, chairman of the executive committee. (Stone would later succeed Wofford as president, an office he held from 1952 through 1972.) [3]

A nonprofit corporation, the USET depends almost solely on membership dues and individual and corporate contributions for revenue; unlike many foreign national equestrian federations, the USET receives no federal governmental subsidy. The USET does receive allocations from the USOC, but these allocations amount to just one-tenth of its operating budget — which, for 2000, is close to $9 million, according to USET executive director Robert Standish. "Every cent" of that $9 million "is applied toward the fielding, funding, training, and development of the very best possible horse-rider and horse-driver combinations to represent the United States in international competition," Standish explained. "We pay for the {Team} veterinarians, the transportation costs, and the coaches for each one of these teams."

The USET's involvement in international equestrian competition reaches far beyond the Olympic Games — and it fields teams for more types of competitions than the three Olympic disciplines. "The primary competitions that USET is involved in are the Olympics, the Pan Am Games, and the World Equestrian Games. Then each year we do a series of international {competition} tours, with the ultimate goal of preparing our horse-rider combinations to be competitive in those {primary} competitions," Standish said. And the USET, like the FEI, is involved in international competition for six equestrian disciplines — except that the USET's sixth sport is reining instead of vaulting.

PRINCESS ANNE

Olympic three-day eventing has decidedly royal connections. England's HRH The Princess Royal, otherwise known as Princess Anne, became the first member of the British royal family to compete in an Olympic Games when she rode Goodwill in the three-day event at Montreal in 1976. The pair took a hard fall at a zigzag fence when the ground gave way on takeoff; Princess Anne sustained a concussion but completed the competition.

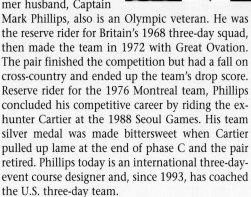

Princess Anne also served as FEI president from 1986 to 1994 — following in the footsteps of her father, HRH Prince Philip the Duke of Edinburgh, who served from 1964 until 1986.

Princess Anne's former husband, Captain Mark Phillips, also is an Olympic veteran. He was the reserve rider for Britain's 1968 three-day squad, then made the team in 1972 with Great Ovation. The pair finished the competition but had a fall on cross-country and ended up the team's drop score. Reserve rider for the 1976 Montreal team, Phillips concluded his competitive career by riding the ex-hunter Cartier at the 1988 Seoul Games. His team silver medal was made bittersweet when Cartier pulled up lame at the end of phase C and the pair retired. Phillips today is an international three-day-event course designer and, since 1993, has coached the U.S. three-day team.

As a designated national governing body (NGB) for equestrian sports, the USET answers to the USOC when it comes to Olympic and Pan American Games matters. (World championships — in the case of equestrian sport, the World Equestrian Games — are held independent of IOC and NOC control.) And the USOC is a hands-on organization, according to Standish, who formed a USET division exclusively to serve as the USOC liaison. "They (USOC) are the governing body for all sports in the U.S. as it pertains to Pan Am and Olympic Games. Any type of selection procedures we come

USET executive director Robert Standish (top); Kate Jackson, secretary-general of the AHSA and its former executive director (above).

up with has to be approved by them. Our entire interface with the Olympic Games organizing committee is done via the USOC." As an example, he said, the USOC sponsored a trip to Sydney in November 1999 so that "team leaders" from the various summer sports could scrutinize the competition sites, evaluate and choose among accommodations, and learn the various policies and procedures of the Sydney Organizing Committee for the Olympic Games.

A "discipline director" or "team leader" shepherds each USET discipline through the various approval processes and is charged with executing the programs developed by each discipline committee. Explained Standish, "They are responsible for guiding the discipline committees in the development of budgets for that program each year, and they're also responsible for fulfilling the markers and milestones that we've set in our high-performance plan — a USOC-mandated long-term strategic plan — that we have to submit to the USOC for each quadrennium for the Olympic disciplines. If we don't meet those goals, we are subject to possible loss of grants that come through the USOC."

Three capable individuals direct the Olympic disciplines.

Jim Wolf brings experience as both a competitor and an administrator to his position as USET three-day-eventing team leader. He's managed an eventing facility and has worked for American eventing stars Bruce Davidson and David and Karen O'Connor. He has held his current position since 1993 and also served as *chef de mission* for the USET's entire equestrian delegation at the 1996 Atlanta Olympic Games.

Sally Ike, herself a USET three-day-eventing veteran, has been show jumping's team leader since 1989. She has served as *chef d'équipe* of several show-jumping teams and also is an FEI steward for show jumping and eventing, a national (AHSA-rated) jumper and combined-training judge, and a combined-training technical delegate.

The USET's newest team leader, dressage discipline director Maureen Pethick, joined the Team in 1997. She brings academic and professional experience in business and finance, as well as in-the-saddle knowledge of dressage, to her position.

The American Horse Shows Association

The USET's partner in getting horses and riders to the Olympic Games is the American Horse Shows Association (AHSA), the national governing body for equestrian sport. The AHSA is by far the widest-ranging equestrian organization, in that it governs the greatest variety of breed and discipline competitions: from the Olympic disciplines to show hunters and English pleasure, and from Morgans and Saddlebreds to Welsh ponies and Paso Finos. The organization's many committees write and enforce competition rules, including strict policies regarding the use of drugs and medications at recognized competitions; sanction competitions; train and certify judges and other competition officials; and organize and administer year-end awards programs and other national championships, among other duties. The AHSA generally follows the FEI's lead in terms of rules and procedures for the FEI disciplines.

"The AHSA is kind of like the FEI; it's more structured toward rule-making and enforcing fairness of a competition country-wide, whereas the FEI is worldwide," explained Kate Jackson, the AHSA's executive director from 1996 to 1998 and currently its secretary-general. "The USET is more like the USOC, focusing on our representation at Games and on winning medals."

In her position, Jackson said, she "work{s} with the FEI on rule changes; we're working now on getting some consistency across disciplines for veterinary examinations, horse examinations, that sort of thing. It's a more global view rather than

{just} representing our country. The AHSA and the FEI are more of a pair, whereas the USET and the USOC would have the same complement. That's not to say that we're not totally supportive of our riders, but ours is a slightly different role."

In truth, the AHSA's and USET's roles in the past have overlapped, a situation that has created friction between the organizations and fueled reports and rumors of one group's trying to usurp the other's authority or to gain sole status as equestrian sports' national governing body. For now, though, a carefully worded truce is in effect in the form of the AHSA/USET Operating Agreement, which has been in effect since 1997. As a result of the agreement, the AHSA now staffs an International Services Desk at USET headquarters in Gladstone; each organization now names individuals to the other's board of directors; active athletes and USET trustees serve on AHSA hearing-committee panels for the hearing and resolution of disputes and grievances; and active athletes are represented on the joint AHSA/USET Credentials Committee, which reviews horse and rider qualifications.

Jackson and Standish regard the operating agreement as a positive step for their organizations and for equestrian sports in the U.S. "It's my perception that the communication process has been simplified," said Standish. "I would like to think that it's made it easier for both organizations to function without stepping over one another. I think the staffs of the two organizations work together beautifully…In the long term, I'd say the athletes have probably been served better."

So why all the reports of squabbling? "I think the recent controversies that have been tossed back and forth in the press are due to the fact that we are an anomaly in the eyes of the USOC," said Standish. "They look for one national federation...The AHSA-slash-USET does present an anomaly in the fact that the USET performs the functions of supporting the Olympic involvement, while the AHSA provides rules and regulations for the national sport as well as the drugs and medications {policies} and the hearing procedures. There have been opinions put forth from the USOC's Members and Credentials Committee that they would like to impose the singular-body pattern that's currently implemented in the other sports."

The terms of the AHSA/USET Operating Agreement will remain in force until after the 2000 Sydney Olympic Games, at which time the USOC will hold a "compliance review" with AHSA and USET representatives to evaluate and determine how best equestrian sports and teams should be governed and fielded. [4] It's a process that has the potential for profound implications and one that's sure to attract keen interest, speculation, and debate for some time to come.

The Team-Selection Process

So who picks Olympic-team members, and by what process? The answers to these questions have changed significantly since equestrian sports joined the modern Games in 1912. The selection processes themselves constitute a mini-summary of how horse sports have evolved, particularly in the U.S., and how financial issues have become seemingly inextricably intertwined with athletic aspirations. They also are a testament of sorts to the enduring power of the Olympic Games as a symbol of sporting achievement to which many aspire and so few attain.

The Army Years

Olympic-team selection was once a non-subject. There was no debating or second-guessing the selection by the commanding cavalry officer of the men (only men could serve in the cavalry, of course) and the horses who would represent their countries in Olympic competition. What's more, even the riders themselves had no say as to which horses they rode; the matches were made strictly according to the commanding officer's opinion as to which men did the best with which mounts. And being the military, of course, orders were to be strictly obeyed.

The Early Civilian Years

After the cavalry became mechanized and the Army no longer assumed responsibility for select-

ing and fielding equestrian teams for international competition, no structures or organizations existed to take its place. Enter the newly formed civilian equestrian association that came to be known as the United States Equestrian Team. The loss of the military stronghold on horse sports presented both opportunity and challenge: opportunity, in that the pool of human and equine talent had suddenly exploded in size to encompass the civilian sector as well as veteran cavalrymen and their mounts; and challenge, in that suitably experienced coaches and selection procedures needed to be identified and brought on board.

Luckily for the USET, several outstanding coaches were recruited and went on to select and train some of America's most legendary riders and horses; and, lured at least in part by the prospect of an attractive income-tax write-off, a number of well-to-do horse owners lent or donated talented mounts to the Team.

For more than three decades after the USET's founding in 1950, Team coaches, such as show-jumping coach Bertalan de Némethy and eventing coach Jack Le Goff, had complete say over which riders and horses were selected to train with the Team, who made the Olympic and other teams, and even which horses they rode — a system not entirely unlike that of the Army equestrian teams. The coaches knew every strength, flaw, and quirk in their human and equine

The early U.S. Olympic teams were composed with members of the military.

charges — Le Goff boasts that he could identify the Team's event horses, blindfolded, merely by running his hands down their legs — and thus were best equipped to recommend the strongest group of medal contenders, the logic went. And for many years, the USET's success record supported the subjective selection system.

The Numbers Game

It all came to a halt in 1989, when a jumper rider who was passed over in a team-selection process brought legal action against the USET. As the USET's Standish explained, U.S. tort laws, which state that the defendant in a lawsuit must pay his or her own court costs, forced the Team to spend "hundreds of thousands of dollars" defending its position in this and other cases — ultimately successfully, but with an understandable desire not to have to repeat such a process. The days of subjective team selection — at least in show jumping — were over.

Other factors also affected the USET's decision to switch to an objective selection process for jumpers. "Probably one of the biggest factors causing this change was the tremendous increase in purse dollars, along with the tremendous increase in the cost of horses," Standish said. "A good Olympic mount is probably a seven-figure horse. Given those considerations, people began to think more about the money — and, given the fact that so much was invested, people were looking for ways to avoid the subjective selection process."

The USET has and will continue to grapple with the selection-procedure issue, striving to find the right balance between subjectivity and objectivity for each discipline. In the case of show jumping, complete objectivity is the only

method deemed capable of withstanding legal challenges. As a result, the Team now uses a computer list to track show-jumping competitors' standings, and Olympic-team contenders must compete in a series of head-to-head trials.

Veteran Olympian William Steinkraus has seen the USET's selection process evolve from a U.S. Olympic Committee-mandated numerical system, to the hybrid objective-subjective system used with great success during his years at the USET's helm, and back again. He was USET chairman during a tempestuous period in the Team's history: the late 1980s, during the period of challenge to the subjective team-selection process. He doesn't think the numerical system now in place for choosing members is entirely positive.

"The first Olympics I followed really closely were the 1948 London Games, and I can remember my shock when Harrison Dillard, then the world-record-holder in the hundred-meter hurdles and the winner of eighty-two consecutive hurdle races or sprints, hit a hurdle in the Olympic trials and failed to make the team. The best hurdler in the world was left off our team, and I thought a selection method that could produce so unjust and arbitrary a result was both wasteful and excessively rigid. When you applied {a purely objective process} to a sport as complex as ours, I considered it totally irrational and fought to get it changed. After 1956, we persuaded the USOC to accept an alternative — filtering the raw trials numbers through the collective intelligence of a highly qualified selection committee — and this method produced for us a very successful Olympic record over a long period of time. I wish it were possible to still use such a method, as almost all of our leading rivals do, for

I think the results show that there is no question as to which selection process makes better use of our outstanding raw material. So-called 'objective' selection still has its advocates, but for a complex sport like ours it is so simplistic and clumsy that it constitutes a very serious competitive handicap, and I think that's a shame."

Standish said the American selection system is a frequent topic of conversation among his contemporaries at the various international conventions he attends. "They're really quite amused at what the Americans have to do and what we're subjected to. In some cases, we're actually ridiculed," he said, noting that other countries don't face the specter of lawsuits as does the United States. "Nevertheless, this is the situation under which we live, and we have to make our best efforts to live under it instead of bemoaning the fact — because I don't think that's going to change unless there's complete tort-law reform here."

The Show-Jumping-Team Selection Process

The show-jumping-team selection process has already evolved in the four years between Atlanta and Sydney, to move away from "the long series of trials that were held at Gladstone for the 1996 Olympics," as Standish explained. A two-phase process will determine the team for the 2000 Sydney Olympics. The first phase consists of screening trials at the Bayer/USET Festival of Champions in the spring at Gladstone, which determines the top twelve qualifiers. Then those top twelve qualifiers matriculate to the phase-two selection, which takes place on the West Coast. The results of five trials during phase two will determine the eventual squad of four for Sydney.

The Eventing-Team Selection Process

U.S. three-day eventing tried to follow show jumping's lead and used a numbers-only selection process to pick the 1992 Barcelona Olympic

William Steinkraus, shown with Olympic show-jumping rider Greg Best, questions the "objective" system used for U.S. team selection.

squad — an experiment that Standish called "a dismal failure. That was their worst year ever." (It didn't help, he added, that the '92 eventing team had only limited coaching, from U.K.-based Coach Lars Sederholm, another situation that was swiftly corrected after Barcelona with the hiring of Captain Mark Phillips of the U.K.)

Eventing has developed a combination subjective-objective selection system that appears well-suited to the sport's unique physical demands. After Barcelona, Louise Meryman, then chair of the USET Three-Day Event Active Riders Committee, asked 1984 Olympic team gold and individual silver medalist Karen Stives to chair a five-member selection committee. Stives, then the common member of the Team's eventing, selection, and executive committees, helped to develop

43

a unique evaluation process that incorporated competitive and veterinary know-how into a framework of performance at qualifying events. [5]

"Selectors are charged with evaluating the horses' performances at qualifiers — they're not actually called trials — and then we have a final mandatory outing after which the actual squad is selected," Standish explained. "Soundness is such a critical element in eventing that it would be almost ridiculous to select a horse through a series of trials and then have a soundness issue keep that horse from making the trot-up at the Olympic Games. Obviously, there is some subjective evaluation by the selectors and by a team of veterinarians who work in that process. Also, {they consider} the ridability of the horse: How is he going over courses? The only way you can make that determination is to evaluate him over past performances."

The Dressage-Team Selection Process

As Standish points out, dressage is subjective by its very nature: Judges' evaluations, which are essentially opinion, determine the winners. Because subjectivity is already such a big part of the mix, and because the USET dressage riders have never had one team coach, U.S. Olympic and other dressage squads have always been chosen via an objective system: competition results. "If an individual is able to stay consistently at a seventy percentile {score}, obviously {that score} is better than average," Standish said. "We've put together a series of qualifiers and then a final selection trial (at Gladstone, during the Festival of Champions)." The top four finishers at the selection trial go to the Olympics.

Standish acknowledged that "There have been

situations where I've been advised…that we have left our best horse-rider combination at home because of a fluke — somebody opened an umbrella or something and spooked him across the ring. Had the USET been given any subjective latitude, we probably would have made another determination {in the case of such events}; but obviously, in a country as litigious as the United States, that would certainly be challenged."

The *Chefs d'Équipe*

If American competitors are not the envy of the world when it comes to the processes by which Olympic teams are selected, they can take some comfort in knowing that, if they make the team, they'll be looked after in a way that's second to none, thanks to the tireless efforts of the *chefs d'équipe*.

The job of a *chef d'équipe* is "to be the go-between for the riders and the organizers, and the riders and the judges," said three-time Olympian Jessica Ransehousen, who has served as *chef* of the U.S. dressage team since 1990. "You have to go to the meetings, you have to be there for the draws (that determine the order of go). The *chef* is responsible for the athletes' behavior and for making sure they get where they're supposed to go, when they're supposed to get there. You have to do the things that pertain to your job, and do them very well, and be very tenacious and tough about it. You'll have quite a few meetings with the technical delegates, with the judges, with the organizers, before and during the Games. You have to be very much on top of the things that you feel strongly about."

Ransehousen wasn't shy about asserting herself when, at the 1992 Games, some well-meaning

Spanish stewards tried to enforce the letter of the law. "With the terrible heat in Barcelona — which, by the way, was far worse than Atlanta — we would have the grooms bring ice and alcohol and water to the arena, and we'd wash the horse down during the workout. Almost every time we would do it, a steward would run over and say, 'No, no, you can't do that' — all in Spanish, mind you — 'There are wash stalls in the stable area for horses to be washed.' We even had to get the international steward to tell the Spanish stewards it was okay for us to graze our horses."

Having competed in the Olympics in the days when competitors were more likely to be left to fend for themselves — Ransehousen was just twenty-two when she rode in her first Games in 1960 — she gladly accepted the invitation of the late Fiona Baan, then the USET's director of dressage, to *chef* the U.S. dressage squad for the 1990 World Equestrian Games in Stockholm. "That was one of the things I swore in my life: that if I ever had anything to do with anybody else, I would make sure that everything ran pretty well," she said. And she logs plenty of miles doing just that: scoping out the warm-up areas, finding out where her riders prefer to school, tracking them down before their tests so they don't have to keep looking at their watches, hunting down the veterinarian and the farrier as needed.

Ransehousen's counterpart on the three-day-event team, Captain Mark Phillips, does double duty as coach and *chef*, as team coach Jack Le Goff did before him. On the show-jumping side, coaching and *chef*-ing duties are split more or less evenly between good friends and fellow Olympic veterans Frank Chapot and George Morris. Chapot is billed as the *chef* and Morris, as the

assistant; but in practice, they divide the jumping team's grueling travel and competition schedule so that both aren't on the road all the time, with the two men working together only at championship competitions. At the Olympics, for instance, "Frank is more the *chef d'équipe* and I'm more the trainer," said Morris. "But we both do the same thing, we both watch the riders school, we both make suggestions."

Even the most successful riders want and need the support of a *chef*, Morris said. "Whether it's a rider

British Olympic veteran Captain Mark Phillips is the current chef of the U.S. three-day event team.

just taking his first lesson or somebody on the big team going to the Games, the most important thing is confidence. Whether it's Anne Kursinski, Michael Matz, whomever you want to mention, those people want confidence. They want support. They want reinforcement. They want reassurance walking the course. They want people to watch the other riders and give them an accurate description of how to ride the course. They want to know that you know."

Chefs d'équipe aren't exactly volunteers — the USET pays them $250 a day when they're on the job, and the various championships organizations pay their expenses — but they're not getting rich doing it, either. Clearly, these *chefs* serve up a lot of love of their sports and their country along with their advice and experience.

CHAPTER THREE

Are the Olympics Good for Horses?

The horse is our partner in all equestrian endeavors, whether those endeavors are going for Olympic gold or simply enjoying a leisurely trail ride. That's all well and good, but of course nobody asked the horse if he wanted to come along. And there's the rub, so to speak: Horses live in stalls, travel in cramped metal boxes, and exert themselves in all kinds of weather not really of their own volition, but because that's the hand they're dealt in life.

By most measures, though, elite equine athletes lead a pretty good life. They usually receive the best of treatment, care, feed, training, and equipment. Still, showing and travel schedules and the demands of Olympic-level competition are tough on even the hardiest horses. And if you can't imagine getting through a grueling day without popping a couple of aspirin or Advil tablets, just consider the fact that horses at the Olympics are permitted no such substances whatsoever to ease their aches and pains.

But through the efforts of concerned veterinarians and industry supporters, many top horses are managing to stay sound and healthy for competition without medication, thanks in part to an array of joint-health products, non-medicinal techniques such as massage, and other cutting-edge health-care measures. Before the 1996 Games in hot, humid Atlanta, a trio of veterinary researchers spearheaded a comprehensive heat-stress study that resulted in significant changes' being made both on course and behind the scenes at the three-day event — arguably the most successful Olympic three-day event ever. For the Sydney Games, those same researchers are tackling another perennially problematic issue — transport — and are publicizing findings that will help keep horses safe and healthy not only on the long journeys to and from Australia, but in trailers and vans all over the world.

Still, the fact remains that equestrian sports have come under fire from various animal-rights and animal-welfare groups. It's not difficult to grasp how a casual spectator could be alarmed at the sight of horses falling on cross-country, for instance. Equestrian organizations strive to ensure that inhumane treatment of horses does not go unpunished. But it's a fine line that horse enthusiasts walk, and one that shows few signs of growing easier over time. Perhaps horse sports' best hope lies in a proactive approach to educating the press and the public, as was done with considerable success in Atlanta in 1996. To that end, this chapter will take a look at the concerns of animal-advocate groups and the steps equestrian organizations have taken to help keep horses and horse sports safe and sound. We'll also explain the ways that FEI veterinary regulations and issues have evolved as well as the roles of the various team and Olympic veterinarians and veterinary committees.

Olympic horses receive mandated veterinary inspections and scrutiny.

CHAPTER THREE

Humane Issues

All equestrian-sports enthusiasts profess to love horses and to be concerned for their health and welfare. But some animal lovers have difficulty humane treatment. Others take their case quite a bit further, arguing that it is wrong to use animals in any way, be it for companionship, sport, food, or clothing.

Dramatic-looking falls and crashes tend to incite animal-welfare and animal-rights groups.

reconciling verbal proclamations of affection with the dramatic-looking and at-times serious falls, crashes, and other mishaps that do occur in the course of equestrian competition.

A variety of animal-protection groups exist throughout the world. Some state as their purpose a desire to protect the welfare of animals: to make sure that all animals, from Olympic horses to household pets, receive adequate care and

Horse sports — from the Olympic disciplines and fox hunting to rodeo and gaited-horse showing — have come under fire by animal-welfare and animal-rights organizations. Several prominent horse-industry experts, including a number of Olympic veterinary officials, have dealt with protests by animal-rights groups. Although they perhaps did not welcome the scrutiny at the time, they have responded by taking steps toward elevating the Olympic equestrian disciplines above reproach — at least in terms of animal-welfare issues.

Some animal-rights groups, such as the People for the Ethical Treatment of Animals (PETA), state as their mission that they wish to see all uses of animals cease, including the use of horses for sport. It is difficult for equestrian-sport enthusiasts to find any common ground in a view that is so radically opposed to their own; but perhaps, as with other similarly charged issues, education can play a role in narrowing the gap. Thanks in large part to the efforts of veterinary researchers and high-profile horse-sport organizations such as the FEI, word is beginning to get out to the general public that a well-cared-for, carefully schooled, elite equine athlete loves his job in much the same way that the drug-sniffing dog or the guide dog loves his work. Most creatures — including human beings — like to feel a sense of purpose in life. At its best, an Olympic horse's purpose is to help express the ultimate in human-animal partnership and, in the process, to help his rider, trainer, and handlers become better people.

Animal-Rights Protests and the Olympics

In his memoirs, *Olympic Vet*, Joseph C. O'Dea, DVM, the U.S. Equestrian Team's veterinarian from 1955 through 1975, described an animal-rights protest that nearly resulted in horse sports' being banned from the Games. O'Dea officiated at the 1956 Games in Stockholm, at which the three-day event was marred by accidents on steeplechase and cross-country due in part to treacherous footing caused by downpours before and during the Games following a serious drought; and in part, he said, to competitors and horses' lack of preparation for the level of competition. He wrote:

The media fanned the situation to the detriment of the sport...{E}very faux pas on course was recorded from multiple angles and the bloodiest, most exaggerated pictures were carried in the press. To the anti-blood sports people, the circumstances did not go unnoticed.

Late in the following winter, {USET president} Whitney Stone called to alert me that Avery Brundage, the American President of the International Olympic Committee {IOC} had a serious problem and would be calling on me for help. An agitated Brundage explained that the IOC was being sued by a consortium of anti-blood sports organizations in Europe. As a result of the unfavorable media coverage at Stockholm, there was strong sentiment in the IOC that the equestrian sports should be dropped from the Olympic roster. [1]

O'Dea responded to the IOC's concerns by preparing a brief stating that Olympic competition and rules meet FEI-approved standards of difficulty and that each country's national federation is responsible for selecting teams that are up to the challenge. He further argued that equestrian sports have a historical right to be part of the Games. The brief worked: The animal-rights groups dropped the lawsuit, and the IOC kept horse sports in the Olympics. [2]

Current FEI Veterinary Commission president Professor Leo Jeffcott also has had to fight a legal battle concerning Olympic equestrian sports. "My last day in Atlanta {at the 1996 Games} was in the district attorney's office because of a legal challenge to Georgia law. The Humane Society of the United States (HSUS) and its counterparts in other countries have taken particular exception to eventing and have tried to mount campaigns to stop it. In the Georgia case, the HSUS said that eventing was cruel as a result of running the horses in the Olympics in Atlanta. They just showed a video of all the horses that fell. The DA threw the thing out, us {the FEI} having given the correct evidence (a balanced look at the competition).

"Some of these societies won't give up and won't look to the improvements that are being made, and feel very strongly that they need to ban, if possible, these sorts of competitions," said Jeffcott. "On the other hand, organizations like the UK-based International League for the Protection of Horses and the Royal Society for the Prevention of Cruelty to Animals are very pro-the-improved-welfare that goes along with international equestrian competition."

To help publicize the veterinary community's research on heat stress, conducted before the 1996 Atlanta Olympics (see "Too Hot to Handle?" later in this chapter), American veterinarians A. Kent Allen and Catherine Kohn held a second pre-Games press conference, which was deliberately scheduled "before the animal-rights groups gave theirs," recalled Allen, veterinary coordinator in 1996 and foreign veterinary delegate for the 2000 Games. The crux of his and Kohn's presentation: "Here's what's going on. Look at how much work's been done, and, frankly, these horses are very well cared for and very well scrutinized.

"Looking back at those Olympics, that's what our research group feels most proud about: that we took what was predicted to be the single

High-tech misting fans helped cool horses (and humans) at the 1996 Atlanta Olympics.

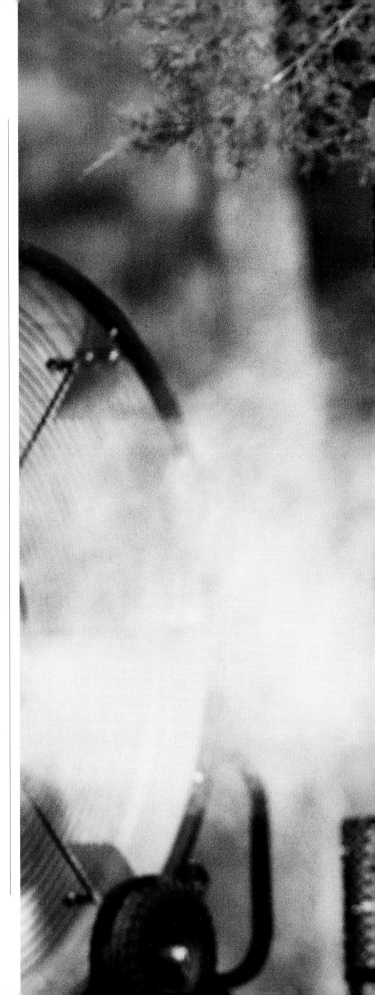

biggest disaster in equestrian sports and turned it into a non-event, from our standpoint. And that's the way it should be: It should just be safe for the horses."

Health and Welfare Issues

From the early days of modern Olympic equestrian competition, at which veterinary supervision was minimal, veterinary care and regulations have increased in sophistication and com-

We have an obligation to see that our horses are properly used — never abused — and that their lives are made as easy as we can make it for them, keeping them as physically fit as we can and helping them to do the job. That has to be our mission.

— Joseph C. O'Dea, DVM, former USET veterinarian and member of the FEI Veterinary Commission

plexity. Team veterinarians today must concern themselves not only with such matters as acclimating horses to atmospheric conditions and treating illnesses and lamenesses, but also with how to treat their charges without the use of the many FEI-prohibited drugs and medications.

Altitude Adjustments

If you've ever hiked in the mountains, or even just visited a town located in a higher altitude than you're accustomed to, you know you're likely to huff and puff for a few days until your body adjusts to the thinner air. The American horses were faced with a significant altitude-adjustment challenge at the 1968 Games in

8,000-feet-above-sea-level Mexico City. As he recalled in *Olympic Vet*, Dr. Joseph O'Dea devised a way to measure the horses' blood oxygen, which diminishes considerably in high altitudes. He recommended a step-by-step approach: hand-walk for two or three days after arrival, and begin work under saddle after three or four days, depending on the individual horse's adjustment rate. The approach worked, and the U.S. horses showed no signs of the hypoxia, colic, and "severe physiologic disturbance" suffered by "more than a few" horses from other countries that did not take such precautions. [3]

The War on Drugs

The FEI's policy of drug-testing horses for prohibited substances (today's horses must show on no medications whatsoever) is actually fairly recent: instituted — in policy, at least — for the 1972 Munich Games. The FEI drew up a medications rule, created a veterinary committee to be chaired by a French veterinary-school professor, and established sampling and testing procedures.

USET veterinarian O'Dea took pains to ensure that the Americans understood and followed the rule, and he naturally assumed that the other participating nations were doing the same. An incident in Munich, however, proved otherwise.

The American jumper Sloopy, ridden to a team silver and individual bronze medal at those Games by Neal Shapiro, lacerated a pastern, wrote O'Dea in *Olympic Vet*; and another veterinarian administered the anesthetic Lidocaine — an FEI no-no — in preparation to suture the wound. O'Dea was naturally dismayed at the veterinarian's action until "(USET three-day-team coach and *chef d'équipe*) Jack Le Goff popped in and confirmed to us that he had learned from the French team veterinarian that there would be no testing. He shrugged, 'Everybody knows it.' The truth was that everybody did not know it. The French and their cronies had been given a special advantage by their professor. A member of the French delegation who had been tipped off by the professor had relayed the information to the French team veterinarian early on." [4]

French officials, the FEI, and O'Dea, among many others, were horrified at the incident and resolved to make sure it wasn't repeated four years later at the 1976 Olympics in Montreal. By that time, O'Dea was in an even better position to make good on his promise, as the FEI had appointed him FEI veterinary technical delegate for those Games. [5]

According to O'Dea, the FEI realized before the 1972 Games that medications abuse was rampant in horse sports and sought to bring it under control. After much debate, the Federation passed a rule at its 1970 General Assembly banning all drugs during competition except for the non-steroidal anti-inflammatory drugs (NSAIDs), the best-known of which is butazolidin or "Bute." [6]

FEI drugs-and-medications regulations have since become even more restrictive, with even "Bute" and other NSAIDs now on the list of prohibited substances. O'Dea was a member of the FEI's Veterinary Commission at the time of the 1987 meeting of the Federation's General Assembly, during which a motion was made to repeal the existing medications rule — a move that would ban the use of all medications, including Bute, at FEI-sanctioned competitions. O'Dea recalled the events in *Olympic Vet*: "All votes were in favor except mine. My fellow com-

missioners were aghast at my nay...{The concept of a total ban} was wrong by every yardstick of good regulation and fair play." He was pleased when the motion was tabled, hoping that the delay would allow more study and discussion and the presentation of a "feasible alternative." [7]

In his argument against a ban, O'Dea pointed out that

The original 4-microgram residue level for PBZ {Bute} had worked well and had protected the sport against the abusive use of the drug. In time, however, the testing chemists started to recognize a suspicious residue pattern in the tests and alerted the FEI.

When PBZ is metabolized or broken down in the horse's body, the residue consists of whole PBZ, a metabolite named Oxyphenbutazone (OPBZ), and an alcoholic metabolite which is of little practical significance...{T}he laboratory tests revealed that the levels of the metabolite...OPBZ were often out of ratio to {those of} whole...PBZ{,} sometimes substantially exceeding the whole PBZ level...OPBZ has almost the same therapeutic effect as does PBZ... Investigations confirmed that some horsemen were attempting to intensify the approved therapy with PBZ by supplementing it with OPBZ. [8]

O'Dea and his fellow members of the FEI Veterinary Commission knew that the pharmacologic effects of Bute and/or OPBZ cease at levels below 2 micrograms per milliliter of plasma. They proposed a rule to permit residue levels of

Bute or OPBZ not to exceed 2 micrograms/ml. The FEI adopted the rule in 1988 "and it worked well. A few professional horsemen and their veterinarians objected, seemingly incapable of working within the rule or unwilling to do so. Little did they realize how destructive a total ban could be." [9]

Despite O'Dea's objections, that "total ban" did indeed later become FEI law — a regulation that remains on the books to this day. His fears of a ban's detrimental effects on equine welfare have largely failed to materialize — in large part, he claims, because the ban has a de facto tolerance level of 2 micrograms/ml, ironically the same level he proposed back in 1988.

"We know that, at two micrograms per milliliter of plasma, the pharmacologic effect {of Bute} extinguishes," said O'Dea. "You still have a residual therapeutic effect, of course; that's what you want to get in the first place. But you have to have a line that you can actually control, and we know that we can control at two-microgram levels — at the extinguishing point — through laboratory testing."

What are the practical implications of Bute's extinguishing effect? In short, that a true zero-tolerance policy is almost impossible to enforce, said O'Dea. "Say an event horse gets banged up a bit on cross-country. He could have a dose of ten cc (ten milligrams) before six o'clock that night, and he would be under the two-microgram level by competition time the next day. In other words, he would have had the humane, desired, beneficial effect — to take care of those little bumps and bruises of competition — but he would not be performing under the influence of a drug." In practice, he believes, the FEI and its

veterinarians "agree with the two-microgram level. If {a horse tests} under the two-microgram level, they don't call it a positive." In other words, "It appears to many {competitors and officials} that a margin of tolerance is given in the reading of the positives."

Professor Leo Jeffcott of England's University

of Cambridge, chair of the FEI Veterinary Committee, official veterinarian for the 1988 Seoul Games, a foreign veterinary delegate for the 1992 and 1996 Games, and president of the FEI Veterinary Commission for the 2000 Sydney Games, disagreed. "I'm obviously interested in the welfare of the horses, and you can argue that these drugs will actually be to the benefit of the horses; but we have to have a level playing field, and so we have to have a black-and-white situation. We can't have, 'We'll just have a little bit of that, and that will be OK.' We've got to have 'Allow it or not allow it.' My job is not necessarily to agree with whether we should be giving

the first place," Jeffcott pointed out. He's proud of the strict enforcement program and said that, as a result, "the sport is considered to be in a very much better state than some of the examples we've had recently in cycling and football and weight-lifting and that sort of thing. It's a pretty clean sport."

more drugs, or letting more drugs through, or raising the threshold, but to try and be sure that what we are doing is fair and satisfactory for everybody.

"The drug-testing program is meant, not so much to catch people out, as to prevent people's wanting to do it {administer drugs to horses} in

Before the advent of air travel, equine competitors journeyed by ship.

Getting There Is Half the Battle

Transport, regardless of by what method, is stressful to horses. From the days before air travel, when horses traveled by boat to reach competitions on faraway shores; to modern times, when horses and riders alike rack up their share of frequent-flyer miles, Olympic Games-bound mounts have endured their share of travel delays, cramped conditions, stale air, weather-related difficulties, and trip-related illnesses.

More Leg Room, Please

As O'Dea recounted in *Olympic Vet*, the confined quarters of the shipping box themselves can cause a horse to panic and scramble. The USET veterinarian faced a particularly harrowing situation en route to the 1964 Tokyo Olympic Games, when J. Michael Plumb's three-day-event

mount, Markham, panicked in midair. The horse had recently suffered a bad experience on a van ride, and evidently the turbulence the Super Constellation propeller-driven aircraft encountered on the flight from New Jersey's Newark International Airport triggered bad memories. Markham became increasingly uncontrollable;

and sedatives, twitching, blindfolding, and other attempts at restraint had little effect. The horse managed to get his front feet over the front panel of his shipping box — which was considerably smaller and more flimsy than today's "air stables" — and began bashing the aircraft's ceiling panels. The flight engineer ordered O'Dea and team coach Bertalan de Némethy to do something, and De Némethy reluctantly instructed the veterinarian to administer the lethal injection. [10]

The only bright spot in the sad episode, O'Dea recalled, was the calm behavior of Markham's neighbor, the event horse Grasshopper. The Anglo-Connemara gelding "kind of looked at {Markham's hysterics} and said, 'You big dummy, what the hell are you trying to do?' He didn't break out and get all worked up. And it's helpful that he didn't because we had other horses that were behind Markham, and it could have gotten doubly serious."

Fortunately, "air stables" have become roomier, so tragedies like Markham's are less likely to occur today. "In those days," O'Dea said of air transport in the 1950s and 1960s, "the fronts and the backs of the boxes were not {permanently} in place, so you walked horses up a gangplank onto the airplane and then walked them all the way through the boxes until you got to the first set in place. Then you put up the front and back partitions and bolted them in place. Today, the boxes are like standing stalls in a horse trailer.

"When we went {from the smaller, older propeller-driven aircraft} to jet airplanes, we got the 'astro' boxes, which have more room. When a

Air shipment of horses has become commonplace and more comfortable for the equine passengers.

Travel by land, air, or sea is stressful to horses. Researchers' recommendations for reducing transport stress will help Sydney-bound equine competitors.

horse got his butt against the side of the stall partition in the old, narrow boxes, he would start to scramble to get upright. He would just keep on leaning more and more. We don't have that problem with the astro boxes because they've got enough room."

Recent research has produced new insights into the stresses of transport, as well as practical suggestions for helping to ensure that horses in transit — whether they're headed to the 2000 Sydney Olympics or to the next town — arrive at their destinations as healthy as when they left home.

Catherine Kohn, DVM, president of the FEI Veterinary Commission for the 1996 Games; Kent Allen; and Jeffcott together were concerned about the effects the very long journey to Australia will have on this year's Olympic horses, as practically all will have to fly nearly halfway around the world to get to Sydney.

"We {in North America} face {having to ship horses by air} frequently because we have horses that fly to England and Europe and compete," Kohn explained. "This is a much longer trip." The three experts, who had worked together previously on the successful heat-stress studies conducted before the 1996 Atlanta Games, began discussing their concerns and realized that "There's a lot we don't know about the effects of transport on horses. And we've got horses shipping to Sydney for the Olympics, but we also have 4H kids putting their horses on trailers every day; and there are lots of people who ship across country."

As they and their horse-industry supporters had done with the heat-stress study, Kohn and her colleagues tapped into others' generosity to obtain the needed funding for their research project. The Massachusetts Society for the Prevention of Cruelty to Animals sponsored a transport-stress seminar in March of 1999, which "brought together people who had done work in transport {research} from around the world," said Kohn. "We had five state-of-the-art papers that reviewed the literature. And, with a sort of collective wisdom, we came up with guidelines for transport...We also suggested what the research priorities should be in order to learn more and possibly improve our methods of shipping horses."

A Breath of Fresh Air

The researchers' primary goal: to learn more about the causes of respiratory ailments and "shipping fever" that plague transported horses. Said Kohn, "We think that the quality of the air in the transport vehicle is a very big contributing factor in challenging the horse's respiratory system. We know that a horse has to be able to clear his airway of all the particulate matter he's inhaled, and that he can do that only by putting his head down. But when you tie his head up in a horse trailer, he can't get his head down. Some work done in Australia and Washington state suggests that, the longer you tie a horse's head up, the more bacteria and particulate matter find their way into the lungs.

"The other thing we're concerned about is the quality of the air," Kohn continued. Exhaust fumes, pollution, dust from the road and from hay and bedding — all are bad news for a horse's respiratory system, and their effects are worsened when the vehicle is stationary.

"I think the key will be: Can we develop something that is better ventilated?" Allen added. "We don't even understand the ventilation system — how the air flow works. It's very complex aero-

dynamics. You would think it would be simple, but it's not. A researcher is trying to design a model that will mimic the conditions of road and air transport." When the research is completed, Allen predicts, "I think you'll see changes in the design of air stables and changes in trailer design."

Rest for the Weary

"We've already learned that, if horses are going to travel for ten to twelve hours, they really need an overnight — six to eight hours to recover from the stresses," Allen said. "Many people used to think that you could simply stop for a half-hour every few hours to give the horses a break. The research proves that doesn't given them enough of a break; they don't recover."

Quarantine

Depending on a given country's indigenous equine diseases, that country passes laws mandating a quarantine period for horses imported from other parts of the world. With the numbers of countries represented at the Olympic equestrian events, it stands to reason that importation and quarantine can be thorny issues.

Horse enthusiasts who are looking forward to the 2000 Sydney Games may not realize that, technically, the equestrian Olympic events should have been held in Australia once before, in 1956, when all the other events of that Olympiad took place in Melbourne. But "because of the restrictive animal import requirements then in force in Australia,"[11] the equestrian events were held in Stockholm, Sweden.

Evidently the situation has changed enough to allow the 2000 Games to proceed intact in Sydney, but Australia's restrictions still pose a challenge to veterinary officials. As Jeffcott explained, "The quarantine is governed by the country that's running the event. So in the case of the 2000 Games, the Australian Quarantine and Inspection Service (AQIS) set down standards of what they require. They require most horses from countries that have no serious disease problems — the U.S., most of Europe, certain parts of South America and Asia — to do two weeks' quarantine in their own country. Then most horses will fly to Frankfurt and then to Sydney, where they will have to do fourteen additional days of quarantine.

"Because all the horses can't come in on one day, they're coming in in five days, in sort of batches of fifty or sixty," Jeffcott continued. "The horses that come in on the first day will probably actually have about nineteen days of quarantine, whereas the horses that come in on the last day will have fourteen days." AQIS has deemed the entire area of the Olympic equestrian venue a quarantine zone, so no non-competing horses will be permitted within the borders. Any competing horses that are stabled in Australia at the time of the Games will be allowed into the compound after the fourteen-day quarantine period has ended.

"Australia is free from most equine diseases," said Jeffcott. "For example, they don't have equine influenza; you don't have to vaccinate your horse against it. This creates quite a problem for international competitions because the Australian horses aren't vaccinated, but they can't compete in FEI events unless they're vaccinated. All the Australian horses that are going to compete in the Sydney Olympics will have to be vaccinated beforehand with specially imported vaccines; that's how seriously the Australians take the issue of disease spread."

The Aussies aren't exaggerating the dangers: A disease outbreak almost shut down the 1992 Olympics in Barcelona. Cases of African Horse Sickness cropped up in southern Spain in 1989 and 1990, said Jeffcott; had the outbreak proved uncontainable, it would have been impossible to hold the equestrian events in Barcelona. Fortunately, though, the area of the outbreak was a considerable distance away from the Olympic city; and organizers were able, in part by enacting some special restrictions, to create a large disease-free zone so the Games could proceed.

Too Hot to Handle?

With the exception of the 2000 Olympics in Sydney, which start in September to allow for the southern hemisphere's "reversed" order of seasons — winter in Australia is summer in North America — the summer Olympic Games generally are held in just that: the good old summertime. Add to the usual July-August time frame the fact that most cities that host summer Games are in warm locales to begin with, and you have a potential recipe for heat-related health problems if you're not lucky enough to be involved with a sport that's held in the water or in an air-conditioned arena.

Because of the demands of speed-and-endurance day, the three-day event tends to be the most scrutinized of the three Olympic equestrian disciplines in terms of the horses' health and welfare. When a horse falls on cross-country or finishes the course in an apparent state of exhaustion, the incident makes the news. In Barcelona in 1992, the three-day event made the news a lot, to the consternation of Jeffcott and many others in the horse world.

"We had some very bad press as a result of the fact that the weather was pretty hot and a couple of horses did get overtired," Jeffcott recalled. "It was a great shame, really, because it wasn't the media's fault; the information from the veteri-

Jeffcott as if "the press didn't wish to know that. They reported in the Scandinavian press that two horses were dead; they showed in the {London} *Daily Telegraph* the Russian horse upside down, being anesthetized, looking as if it was dead...Everyone was saying that {the three-day event in} Barcelona was a disaster."

nary {contingent} was just not presented. After the speed and endurance, a colleague and I sat for an hour at the press office waiting to be interviewed, to tell them in fact what a great day we'd had: Despite the heat, the horses had all got 'round; we'd had two tired horses but they'd been treated; we'd covered everything and it was all pretty good." Unfortunately, it seemed to

An event horse's team wastes no time in cooling down the athlete.

Jeffcott and other veterinary experts resolved not to allow the 1996 Games — to be held in notoriously hot, sticky Atlanta, Georgia — to become a repeat of the events in Barcelona. So, even before naming of the veterinary officials

61

and committees for Atlanta, Jeffcott, Allen, and Kohn formed an ad hoc task force to study the effects of heat and humidity on the exercising horse — and, they hoped, to come up with practical recommendations for keeping Atlanta's equine athletes safe and healthy.

According to Kohn, the researchers wanted to learn the answers to three questions:

1. What is the effect of environment on performance?

The best-cared-for athletes at these Olympic Games are going to be four-legged instead of two-legged.

— A. Kent Allen, DVM, at a press conference before the 1996 Atlanta Games

2. In what ways can the exercise regimen or the competition rules be altered to compensate for hot-weather conditions?

3. What other measures can be taken to enable a horse to cope with heat and humidity?

As Allen recalled, the research project "began to take on a life of its own" as additional veterinary experts and horse-industry groups began to get involved. One of the researchers' concerns was funding, as "there are fairly meager resources in equine research. As it turned out, {the late USET veterinarian} Marty Simensen and {former American Horse Shows Association president} Jane Clark were able to get significant money out of the AHSA. The FEI put money in; the U.S. Combined Training Association put money in; everybody who was involved in the horse industry — particularly those who had an interest in three-day eventing — really got involved.

"As it turns out, the research went great: We were able to get it done at an affordable price," Allen said proudly. "When we got done, we probably knew more about the effects of heat and humidity on the exercising horse than the body of knowledge preceding us for the last hundred years."

So what did the researchers learn? "We were able to take some old myths and debunk them, such as the notion that you can't put cold water on a hot horse's buttocks," said Allen. The study showed that a hot horse will not tie up or suffer other detrimental effects previously thought to be related to cold-water application. "We were able to look at how hot the actual muscles get — up to 107, 108 degrees Fahrenheit — which is one of the reasons you really need to work hard at cooling them down." The research team discovered that heat has a greater effect on horses than it does on humans because of horses' increased surface-to-mass ratio, he added.

"We came up with a new formula for calculating a heat index for horses" using factors such as the heat, the humidity, the wind speed, and the solar radiation, Allen explained. The veterinary researchers used as a jumping-off point the U.S. Marine Corps' heat index for humans. "We had to adjust it, but we learned that we could take a set of environmental circumstances and directly calculate the time of day that the effects would be less on the horse. That's why we started the cross-country {in Atlanta} at seven o'clock in the morning and had it all finished by eleven-thirty."

Still, cooling a horse who's just run a cross-country course in the Atlanta summer heat, in pea-soup-thick humidity, is no small feat. To help prevent horses from overheating in the first place, the researchers recommended rule changes in the speed-and-endurance competition itself. "We shortened the endurance test by about twenty-two percent," said Kohn, "and we had a few fewer jumps than normal. We also added two mandatory rest pauses during phase C {the second roads-and-tracks phase, before the cross-country phase D}. So when the horses got to the end of the roads-and-tracks, they were in very good shape. I actually remember one competitor who was annoyed because his horse was so fresh {before cross-country} that he couldn't hold him at the start, and he didn't do very well. We thought that was a good problem to have."

Another first-time strategy that benefited horses and humans alike in Atlanta was the use of misting fans. "They're not like an ordinary fan that you hook up with some water nozzles," Allen explained. "You have to pressurize the water up to at least 150 pounds per square inch and blow it out through a very fine nozzle." The fans consume very little water — only a gallon and a half per hour — and the mist they produce is so fine that it flash-evaporates, with the evaporation cooling even the humid Atlanta air. "If you stood ten feet away from those fans, you never got wet!" said Allen. "But they can be very effective in cooling large areas out in the open."

The misting fans in Atlanta proved so effective that they're now used to cool horses in a multitude of hot-weather activities, from endurance-riding competitions in Saudi Arabia to Quarter Horse shows in Oklahoma City, Oklahoma, said Allen. The Olympic veterinary researchers didn't invent the misting-fan technology — the fans were already in use in feed lots, on poultry farms, and at sporting events in the desert Southwest — but their application had not been widespread because it had been believed that they would be ineffective in humid climates.

Catherine Kohn, DVM, headed the veterinary commission in Atlanta and conducted groundbreaking research on heat stress and transport.

Proud of their accomplishments and confident about the welfare of the horses at the 1996 Games, the lead researchers were eager to share their work with the press. The American Association of Equine Practitioners sent Allen and Kohn to a course in media relations. Allen recalled a particularly large press conference held before the Games. "There were, like, sixty cameras in there and people from all over the world reporting. All the speakers except me were MDs. They're talking about their plans for the Games, and they've given me this one little fifteen-minute time slot. I stepped up there and showed them all the research we'd done, and they were absolutely blown away. They had no clue the veterinarians had done all of this work.

"I had all the MDs coming up to me afterward and saying, 'That's amazing that you guys did all that! The fan idea is a really good one; have you tried it?' I said, 'Yeah, we've been doing that for two years.' And I got to use my little line, which got used multiple times during the Games: that the best-cared-for athletes at these Olympic Games are going to be four-legged instead of two-legged."

Allen's prediction came true: As Kohn put it, "We just didn't have horse problems; we really didn't. I know that the chief physicians were treating people for heat problems, but we weren't treating horses for heat problems. I have some cute photos of the three-day dressage judges standing in front of the misting fans to get cooled off."

Additionally gratifying to Kohn is the fact that the heat-beating strategies developed for the Atlanta Olympics have continued to be employed at hot-weather equestrian competitions. "At the 1999 Blenheim three-star event in the west of England in September, it was unseasonably hot and they elected to use the additional phase-C-halt principle. I don't think it had ever been done in Europe before. It worked extremely well.

"I think none of us would suggest that we use hot-weather venues for big competitions," Kohn concluded, "but we do feel that we have some good strategies now for assuring horse safety as well as meaningful sport."

The Weight Rule

As if heat and humidity and the demands of cross-country day weren't challenges enough for event enthusiasts and veterinary experts, the sport of three-day eventing has had to deal with yet another equine-welfare issue: the weight rule. Until 1998, FEI eventing rules specified that horses must carry a minimum of 165 pounds on speed-and-endurance day. (A similar rule for show jumpers had been abandoned years before.) The weight rule was a leftover from the sport's military roots: Eventing was an endurance test of cavalry horses, and "no horse that couldn't carry 165 pounds was worth keeping," according to former FEI Three-Day Event Committee chairman Hugh Thomas. [12]

The rule drew criticism from experts, including Dr. Joseph O'Dea, who argued that the addition of "dead weight" (in the form of lead weights in saddle-pad pockets) compromises horse and rider safety and increases the likelihood that he'll hit the fence and possibly take a fall — not to mention the potential for damage to joints and soft tissues when all that extra weight lands on his front legs.

Research by noted equine biomechanics expert Dr. Hilary Clayton bore out O'Dea's beliefs. In 1995, with input from O'Dea, Clayton designed a study to test dead weight's effects on event horses. Three experienced event riders — all small, slender women — rode a total of six experienced event horses in simulated speed-and-endurance-day conditions, then jumped a three-and-a-half-foot table with and without a forty-pound weight cloth. Clayton attached reflective markers to the horses' joints and videotaped the jumping efforts, later computerizing the videos and plotting the jumping arcs. Her research showed that the added weight had two major effects on the horses' jumping efforts: It caused them to make shallower jumps, apparently because it hampered their power and thrust on takeoff; and it caused them to land with considerably more force on the leading foreleg. [13]

Armed with the study results, Canadian Equestrian Team veterinarian Dr. Alan Young, then a member of the FEI Veterinary Committee, convinced the Federation's Three-Day Event Committee to reduce the weight requirement from 165 pounds to 154 pounds for the 1996 Olympic three-day event. Realizing that keeping a weight rule on the books had the potential to spark a protest by animal-rights groups should a lead-weight-carrying event horse become injured, the Three-Day Committee abolished the weight rule altogether as of January 1, 1998.

Veterinary Officials and Committees

Doctors, athletic trainers, and other medical personnel may abound at all other Olympic events and venues; but DVMs, not MDs, prevail at the equestrian sites. In attendance are FEI-appointed veterinary officials as well as each nation's team veterinarians, each of whom has a distinct set of responsibilities. Here's how the roles break down.

FEI Veterinary Committee

One of the FEI's "standing committees," this group is responsible for developing veterinary regulations for Olympic Games, managing horse inspections and examinations at FEI-sanctioned competitions, controlling disease, and dealing with the various countries' quarantine regula-tions. A three-member Medication Subcommit-tee, which focuses strictly on the issues of drugs and medications regulation, advises the Veterinary Committee.

Jeffcott chairs the Veterinary Committee and, as the chair, also is a member of the FEI Bureau. Allen is a fellow current Veterinary Committee member.

FEI Veterinary Commission

Jeffcott heads the four-member commission that is overseeing all equine-health matters at the 2000 Sydney Games. Assisted by Allen and by two Australian veterinarians, Jeffcott will "make sure that the welfare of the horses is satisfactory, that the facilities are being looked after, that the veterinarians who are involved with the horses are up to scratch, and assisting them if they need anything. We're there to see that the veterinary regulations are properly adhered to."

Jeffcott emphasized that the Veterinary Commission is not a policing group. "Our job is to see as many horses as possible compete and finish. We're not trying to put horses out. But if we are concerned that there's something wrong, or that there's been an infringement of the rules, it's for us to report to the ground jury.

"We need to ensure the health of the horses," Jeffcott continued. "As horses come in from around the world, they could possibly bring in infectious disease, or they may have injured themselves on the journey and the team vet hasn't had a chance to see it; so when they arrive, a veterinary examination of all horses is carried out. We also have the responsibility of making sure that the horse that comes in is the right horse: We have to check the passports and check

Veterinary coordinator Kent Allen discusses the three-day event course at the 1996 Atlanta Games.

the horse's identification against the passport.

"We also have to organize the surveillance of horses throughout the event, particularly the speed-and-endurance portion of the three-day event. We make sure that there are enough vets at the fences and that we have a team at the ready to deal with any emergencies."

Last, said Jeffcott, "We have to ensure the horses' fitness to compete. All horses that compete in Olympic disciplines undergo a veterinary inspection before and during the competition.

"It sounds rather bureaucratic," Jeffcott concluded, "but we're there, not to do a lot, we hope, but to be there should there be any problems. We're the official side; we're there as the veterinary representatives of the FEI, to ensure that the welfare and safety of the horses is OK. Then, at the end, we have to report back to the FEI that everything was all right — or, if it wasn't all right, what went wrong and what should happen in the future."

Allen, who served as veterinary coordinator for the 1996 Atlanta Olympics (see below), said that "with this sort of Veterinary Commission (the lineup for Sydney), which is a very experienced one, we all coordinate and we all work together, so there is less assignment of specific roles. Probably the single exception is that, at veterinary inspections for eventing, the foreign veterinary delegate is the only one allowed to stand on the line with the ground jury. The other members of the Commission stand back from the line and observe but don't have any direct comment" as to whether a horse should pass or fail. "With the jumpers and the dressage, we operate as a group. The veterinary rules have evolved over the years, and they've occasionally evolved in slightly different directions."

Veterinary Coordinator

Unlike the members of the Veterinary Commission, who are appointed by the FEI, the veterinary coordinator is hired by the Olympic Games' organizing committee. Kent Allen was the veterinary coordinator for the Atlanta Games, and Nigel Nichols is the veterinary services manager (as the position is being called) for Sydney.

"The veterinary coordinator doesn't have a direct impact on the competition," Allen explained. "In other words, he or she can't throw a horse out of the jog, as the foreign veterinary delegate can." Instead, the coordinator's role begins approximately two years before the start of the Games, and that person works more or less full-time to organize all of the veterinary services and to ensure that the facilities and supplies are adequate and sufficient.

The coordinator "gets the facility, organizes the vets and the students and the scribes — everybody who's needed, gets all the equipment in, organizes the hospital and the running of the veterinary side of the stables," explained Jeffcott.

American Horse Shows Association secretary-general Kate Jackson, who organized the equestrian events for the Atlanta Games, said that, thanks to Allen's efforts as veterinary coordinator, "We had a small, fully equipped equine hospital at the venue. He got all this equipment donated. He was really my star; he was so great."

National Team Veterinarians

"The team veterinarian is absolutely crucial to any of the teams competing because he has to look after the horses and present them in the right condition to be able to compete," said Jeffcott. The team vet does any hands-on ministration — but, as Jeffcott emphasized, with the knowledge that certain kinds of treatment might necessitate a horse's removal from the competition. "We won't say that no medication can

occur during a competition," he said, "but it is limited, and it has to be authorized" by the Veterinary Commission. "So if a horse has a cut, or it has a little problem in its eye, or a minor skin irritation, we would probably allow that to be treated; but if a horse has colic or a circulatory problem or something like that, we probably would say to the team veterinarian, 'If you want to treat this horse, you have to eliminate him. The drugs he's going to get could affect his performance; and if he's that sick, he shouldn't be competing.' "

Most nations send at least one veterinarian per discipline, so that the jumpers, eventers, and dressage horses each have their own veterinarian.

Preparing for an Olympic Games or any other international equestrian competition requires a massive cooperative effort by veterinarians from around the world, and the horses are better off because of it. According to Jeffcott, the training of officiating veterinarians — in duties from conducting horse inspections to the general surveillance of horses during all phases of competition — has improved in recent years. Jeffcott himself gave an FEI-sponsored course to event veterinarians during the September 1999 "test event" in Sydney, and fifty-three veterinarians from nine countries attended. [14]

"Some of these courses have received assistance from the Olympics, so there's a bit of an Olympic link there," Jeffcott said. "And the other thing that has assisted veterinarians is that there seems to be a better acceptance and emphasis on research that can be of help to equestrian competition. I think that's very healthy, from a veterinary point of view."

Most important, it's healthy for our horses.

67

Those Who Went Before Us

In the past 100 years, horseback riding and equestrian sports have changed immeasurably — arguably more than in the preceding 2,000-plus years that riding and horsemanship have been practiced and documented. The reason for the change can be summed up in one word: mechanization.

The horse is the original sport-utility vehicle. Until the invention of the automobile, he was a means of transportation and freight, a farming tool, an instrument of war and peace, a sporting

The U.S. Army equestrian team departing New York for the 1924 Paris Games. Opposite: Brigadier General Harry D. Chamberlin, the greatest horseman and trainer of the Army equestrian years.

partner, a source of entertainment, and a companion, to name a few. Horsemanship's roots were eminently practical: If you couldn't ride well and didn't know how to care for your horses, you risked the welfare of your business, your family, and perhaps even your country.

Much of the horse's practical usefulness evaporated with the advent of the automobile. As cars and trucks replaced horses as means of transportation and instruments of battle, the armed forces, among many other sectors, no longer needed their mounts or to teach their personnel to train and ride them. The U.S. Cavalry, renamed "Armor," was soon powered by tanks and Jeeps; even its magazine, *The Cavalry Journal*, was rechristened *Armor* to reflect the changing times.

Although horses continued to work for a living in some sectors of society, their primary *raison d'être* changed abruptly from business to pleasure. Many of the developments of the 20th Century, including the loss of open space to development and the rising costs of real estate, helped to transform horse ownership into a luxury. Horseback riding and horse showing became leisure pastimes of the well-to-do, and horse sports — particularly the English-riding disciplines — soon acquired an image of privileged pleasure, with price tags to match. This image has become so well-entrenched, through *Town & Country*-type advertisements and photographs of the late Jacqueline Kennedy Onassis and other celebrities on horseback, that it may be difficult for people born in the latter part of the past centu-

The U.S. Army Olympic team poses at the stadium entrance at the 1912 Stockholm Games.

ry to imagine that horse sports were ever regarded any other way.

Can you imagine, for instance, having to take riding lessons as part of your schoolwork? Having to study basic horsemanship, horse management, and veterinary care? It may sound like a horse-crazy schoolgirl's dream, but for almost 150 years it was just part of the demanding academic curriculum at the U.S. Military Academy at West Point, New York, America's service academy for Army officers and the alma mater of many legendary military leaders and statesmen, including Generals Robert E. Lee and George S. Patton and Presidents Ulysses S. Grant and Dwight D. Eisenhower.

The Army's Equestrian Tradition

One hundred years ago, the U.S. military was not nearly as large as it is today, and most of America's military officers were products of the nation's service academies. The majority of Army officers were USMA graduates, and, therefore, received the same undergraduate academic, military, and physical training. Learning to ride was an important part of a cadet's physical and professional training, according to U.S. Army Lieutenant Colonel Louis DiMarco, USMA class of 1981. DiMarco is a modern armored cavalryman and military historian who's currently on the faculty of the Army Command and Staff College at Fort Leavenworth, Kansas, not far from the site of the former U.S. Army Mounted Service School at Fort Riley, Kansas, so named from 1905 to 1920 and then known as the Cavalry School from 1921 to 1947.

"Riding was mandatory at West Point until the early 1950s," he explained. Cadets, many of whom had never been on a horse before they came to the Academy, learned to ride in the enormous four-story-high riding hall on the banks of the Hudson River — now converted to an academic building and known as Thayer Hall.

Having chosen a military occupational specialty in a "service selection" process before graduation from the service academies, newly minted officers learned basic soldiering skills and leadership and then went on to specialized schools for advanced education. One such school was the cavalry school, and it was at Fort Riley that cavalry officers immersed themselves in a year-long study of horsemanship, equitation, and horse management, as well as schooling in weapons and military tactics. The cavalry school operated horseshoeing and saddlery schools, and officers were expected to learn how to shoe their own mounts and to develop advanced knowledge of equine anatomy, disease, lameness, and treatment — as well as, of course, how to ride well.

"Soldiers (low-ranked enlisted cavalrymen) generally were beginner riders; they didn't need to ride well," said DiMarco. "Sergeants (mid-ranked enlisted men) were journeymen horse-men. They had a lot of other horse-management responsibilities: keeping the stables squared away, as well as taking care of the soldiers and horses and teaching basic military skills, including horsemanship. They were very capable horsemen. But the officers were expected to be experts, and they received formal equitation training throughout their careers."

About fifty-five officers a year attended the cavalry school at Fort Riley, "and the top twenty percent of each class — ten or twelve officers — was selected to stay for a second year for what was the premier American horsemanship program: the advanced course in equitation," DiMarco said. "They did nothing for that year but study horsemanship, and they pursued no military training that was not related to equitation. At the beginning of the year, each officer was assigned four horses: a green polo pony, a green jumper, a remount, and a seasoned old jumper. They had to train and care for those horses, the objective being to get the maximum performance out of those four very diverse types of horses. When an officer had successfully completed the advanced course, he was qualified to work in the remount service — buying horses for the Army and supervising the training of Army horses — and to become the chief of equitation in a three-thousand-horse-regiment cavalry unit."

To the cavalrymen, "The horse was a lifestyle," said DiMarco. "They rode more than one horse five days a week at work, for at least one to two hours a day. It was not uncommon for them to be in the saddle for eight or twelve hours a day for weeks at a time if they were in the field or doing some kind of mounted training. On weekends, they did foxhunts, horse shows, drag hunts, polo.

Their kids rode; their wives rode. Most cavalry officers owned one or two horses privately, in addition to their Army-provided troop horses."

The Army's selectivity and intensive training produced what at that time were the nation's finest horsemen — almost certainly the only American riders who were ever afforded the opportunity to study the European classical-riding tradition in the great equitation schools of France and Italy as part of their professional development. (It was during such educational opportunities that U.S. cavalry officers learned the revolutionary forward-seat jumping style as pioneered by Captain Federico Caprilli of the Italian Cavalry School.) Military and cavalry traditions were strong in most developed nations and so, just as in the United States, the best riders were those in uniform. So strong were the ties between top-flight horsemanship and the military that, when the International Olympic Committee voted to institute equestrian competition, the rules of Olympic horse sports permitted only military officers and military-owned or -affiliated mounts to compete.

The Army Goes to the Olympics

In January 1912, just six months before the inaugural equestrian competition to be held at that year's Olympic Games, the U.S. War Department published Special Order No. 20: that the cavalry should select and prepare a team of horses and riders for the competition. Fort Riley was the obvious choice for the training headquarters, and five Army officers — headed by Captain Guy V. Henry, Jr. — and eighteen horses began the intensive and daunting process of training for the Games. They faced more than a

few obstacles: a short time in which to prepare, a severe Midwestern winter, an allotment of just ninety minutes a day in which to school in the post's riding hall, and no let-up in the officers' regular military duties and obligations. [1]

Captain Henry and his colleagues knew the road to the Olympic Games would be an uphill climb. The Army had traditionally fielded a horse-show team that competed at the prestigious indoor competitions, such as the National Horse Show in New York and the Washington International Horse Show in Washington, D.C.; but those shows offered only show-jumping competition — no eventing or dressage, which, of course were to be part of the Olympic Games — and "the standards were not anything near comparable to Olympic standards," said DiMarco. With no formal dressage or eventing training or competitive experience, the cavalrymen had to draw on their European exposure and their "horse sense" to prepare for the most formidable challenge of their equestrian careers — and one that, they knew, the entire world would be watching.

The Olympic hopefuls faced another significant challenge: a lack of funding. "The Army Olympic teams themselves received no government funding," explained DiMarco. "So the chief of cavalry established a fund and had to raise money through private channels to finance the team's training and expenses and to pay to send the horses and riders to the Games.

"The cavalrymen would call on the senior civilian horsemen around the country to help organize and support fund-raising tours of the Army horse-show team. One person would donate stabling for the horses; another would donate rooms for the riders; a city would donate the use of its stadium for the show; the local equestrian organizations would provide the manpower to get the stadium ready. The Army guys would roll in and put on their exhibition, and most of the money raised would go toward financing the team's Olympic expenses."

Lieutenant Colonel Charles L. Scott described such a tour — a fund-raiser for the 1936 Army Olympic equestrian team — in an article published in the May-June 1935 issue of *The Cavalry Journal*: "General R. H. Tyndall, Commanding 18th Division, National Guard, had reported to General {Guy V.} Henry that he thought Indianapolis and surrounding cities would welcome the opportunity to cooperate with the Chief of Cavalry." The organizers, spearheaded by 1936 Olympic-team trainer Captain William B. Bradford, arranged for a ten-exhibition tour in five cities: Detroit, Cleveland, Louisville, Indianapolis, and Cincinnati.

Accompanied by an announcer who explained the fine points of equestrian competition to the audience, five cavalry officers and four dressage horses, eight event horses, and six jumpers traveled from city to city, showing their stuff. The exhibition program consisted of an opening ceremony, with music provided by a local band; a parade of all horses and riders; a "school ride" demonstrating the three gaits and basic flatwork; longeing over fences; an Olympic-level dressage exhibition; "All-Around Equestrian Championship jumping"; a dressage exhibition by a Field Artillery School dressage horse; "Prix des Nations jumping"; and a "farewell salute" and closing ceremony. (In his official report on the dressage team's performance at the 1936 Olympics, Major Hiram Tuttle criticized the exhibitions as a waste of valuable training time and a disruption to the schooling routine.)

With at most two days between appearances and a tight travel schedule, the exhibition horses and riders were understandably fatigued at the conclusion of the two-week tour. Bradford took a pragmatic view of the stresses, telling writer Scott, "Of course, they are all tired; they are probably going to get a lot more tired during the 1936

Key riders on the 1948 U.S. equestrian team (from left): Frank Henry, Jonathan Burton, Bob Borg, Earl "Tommy" Thomson, and F. F. Wing.

Olympic Equestrian Events. We have called this tour a 'tryout' as well as an exhibition, and I welcome this opportunity to see if any horse or rider will fall down because of fatigue."

In an editorial aside that foreshadowed an important development in American horse sports, Scott wrote of the tour: "We all know that spectacular jumping is highly popular, but it was both surprising and highly pleasing to see...how readily the average spectator learned the really fine points of dressage riding and how strongly they showed their appreciation of this most advanced form of equitation art. The passage, the piaffer, the pirouette, and the change of leads never failed to bring forth a thunder of applause at all the exhibitions...I predict a strong and insistent demand for this form of equitation work throughout this country; any large horse show that omits it in the future will indeed be shortsighted." [2]

The Army Years: Olympic Highlights

The military dominated the Olympic equestrian events of the first half of the 20th Century, in terms of both its competitors and its overshadowing events. Two world wars forced the cancellation of the 1916, 1940, and 1944 Olympic Games; and Adolf Hitler used the 1936 Berlin Games as a propaganda tool for Germany's Nazi regime. But the Olympic Games and the ideals for which they stand survived the decades of turmoil and tragedy, and the U.S. Army equestrian teams made history as they rose above inexperience, limited funds, questionable judging, and other obstacles to claim their share of medals and prove that American horsemanship and military power were worthy of respect on a world stage.

Before equestrian sports were officially added to the Olympic competitive roster, however, they were included in the Games as exhibition events. In his memoirs, *A Brief Narrative of the Life of Guy V. Henry, Jr.,* [3] the former Army equestrian-team captain recounts some key events leading up to the debut of equestrian competition in the modern Olympic Games as well as his own experiences.

A great deal of interest in horsemanship was being aroused throughout the military service in about 1910, especially due to the instruction in the MSS (Mounted Service School) and at West Point...In about 1905 the New York horseshow had started to invite foreign military teams to come to the show to participate in jumping contests. The U.S. Army had participated as individuals with very unsatisfactory results. Neither our horses nor riders could compare with the foreign teams. All of this had stirred up the rich horsemen of the country, who collected a fund of somewhere in the vicinity of $20,000 for the purchase of horses to mount U.S. officers on.

That $20,000 soon was spent, as "{Chief of Staff} General {Leonard} Wood accepted for the United States an invitation for a United States Army team to participate in the International Military Contests which were to be held in the Olympia in London in 1911 during the gala festivities connected with the coronation of King George V." The Army purchasing group bought "a number of spectacular, crazy jumpers" in Virginia — reputed to be the best source of jumpers, but whose training consisted of little more than "putting a little negro on the horse and an individual with a good blacksnake whip behind the horse to drive the animal over the jumps" — also "a horse named Chiswell, purchased in Long Island, whom I rode for years and who became an internationally known horse especially in 'Charger Classes' and 'Military Classes' in which the obstacles were not to exceed four feet in height."

The purchase of the "spectacular, crazy jumpers" and the talented Chiswell completed, Henry had his work cut out for him.

Stockholm 1912

Following a decent but unplaced exhibition at the Olympia, at which Henry and Chiswell took the sole ribbon of the U.S. competitors, Henry was given the task of organizing and training the U.S. team for the 1912 Olympics. ("All this work, of course, I had to do in addition to my duty as Senior Instructor of the MSS," he wrote matter-of-factly.) From the pool of available talent, Henry selected his three-member Olympic teams. The members of those teams included First Lieutenant Benjamin Lear, Jr.; First Lieutenant John C. Montgomery; First Lieutenant Ephraim F. Graham; First Lieutenant A. L. P. Sands; and Second Lieutenant John G. Quekemeyer; the cavalry-owned mounts Bill Stone, Chiswell, Connie, Deceive, Fencing Girl, Mabel Anderson, Norma S., Nymph, Poppy, Prim, Quandry, Roustabout, Seroptic, Sin Glen, Stratta, and Timber Lost; and three privately owned horses: Henry's Bazan, Montgomery's

The U.S. Army equestrian team arrives for the 1936 Berlin Games.

Lady Foxhall, and a Lieutenant Watson's Chesapeake. [4]

In his 1931 *Cavalry Journal* article, "Army Equestrian Teams in Past Olympic Games," Major William M. Grimes wrote that Olympic hopefuls squeezed in their training sessions for the Games around their regular military duties. "A great deal of the training of this first Olympic team took place at four in the morning," he wrote. "Those readers who have spent a winter in Kansas will know what that means!"

In June 1912, a short six months after their training commenced, the entire U.S. Olympic contingent — all the athletes as well as the equestrians and their mounts — embarked on the S.S. *Finland* in New York for the fifteen-day journey to Stockholm, Sweden. They arrived on June 30 after a monotonous and somewhat arduous journey, and the American horses were stabled with a Swedish artillery regiment. Thirteen

days later, the Games began.

According to Henry's memoirs, "The Olympic games were beautifully run." Henry and Montgomery competed in all three equestrian disciplines — the latter aboard the remarkable Thoroughbred Deceive, the only American horse to participate in all three events.

Colonel Ben Lear (a captain at the time of the 1912 Games), who competed in the three-day event and the jumping events, recorded some

of his Olympic experiences for the 1912 edition of the publication *Rasp*:

The cross-country course, which started after some twenty odd miles of the long distance ride had been ridden, was a reasonably hard test for a good military horse. There were about twenty obstacles in all, probably half of which were small ditches. The first obstacle was a three and one-half foot fence with about a five foot ditch on the near side; it was at the foot of a slight decline and approached rather suddenly. Many penalties were given at this jump...Among the other serious obstacles were three large ditches and an 'in-and-out' over Swedish fences...The bottom of one of the ditches was filled with plank, which frightened many horses and caused quite a number of refusals.

The next morning we found our horses pretty stiff and sore in both legs and feet. Connie was in the poorest condition of any of our horses, while Deceive was barely affected. Chiswell and Poppy showed the hard work, but not so badly as Connie. Fortunately this was a day of rest. The horses were led at a walk for half an hour in the morning and afternoon, and there was a continuation of the massage, bandage and water treatment. The animals were also re-shod, as most of the shoes had been worn almost as thin as paper by the hard macadam roads.

The horses of other countries also

The gold-medal-winning Swedish show-jumping team on parade at the 1912 Stockholm Games.

suffered from the heat and the excessively hard roads. A French horse was nearly dead when it reached the stables at the end of the first day's work. [5]

Henry described his own competitive efforts in the steeplechase phase of the "Military" in those Olympics:

> One of the obstacles was a pretty big bank...I knew Chiswell could not jump it and didn't even want to try. But in that period of my riding career, it was very seldom that I could not force a horse to at least make an effort to do what I wished...I determined that Chiswell was at least going to make an effort to jump this bank. As he took off, my heart was in my mouth, because I knew he could not clear it. However, about like a cat he jumped on its narrow top and down on the other side...When we finished that phase, his eyes were bloodshot and his sides were cut up, but at least we were over. As he was a good, strong horse, he recovered quickly.

Foreshadowing criticisms of nationalism in judging that were to plague international dressage competition for decades to come, Henry wrote of the "training" phase of the "Military" event,

> In the Training Phase we did far better than the German team, but much to our surprise, when the final results were published, the German team was placed second and we were placed third. The nations that followed the French school of equitation such as France, Italy, Spain, and some others, were up in arms over it.

> Those that followed the German school were very satisfied. The majority of the judges represented the German school...It would have been a terrible slap at Germany for a novice team, as was the United State's, {sic} to have come to the Olympics for the first time and to have been placed ahead of the veteran German team in what was considered to be the main equestrian event. This is the only explanation which can be given for why Germany was placed second and ourselves, third.

The European tradition of dressage domination began early, as the Americans discovered in Stockholm. Wrote Lear, "Chiswell put up a remarkable performance, and his rider was heartily complimented by many present upon the work done. However, the horse as an animal did not rank with the magnificent animals entered in this competition by Germany and Sweden, the result being the Swedes won the first three places, Germany the next, Sweden two more and America thirteenth out of twenty-one entering." [6]

The inaugural U.S. Army Olympic equestrian team finished the 1912 Games with impressive results — even more so when one considers the fact that the jumping team consisted of just three members to most other nations' four, meaning that there was no "drop score." Under Henry's leadership, the Americans took home a bronze medal in the three-day event and finished fourth in the *Prix des Nations* (Nations' Cup — the show-jumping competition) — not bad for a team's second-ever experience with international competition.

Antwerp 1920

World War I forced the cancellation of the 1916 Olympic Games, and just eight nations entered the equestrian competitions at Antwerp, Belgium. The U.S. team, managed by Colonel Walter C. Short and captained by Major B. T. Merchant, sailed for Europe in June 1920 and arrived in Antwerp in early July. They then shipped the horses to the Army's German headquarters in Coblenz, where they trained and competed in horse shows in the German cities of Cologne, Bonn, Wiesbaden, and Coblenz to prepare themselves for the Games, which did not commence until September.

The Army riders and horses made a respectable showing in Antwerp, but they were not able to repeat the success of the Stockholm Games. The three-day event team placed fourth; Captain Harry D. Chamberlin, who went on to become one of the most influential horsemen of his era, was sixth individually. The jumping team placed sixth, and the dressage team finished fourteenth.

Major Merchant recorded some of the significant events of the three-day competition:

The 1912 dressage individual gold medalist, Count Carl Bonde of Sweden, on Emperor.

Show-jumping teams parade in the Olympic stadium at the 1920 Antwerp Games.

First phase — fifty kilometers in three and one-half hours, five of which were across country over natural obstacles at rate of fifteen miles per hour. Going very heavy due to rains, obstacles, twenty-four in number, some of them very difficult, particularly a brook with treacherous landing where Chamberlin fell.

...Second phase — twenty kilometers in one hour over roads and bridle paths, the latter extremely heavy going due to rains. The measuring of this twenty kilometers was doubtless done with a very long tape as it was at least three kilometers over the distance. Our men were travelling on a time table and got so far behind between the fourth and fifth control that all of them galloped as fast as possible for the last fifteen minutes trying to get in within the hour. None finished on time.

Third phase — jumping over the course in the stadium. This was an entirely new course to us, and no one knew, at least we could not find out, just what the jumps were to be until the preceding day when we were allowed to 'look' at them.

The course was not the Olympic course we had expected at all, in fact there were but few of the jumps that had any resemblance to the Olympic course that we had been training on. Notwithstanding this our three horses did fairly well, that is,

fairly well considering the horses and {Major John} Barry's broken hand {sustained during the cross-country}…All three of our horses showed the lack of recuperative power possessed by better bred animals. [7]

Paris 1924

The 1920s were proving to be a less-than-stellar decade for the Army Olympic teams. Major Sloan Doak put in the best American performance of the Paris Games, winning a bronze medal aboard Pathfinder in the three-day event. Unfortunately, both the three-day and the jumping teams were eliminated because an insufficient number of horses finished the competitions. The other two event horses, Major John Barry's Miss America and Captain Vernon Padgett's Brown Boy, went lame during the speed-and-endurance; and Padgett's Little Canada and Lieutenant Frederic Bontecou's Bally McShane refused the bank jump in the *Prix des Nations* competition. The Army did not field a dressage team for the Paris Games.

Of the jumping competition, Colonel H. N. Cootes, then military attaché to Austria and Czechoslovakia, wrote: "...{A} thick layer of sand covered the entire course which was from fet-lock to over ankle deep in most places. Therefore, the majority of horses after they made a good performance over the first five or six jumps became so tired that they repeatedly fell or knocked down fences over the remaining jumps." [8]

A group photo (below) from the 1928 Games showing three-time Olympic competitors, including Major Sloan Doak (in uniform). Right: Major John A. Barry on Raven in 1920.

Amsterdam 1928

Walter Short, by that time a brigadier general, again managed the Army team; and Major Sloan Doak, a veteran of the 1920 and the 1924 teams, was named team captain. Like his predecessors, Doak was handicapped by an extremely short preparation time — the orders to prepare a team came eight months before the Games, and the team did not assemble and begin training until just three months before the team sailed for the Netherlands — and the team's lack of training time showed in the results. Major Harry Chamberlin and Nigra produced the best finish in the jumping competition, finishing seventeenth; Doak achieved an identical placing aboard Misty Morn in the three-day event. The jumping team placed ninth, and the three-day team was eliminated because Major Charles George and Ozella failed to negotiate one cross-country obstacle — a particularly disappointing turn of events, as the U.S. team had otherwise been in the lead going into the stadium-jumping phase.

As in Paris, the Army did not field a dressage team.

One very good thing did come out of the team's experiences in Amsterdam: a change in the ways the Army selected, trained, and fielded Olympic teams. At Doak's suggestion — prompted by his observations of the European teams' methods — the cavalry began planning for the 1932 Olympics immediately after the conclusion of the Amsterdam Games, selected and began training its team two years before the competition, chose as team director an individual who would not also be competing, and began allowing riders and horses to specialize in one of the three equestrian disciplines. Doak's recommendations led to the Army teams' becoming more successful in Olympic competition than ever before. [9]

Los Angeles 1932

The Los Angeles Olympics were the first Games ever to be held on American soil, and U.S. representatives of all the Olympic sports naturally were anxious to do well and to make the Games a successful national showcase. The combination of Doak's procedural recommendations and a few other key changes on the part of the cavalry resulted in a significantly improved showing by the American equestrians.

In the four years before Los Angeles, the Army improved its horse-breeding program to produce more successful equine athletes, largely by introducing more Thoroughbred blood. (By the 1936 Games, most American Olympic horses were Army-breds — a far cry from the 1920s and the early 1930s, when most of the Olympic mounts were purchased from outside sources or were privately owned by cavalry officers.)

The cavalry school's advanced course in equitation also made its effects felt by the time of the 1932 Games: Enough officers had completed the course that the graduates constituted a sort of elite pool of horsemen from which the Olympic teams could be chosen. Finally, the Army Olympic team's success was due in no small part to the appointment of Major General Guy Henry, the 1912 Games team captain, as chief of cavalry.

Unfortunately, the 1932 Games took place during the height of the Great Depression. As a result, markedly fewer nations sent teams to the beautiful Riviera Country Club near Los Angeles: Only Sweden and the U.S. fielded teams in all three equestrian disciplines; Mexico sent riders in each event but fielded a complete team only for the *Prix des Nations*; France sent only a dressage team; the Netherlands, only a three-day team; Japan, three-day and *Prix des Nations* teams. The sparse entries led to the inevitable opining that certain teams, including the Americans, placed higher than they would have if certain other countries had been represented. At the same time, some American supporters believed that nationalistic judging kept the U.S. riders from placing as highly as they should have.

Writing in the January-February 1933 issue of *The Cavalry Journal*, U.S. Army Captain Lara P. Good (Ret.) sharply criticized what he believed to have been biased judging at the 1932 Games: "There were three judges in the dressage event: Lt. Colonel Sloan Doak of the United States, Count Bonde, equerry to the King of Sweden, and General Lafont of France, Commandant of Saumur. Mexico was the only competitor that did not have a representation on the jury which made the awards, and as one spectator laughingly remarked, 'Maybe that was why the Mexican competitor was rated last.' " [10]

Good especially disdained the dressage test of the eighth-placed dressage competitor, Lieutenant Gustaf Boltenstern of Sweden and his German-bred gelding, Ingo. His remarks echo the "German versus French schools" dressage-training debate that continues to this day: "Contrary to the French School of the use of the aids without a perceptible effort on the part of the rider, which method was followed by both the French and the American teams...one did not need to be an experienced horseman to note when and how Lieut. Boltenstern applied the aids — he was following his German schoolmasters." [11]

Controversies aside, the Army teams did their country proud in Los Angeles. Major Harry Chamberlin and Show Girl won the silver medal in the jumping competition, with teammate Captain William Bradford and Joe Aleshire placing fourth. (Their other teammate, Lieutenant John "Gyp" Wofford, who went on to become the first president of the U.S. Equestrian Team, fell three times from his mount, Babe Wartham, and was eliminated.) In the dressage competition — and the first time since the 1920 Olympics that the Army had fielded a dressage team — the largely self-taught Captain Hiram Tuttle and his horse Olympic won the individual bronze medal, with Captain Isaac Kitts and American Lady placing sixth and Captain Alvin Moore and Water Pat finishing eighth. But the real accolades went to the three-day event team, which won the gold medal — the first in U.S. Olympic equestrian history. Lieutenant Earl "Tommy" Thomson and the remarkable Jenny Camp also took home the individual silver medal, while teammates Chamberlin and the ex-racehorse Pleasant Smiles were fourth and Captain Edwin Argo and Honolulu Tomboy finished eighth.

Opposite, top: The 1932 U.S. bronze-medal dressage team: Hiram Tuttle on Olympic, Isaac Kitts on American Lady, and Alvin Moore on Water Pat. Bottom: the 1932 U.S. gold medal team in three-day eventing: Harry Chamberlin on Pleasant Smiles, Edwin Argo on Honolulu Tomboy, and Earl "Tommy" Thomson on Jenny Camp.

Berlin 1936

In all of modern Olympic Games history, the so-called "Nazi Olympics" stand out as one of two that were marred by political unrest. (The other was in Munich in 1972, when many of the Israeli athletes died at the hands of terrorists.) Perhaps the most enduring memory of the Berlin Games was the triumph of the African-American track-and-field athlete Jesse Owens, whose four gold medals became a symbol of triumph over Nazi-ism and racism.

All Olympic Games showcase their host cities, but the organizers of the Berlin Games had more on their minds than simple patriotism and commercialism. As Richard D. Mandell related in his book, *The Nazi Olympics*, "Berlin itself had been cleaned and dressed for a whole series of festivals that had the common intention of convincing the Germans and their foreign guests that the new Germany was, as it claimed to be, a savior and a creator of culture. The four million Berliners…had constant instruction from above that they had been entrusted with an obligation to demonstrate the excellence of German National Socialism to the whole world." [12] The city nearly turned itself inside out in its efforts to make the Olympic experience the friendliest and finest ever for visitors, VIPs, and athletes. The Olympic venues, businesses, private homes, thoroughfares, even locomotives — all, it seemed, were decorated with huge white flags, some emblazoned with the colorful Olympic rings, others with the black Nazi swastika.

It was at the Berlin Games that athletic superi-

The 1936 U.S. dressage team entering the Olympic stadium in Berlin.

89

ority acquired racial overtones. Adolf Hitler and his regime wanted badly to prove to the world that the German athletes — the finest of the so-called Aryan race — were indeed the dominant

Captain Carl A. "Rags" Raguse and Trailolka, parting company at the water in 1936.

breed. The Germans did enjoy the greatest success in Berlin — thanks in part to nationalistic judging, some allege — and Hitler "became convinced that his athletes' triumphs were omens, portents whose significance was clear...The ath-

letes were symbolically to embody German physical supremacy." [13]

The equestrian events in Berlin, like all the other sports, were no less politically tinged. The most controversial element of the equestrian competition was the fourth cross-country obstacle, the water jump. Wrote Mandell, "Here there were ghastly spills that ended with wet flailing, thrashing in the mud, and frantic attempts of the furious riders and terrified horses to regain footing." [14]

The jump at first glance did not appear exceptionally difficult: a three-foot post-and-rail fence into what appeared to be about a three-feet-deep pond, then a jump out on the far side of the pond. The first American rider on course, Captain Carl A. "Rags" Raguse aboard the little mare Trailolka, learned the hard way that the obstacle was far more treacherous than it appeared: The water was deeper than it looked, and the bottom of the pond was soft and muddy. Trailolka fell and Raguse went off, but he was able to remount and continue. The next U.S. competitor, Captain John Willems, fared much worse: His mount, Slippery Slim, broke his right foreleg in the fall and had to be destroyed at the scene. Only Captain "Tommy" Thomson, who was lucky enough to go late in the order and so had gotten word not to jump into the part of the water that was causing the problems, made it through the water safely aboard the great Jenny Camp.

To make matters worse, "{R}umors abounded that the German team was well aware of the actual conditions of the pond and intentionally withheld the information from the other teams," wrote Louis DiMarco in "The Army Equestrian Olympic Team: Part 2." [15] "The political atmosphere, the controversy over jump number four, and other questionable judgments by the German officials caused a storm of protest from all eighteen teams. Reinforcing the chilled atmosphere among the equestrian community was {the fact} that, for the first and only time in Olympic history, one country, the host country Germany, captured all six equestrian gold medals."

The U.S. jumping team of Captain Raguse on

The 1936 U.S. equestrian Olympic team.
Top: Willems, Moore, Raguse; center: Isaacson, Curtis, Thomson, Matheson; bottom: Jadwin, Bradford, Tuttle, Kitts, Babcock.

Dakota, Major William Bradford on Don, and Captain Cornelius Jadwin on Ugly could finish no better than fourth. With just three members, the three-day team was eliminated after Slippery Slim broke his leg and did not finish. (Throughout most of the Army-team years, IOC rules specified that equestrian teams must consist of just three riders; the fourth rider was a reserve rider only and competed only if another team member had to drop out before the competition began. The lack of a fourth team member meant that there was no "drop score" and also that one rider's failure to finish caused the team to be eliminated. In some Olympic Games, too few three-man teams finished for medals to be awarded, as happened in the 1932 show-jumping competition.)

The dressage team of Captain C. Stanton Babcock on Olympic, Captain Isaac Kitts on American Lady, and Major Hiram Tuttle on Si Murray, placed ninth. In his official post-Olympic report to Major General Guy Henry, Tuttle wrote

that he had been advised by the German team coach that to win in dressage required European-bred horses, European competition experience, and political clout in the host country; and that, having none of these, the Americans likely

The team-dressage awards ceremony at the 1948 Olympics. The U.S. dressage team later was elevated to silver-medal status upon the disqualification of the Swedish team.

wouldn't fare well. The German coach was exactly right, Tuttle concluded in his report.

London 1948

The Olympic Games of 1940 and 1944 fell victim to World War II. The war years also proved to be a turning point in the fates of the cavalry and the U.S. Army Olympic equestrian teams. The Army formed its Armor Force and graduated its final advanced-equitation class in 1940, and soon it became apparent to the cavalrymen that the horse's military days were numbered.

Even as the cavalry school and Fort Riley exchanged its horses for tanks, its equestrian leaders were charged with fielding for the 1948 Olympics what they knew would be the last-ever Army equestrian team. Veteran horsemen and competitors by this time, the team members went on to achieve the Army team's greatest success in London.

Three of the most experienced horsemen in Army history helped prepare the team for the London Games: Olympic veteran Colonel Tommy Thomson, the team captain; Brigadier General John Tupper Cole, chief trainer; and the legendary General Guy V. Henry, Jr. (Ret.), *chef d'équipe.*

By the time of the London Olympics, most of the Army team's riders and its horses were veterans as well, having originally been prepped for 1940. Despite the horses' advancing age, the teams — the dressage and three-day-eventing teams in particular — made an exceptionally strong showing. (The U.S. teams had had access to captured German horses, but after a training period in Germany they opted to stick with their trusted Army remounts.) The dressage team of Lieutenant Robert Borg and Klingsor (who were

Earl "Tommy" Thomson preparing for the 1948 Olympics on Rattler.

fourth individually), Colonel Thomson and Pancraft, and Lieutenant Colonel Frank Henry and Reno Overdo captured the team silver medal — the highest team placing in U.S. Olympic dressage history. (Some of the silver sheen was dulled by the fact that the U.S. team actually earned the bronze medal. Eight months after the Games, they were awarded the silver after the gold-medal-winning Swedish team was disqualified because one rider was an enlisted man, not an officer as the rules required.) And the eventing team took home its second team gold medal, thanks to the efforts of individual silver medalists

Frank Henry and Swing Low, fourth-placed Lieutenant Colonel Charles Anderson and Reno Palisades, and Thomson and Reno Rhythm. Reno Rhythm was actually Thomson's second-string mount; the team captain generously lent his best horse, Reno Palisades, to Anderson after that officer's mount went lame before the competition. Colonel Andrew Frierson and Rascal were eliminated, knocking the jumping team out of contention; but Colonel Franklin F. "Fuddy" Wing

and Democrat placed fourth individually, with Captain John Russell and Air Mail finishing twenty-first. [16]

The U.S. Army's Fab Four

Many cavalry officers represented the United States in Olympic equestrian competition, some of whom took part in two or even all three disciplines in one Olympic competition with their game mounts. Of all the Army Olympic-team members, though, four arguably stand out as the most influential. These talented and dedicated servicemen, all of whom put their military duties before their riding, left their stamp on American riding and made major contributions to equestrian sport worldwide.

Guy V. Henry, Jr.: Leading the Way

Arguably the most influential cavalryman and horseman of the early 20th Century was U.S. Army Major General Guy Vernor Henry, Jr., who competed in all three Olympic disciplines aboard Army-owned cavalry mounts. He helped his U.S. teammates secure a team bronze medal in the "Military" in the 1912 Stockholm Games and also to place a respectable fourth in the show-jumping event. He went on to numerous other equestrian-related accomplishments, including serving as director of equitation at the U.S. Military Academy at West Point from 1916 to 1918; chief of the U.S. Cavalry from 1930 to 1934; commandant of the U.S. Cavalry School at Fort Riley, Kansas, from 1935 until his retirement

Captain Guy V. Henry, Jr., a member of the 1912 bronze-medal-winning "Military" team (and pictured here with Olympic mount Chiswell), was a consummate horseman.

95

in 1939; an international-level horse-show judge (he officiated at the 1932 and 1936 Olympic Games and for many years at New York's National Horse Show); a director of the U.S. Equestrian Team, the American Horse Shows Association, and New York's National Horse Show Association; first American president of the FEI, from 1931 to 1935; director of equestrian events for the 1932 Los Angeles Games; *chef d'équipe* for the 1936 and 1948 U.S. Olympic equestrian teams; and chairman of the Olympic Equestrian Committee from 1930 to 1960, with occasional duties as the OEC's representative to the U.S. Olympic Committee.

Henry's confidence in his knowledge of horses and horsemanship comes through in his memoirs, *A Brief Narrative of the Life of Guy V. Henry, Jr.*, which he dictated to a military stenographer at the Pentagon, beginning in December 1944. Of his equestrian endeavors, he wrote:

> {I}n August 1902, {I} was sent to Ft. Riley, Kansas, as Squadron Adjutant, Adjutant of the Cavalry Post, and member of the Cavalry Board...I felt that the general horsemanship and horsemastership of our mounted service was considerably below the standard it should be and did not hesitate to say so. Finally this talk had an effect on the Commanding Officer who asked the War Department that it send a then noted horseman of the Army, Captain Walter C. Short, to Ft. Riley. Captain Short...established a horseshoer school and a farrier school for enlisted men. At this point almost all treatment of horses was done within the troop instead of in a veterinarian hospital...I talked so

much on the subject that some others volunteered and finally it was made compulsory for all of the lieutenants of the cavalry and field artillery on the post. [17]

In 1905, Henry and some other cavalry officers "succeeded in getting adopted for the Cavalry, the double bridle" to replace "a very severe single curb bit known as the Shoemaker bit" that led to the Cavalry's being "filled with broken-jawed runaway horses." He also "succeeded in getting the Field Artillery to do away with this severe bit on its teams and replace it by {sic} the straight snaffle bit." [18]

A stint at the famed French Cavalry School at Saumur influenced Henry's opinions on training methods, and he had to draw on his experiences in 1907 when he reported to Fort Riley to become senior instructor of equitation at the Mounted Service School and, as such, to develop a training system for U.S. cavalry officers.

> I had...previously received instructions under a Mr. Edward Anderson of Cincinnati ...{who} was a follower of the great French master of equitation, Bouchet {sic} {Baucher}. I attempted to combine the best that we had in the United States with that of the French cavalry school, the German cavalry school, and that of Bouchet. It leaned, however, to the French system, with the exception of the use of the lower leg, where I followed Bouchet...A progressive system for developing both the horse and the rider was instituted. Instead of the western methods of breaking a horse, the system of gentling the young horse by use of the cavvesson {sic} and longe and then grad-

The 1948 U.S. equestrian Olympic team. Guy V Henry, Jr. (in civilian attire) was chef d'équipe.

ually teaching him to bear the weight of the saddle and rider was instituted, and the student officers were taught the proper use of the aids. [19]

Henry's equestrian accomplishments are so numerous and wide-ranging that one may find it difficult to believe that he found time for still other accomplishments. But Henry, like the other cavalrymen of his day, was an Army officer before all else and, as such, enjoyed a long and distinguished military career with which non-military-history buffs may not be acquainted. Henry's father, Guy V. Henry, Sr., was a Medal-of-Honor-decorated Civil War brevet major general. Guy Jr. was born on January 28, 1875, in a log-

and-canvas hut at Fort Robinson, Nebraska, and was immersed in horsemanship as well as military and cavalry life from an early age. The youngster had his own blue troop's uniform and took part in mounted drills with his father's command, the 10th Cavalry's famed "Buffalo Soldiers." He graduated from West Point in 1894 and, five years later, earned the Silver Star during the Spanish-American War. He later became the first American officer to attend the French Cavalry School at Saumur.

Henry and his fellow cavalrymen loved horses

and horsemanship, to be sure, but their first allegiance was to their country — even if that allegiance meant contributing to the Cavalry's eventual mechanization. The January-February 1965 issue of *Armor* magazine contains "A Salute to a Distinguished Cavalryman: An Accolade to Major General Guy V. Henry, United States Army, Retired, on His 90th Birthday, January 28, 1965," which includes quotes from Henry's 1933 annual report to the Secretary of War: "The time has...arrived when the Cavalry arm must either replace or assist the horse as a means of transportation or else pass into the limbo of discarded military formations."

Henry himself became commander of the Seventh Cavalry Brigade (Mechanized) at Fort Knox, Kentucky, in 1934. He was twice recalled to

Harry D. Chamberlin (above) was a member of the 1932 gold-medal-winning three-day-event team.
Left: Earl "Tommy" Thomson relaxes aboard his legendary cavalry mount, Jenny Camp.

active duty, in 1941 and in 1947, and earned two Distinguished Service Medals for his "contributions to US-Mexican and US-Canadian defense." [20] In his "Salute" in *Armor* magazine, General of the Armies John J. Pershing is quoted as calling Henry "a splendid Commandant"; and General of the Army Douglas MacArthur said Henry was "one of the best officers in the Service." [21]

In typical organized, squared-away military fashion, Henry concluded his memoirs with an itemized summary of what he considered to be the most significant events of his life. Item #4 reads: "In the 1900s, 1910s and 1920s, I completely revamped the horsemanship of the United States Army and, incidentally, largely that of the civilian community." [22]

Confident words from a great military leader and a great contributor to equestrian sport.

Harry D. Chamberlin: A Trainer's Trainer

If Guy Henry, Jr. was at the forefront of the establishment of horse sports and modern equestrian competition, then his protégé, Brigadier General Harry D. Chamberlin, was the greatest horseman and trainer of the Army equestrian years. Although Chamberlin enjoyed his share of Olympic success, captaining the gold-medal-winning 1932 three-day team and garnering the individual silver in show jumping at those same Games, he is best remembered for his contributions to horsemanship — contributions that started in the cavalry but that reached well into the civilian equestrian world and live on through his writings.

A member of the West Point class of 1910, Chamberlin excelled as an all-around athlete, competing in track, boxing, and football in addi-

tion to his equestrian activities. His name was added to the lore of the famed Army-Navy football rivalry when, in the 1908 game in Philadelphia, the starting halfback took possession of the ball after a fumbled punt and made a thirty-three-yard run, setting up teammate Bill Dean's game-winning touchdown. [23]

Chamberlin met and served under then-Lieutenant Colonel Guy V. Henry while on the faculty at West Point. Later, during World War I, Chamberlin saw front-line infantry duty with the 161st Brigade in France. During occupation duty after the war, he rode in his first international competition at the 1919 Inter-Allied Games in Paris, which were held in lieu of the cancelled 1916 Olympic Games. Later that same year, he returned stateside and was assigned to the Horsemanship Department at Fort Riley.

Chamberlin rode on the 1920 Olympic team, and after the Games the Army sent him to Europe for two years: one year apiece at the French Cavalry School at Saumur and at the Italian Cavalry School at Tor di Quinto. It was in Italy that he learned the revolutionary forward-seat style of riding, and he would be the one to teach it to his fellow cavalry officers. The spread of knowledge was delayed for a few years, however. "In typical Army fashion, when Chamberlin came back to the States we sent him to Fort Bliss, Texas, where he played polo for a couple of years," DiMarco said dryly. (An outstanding polo player, Chamberlin coached the Army's champion twelve-goal polo team, captained the twenty-goal-winning championship team, and met Lieutenant Earl "Tommy" Thomson, who would go on to become one of his most successful students of horsemanship.) "The Army tried to avoid allowing guys to spend all their time riding horses. You could spend three or four years at the most at Fort Riley, and then you had to go off and work with troops. So it wasn't until 1927 that Chamberlin was allowed to go back to training horses. His task was to help train the 1928 Olympic team, and that's where his equestrian influence really began."

Chamberlin went on to become the chief of horsemanship at the cavalry school and also served as the school's deputy commander. Most important, though, he taught and trained virtually all of his era's best horsemen.

"He was a student and a trainer and a teacher as much as he was a rider," said DiMarco. By all accounts the most gifted rider and horseman of his day, Chamberlin imparted his knowledge as well as the fruits of his European equestrian education on the Army riders. His philosophies and methods live on in several writings, the best-known of which are the books *Riding and Schooling Horses* (1934) and *Training Hunters, Jumpers and Hacks* (1937). He also wrote the cavalry school's *Manual of Horsemanship*, published in 1927.

A sudden illness forced Chamberlin to return to the States from a command in the Pacific Theater. He died soon thereafter, on September 29, 1944, at the relatively young age of fifty-seven. It seems fitting that he is buried at the Presidio in California, a former cavalry post and his last command.

Earl "Tommy" Thomson: Olympic Success

Earl "Tommy" Thomson achieved the greatest Olympic competitive record of any Army horseman. His Olympic career spanned sixteen years,

during which time he earned a total of five medals: a three-day team gold and an individual silver aboard the legendary cavalry mount Jenny Camp in 1932; a second three-day individual silver in 1936, also with Jenny Camp; and a dressage team silver aboard Pancraft and a three-day team gold aboard Reno Rhythm in 1948. He organized and managed the '48 team, judged at the 1952 Games in Helsinki, and was *chef d'équipe* of the three-day-event team in Rome in 1960.

Like his Olympic teammates, Thomson was a West Point alumnus. He graduated in 1922 and went on to a distinguished military career, earning the Silver Star during World War II as chief of staff of the famed 10th Mountain Division in Italy. After his retirement in 1954 at the rank of colonel, he taught college mathematics and pursued graduate studies before his death in 1971 at the age of seventy. [24]

Harry Chamberlin, who was Thomson's trainer and primary equestrian influence, recognized the potential of the Thomson-Jenny Camp partnership and paired the two for the duration of the mare's career. DiMarco emphasized that Thomson, like all the other subordinate officers at Fort Riley, had no say over his choice of mount. "The riding captain was not only the captain of the team; he was the commanding officer," he explained. "The captain matched up riders and horses, and that was a military order. Tommy Thomson rode Jenny Camp, but that was more a function of the fact that, due to his success, his superiors were not inclined to break up the team."

Hiram Tuttle: Ahead of His Time

The Army's lone dressage enthusiast didn't fit

the cavalry mold. Older than his Olympic team-mates, fated never to rise to the top of the officer corps, Captain Hiram Tuttle developed a passion for dressage when almost no one in the United States had ever heard the word. Despite the lack of qualified dressage instructors, he somehow

vidual bronze medal aboard his horse, appropriately named Olympic, in the highest-ever individual placing in American Olympic dressage history.

"Tuttle did so much with so little and was so little appreciated," said DiMarco. "He was the

managed to teach himself the fine points of classical horsemanship and went on to become this country's foremost dressage rider. He played a major role in the Army team's winning the team dressage bronze medal in the 1932 Olympics in Los Angeles — America's first medal in Olympic dressage — and also claimed the indi-

Captain Hiram Tuttle, who helped the U.S. secure a bronze medal in dressage at the 1932 Games, poses with his horses Vast, Olympic, and Si Murray.

only officer to focus strictly on dressage. Everybody else in the Army world — which in those days meant in America — who did dressage learned what to do and how to do it from him." They also learned from Tuttle's horses, which he owned privately so that he could school them as he pleased and use them strictly for dressage, without the all-around demands that were placed on the cavalry-owned mounts. (Two of Tuttle's horses, Olympic and Si Murray, competed on the 1936 U.S. Army dressage team.)

In some ways, Tuttle was the Rodney Dangerfield character among the cavalry officers: He didn't get much respect. Part of the reason was that most Army riders had little use for dressage's discipline, formality, and lack of excitement. Another part, DiMarco surmises, is that Tuttle was a quartermaster officer. "They're in charge of supplies and filling out forms," he explained. "They're just not the swashbuckling types, as most of the other cavalrymen were." Tuttle's age also set him apart from his colleagues and Olympic teammates: Tuttle was at least ten years older, and his equestrian interests, military field, and academic and professional background — he didn't attend West Point, and he had been a practicing attorney when he joined the Army as part of its emergency expansion before World War I — set him somewhat apart from the others. (He did have one protégé, Major Robert Borg, who led the U.S. dressage team in the 1948 and 1952 Olympics.)

Tuttle continued to ride and care for his horses after he retired from the military, and he never sold any of his mounts. He died in 1956 at the age of seventy-three and was buried in the cemetery at Fort Riley — also the final resting place of his horses Vast, Si Murray, and Olympic. [25]

The Army's Equine Heroes

Many of the cavalry's horses were of indifferent breeding and middling talent, and the success their riders achieved was due in large part to the men's horsemanship skills and scrappy character and to their superb conditioning program. But two Army-owned mounts stand out as the equine stars of their day, and their versatility and hardiness are exceptional even by today's stricter standards.

Jenny Camp

The 16.1-hand, three-quarters Thoroughbred bay mare is indisputably the greatest Olympic mount in U.S. Army history. By the outstanding Army-owned Thoroughbred-Standardbred stallion Gordon Russell, who also sired the Olympic and U.S. Equestrian Team horse Democrat, Jenny Camp — named for the cavalry's "Jenny Camp" horse shows, open to women, children, and enlisted soldiers — carried Tommy Thomson to team gold and individual silver medals in eventing at the 1932 Los Angeles Games and a second individual silver medal in Berlin in 1936.

Like her fellow cavalry mounts, Jenny Camp was no pampered show horse. In an article in *The Cavalry Journal* entitled "Olympic Horseflesh," Major John Tupper Cole wrote, "Jenny Camp was foaled at Front Royal (the U.S. Army Remount Depot in Front Royal, Virginia) in 1926...In 1931 she was Captain Raguse's Olympic prospect in the Advanced Equitation Class, having been transferred from the green polo string. Although she is a frail little thing, she showed wonderful stamina and courage." Cole described the mare's Olympic successes with Tommy Thomson and concluded, "She is now at the Remount Depot at Fort Robinson, being bred in hopes that she may transmit her fine courage and stamina to a better shaped and nicer moving colt." [26]

In another article in the same issue of *The Cavalry Journal*, Harry Chamberlin wrote that "Jenny Camp...has proved herself the miracle horse, in that, as stated by Major Cole, she is on the small side, short-gaited, far from prepossessing from the knee down (particularly in her front pasterns which are quite upright), and undoubtedly the poorest of the three horses {of the 1932 three-day team — Jenny Camp, Pleasant Smiles, and Honolulu Tomboy} in general conformation. Yet she did the best work then and lived to repeat in 1936...{S}he possessed that greatest of all virtues, true *quality*...i.e., great courage. She also has the innate and impossible-to-develop attributes of agility and quickness." [27]

Colonel Fred Koester, a member of the 1932 Olympic equestrian team, eventually purchased Jenny Camp and moved her to his California ranch, where she died in 1958 at the ripe old age of thirty-two.

Democrat

Jenny Camp's half-brother, foaled seven years later, has the distinction of having competed both for the Army equestrian team and for its civilian replacement, the U.S. Equestrian Team. With rider Colonel Franklin F. "Fuddy" Wing, the brown Thoroughbred show jumper was poised for the 1940 Olympic Games before their cancellation. Wing and Democrat competed in high-profile horse shows such as New York's National Horse Show and Toronto's Royal Winter Fair and

finally got their shot at Olympic competition at the 1948 London Games. The then fifteen-year-old Democrat carried Wing to a fourth-place individual finish, the best U.S. placing in the Nations' Cup competition.

Four years later, at the 1952 Olympics, Democrat competed as a civilian for the USET with rider Captain John W. Russell, helping to earn a team bronze medal. He ended his career at the age of nineteen with a string of wins on the indoor-show circuit with the soon-to-be-legendary William Steinkraus and was retired to the Virginia stud farm of then-USET president Whitney Stone. [28]

End of an Era

Just months after the 1948 Olympics, the Army dissolved its cavalry branch. With the cavalry's extinction came the end of the relationship between the military and Olympic equestrian competition.

As luck would have it, though, several circumstances made the transition from military to civilian equestrian team relatively smooth. As DiMarco explained, "The timing was about right. Because of World War II, officers who were young guys in the '30s had reached the end of their military careers by the late '40s. As the cavalry disappeared, most of them were just leaving the Army. By the time international equestrian sports cranked up again in the early 1950s, they were financially secure; they were ready to start second careers; and they were very experienced managers as well as horsemen, so they were in a good position to help organize USET to continue to represent the U.S. in international equestrian sports."

CHAPTER FIVE

Three-Day Eventing

All of the Olympic equestrian disciplines have undergone changes through the years, but three-day eventing perhaps has endured the most ups and downs. The phrase "the thrill of victory, the agony of defeat" is especially true of this high-profile, exciting (some would say grueling) sport, which has known triumphs of courage and athleticism as well as tragic losses of horses and riders in devastating spills. The Olympic arena has seen its share of highs and lows, and those experiences stand out in the minds of many of eventing's most renowned personalities.

Olympic history encapsulates much of eventing's history. The most direct descendant of the cavalry's endurance tests, the three-day event (or "Military," as it was once known) is the grand-daddy of Olympic horse sports. Developed as an all-around test of a cavalry mount's fitness, stamina, jumping ability, soundness, and obedience, eventing is considered the most demanding of the Olympic equestrian disciplines in terms of sheer effort. It is the long-distance marathon to jumping's speed and agility emphases and dressage's power and gymnastic ability.

Eventing Through the Years

At the 1912 Stockholm Olympic Games, the phases of the "Military" competition were held in quite a different order from the dressage-endurance-stadium arrangement of today. (All rules and specifications in this section are taken from *Equestrian Olympic Games: Ancient and Modern*.) [1]

Day 1 consisted of endurance and cross-country: fifty kilometers over roads, five kilometers over a flag-marked cross-country course with natural obstacles. Competitors had four hours in which to complete the two tests, fifteen minutes of which were allotted for the cross-country; finishing under time was of no advantage, but exceeding the time allowed was penalized.

Lawrence Morgan of Australia on Salad Days, the 1960 eventing team and individual gold medalists. Opposite: Alfred Buller of Ireland and Sir Knight into the water at the 1996 Atlanta Olympics.

After cross-country, horses and riders undertook a speed test of 3,500 meters over ten obstacles, with a time limit of five minutes and fifty seconds.

Day 2 of the Military event in Stockholm was

The Military dressage test was similar to the individual dressage test but lacked some of the difficulty: The eventers did not have to perform the figures of eight, flying changes of lead, and

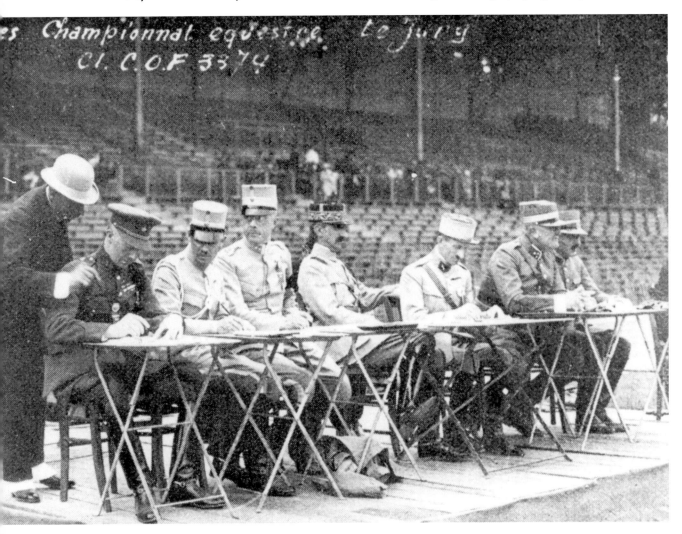

The ground jury for the 1924 Olympic three-day event.

the jumping test, over a course of fifteen obstacles of a maximum of 1.3 meters high or three meters across. Refusals, knockdowns, and other errors were penalized according to *Prix des Nations* competition rules (see Chapter 6, "Show Jumping").

jumping and obedience tests. The scoring system was the same as for individual dressage.

Event horses had to carry at least eighty kilograms (approximately 176 pounds). Any type of saddle was permitted, but use of a double bridle was mandatory. The dress code was "undress (informal) uniform."

A significant rule change was enacted for the

1920 Antwerp Games: The dressage test was eliminated from the event altogether and was replaced by a second endurance test, held on the second day of competition. Competitors did forty-five kilometers of endurance (roads and tracks) and five kilometers of cross-country on day 1, with the cross-country course consisting of eighteen obstacles of 1.1 to 1.15 meters in height. The time limit was three and one-half hours, twelve and one-half minutes of which was for cross-country.

On day 2, competitors did a second roads-and-tracks course of twenty kilometers, with a one-hour time limit. A committee of officials examined each horse as he crossed the finish line and eliminated obviously lame or exhausted horses. Those horses that passed muster went on to complete a 4,000-meter steeplechase course. Speed was rewarded: The minimum speed was 550 meters per minute (mpm; 601 yards per minute), but riders earned half a point for completing the course at a rate of 600 mpm (656 ypm) and a full point if they stepped it up to 650 mpm (711 ypm). Every second over the time limit cost a point. As in all the jumping tests, refusals, runouts, and falls were penalized; a "three strikes and you're out" rule was instituted for Antwerp.

The final day of the Military event in Antwerp was the jumping test. Competitors had three minutes to negotiate a 1,150-meter course with eighteen obstacles at a maximum height of 1.25 meters. Some obstacles were to be taken between two close-set flags; others had to be cleared several times, each time over a different part of the fence. Riders earned an extra half-point for every second they finished under the time limit and lost a quarter-point for every second over. Going off course, refusals, falls, knockdowns, and taking off or landing within the demarcation lines of spread jumps also cost points.

The minimum weight at Antwerp dropped slightly, from eighty kilograms to seventy-five kilograms (165 pounds). The dress code changed slightly, with dark or "pink" (scarlet) coats as well as undress uniform now allowed. White breeches and silk hats were mandatory. No rules, however, governed tack. Twenty-five riders from eight nations took part.

At the 1924 Paris Games, the three-day-event phases were held in the now-standard order of dressage, speed and endurance, and stadium jumping. The competition actually encompassed four days, as the number of entrants (forty-four) was so large that the dressage competition took two days. [2]

For Paris, the eventing-dressage rules specified an arena size (the now-standard sixty meters x twenty meters) and a time limit (ten and one-half minutes) for the first time. Riders could enter the arena at any pace they wished and had to show the following gaits during the test: the "ordinary trot" (rising and sitting), the "slow trot," the extended trot, the ordinary and extended canter, and the walk. Required movements included small circles, the counter-canter, the halt, and the reinback.

Day 2 consisted of seven kilometers of roads and tracks at 240 mpm (262 ypm), a four-kilometer steeplechase at 550 mpm, another fifteen kilometers of roads and tracks at 240 mpm, an eight-kilometer cross-country course at 450 mpm (492 ypm), and a two-kilometer "canter over level ground" at 333 mpm (364 ypm). Total time allowed for the five phases: two hours, one minute, forty-seven seconds.

The dress and saddlery rules for Paris were the same as in Antwerp, with the exception of the dressage: The dressage rules now specified a double bridle and forbade the use of martingales, bearing reins, or bandages. Riders were allowed to wear hunt caps as well as the previously allowed silk hats. A total of thirteen nations took part. [3]

There were few eventing rule changes for the 1928 Olympics in Amsterdam. The dressage time limit was increased to eleven minutes, with competitors docked two points for every second over the limit. The steeplechase speed increased from 550 mpm to 600 mpm. As for the speed-and-endurance scoring, "Calculation of rewards and penalties in connection with the time limits for the three tests had been made very elaborate and was based on a number of tables." [4] The stadium-jumping rules specified a twelve-obstacle course and a pace of 375 mpm, with a half-point deducted for every two seconds over the time limit. The rule changes enacted for Amsterdam remained in force through the 1932 Olympics in Los Angeles.

Rules regarding the administration of performance-altering drugs to horses went on the books for the 1936 Olympics in Berlin. For the speed-and-endurance phase, "Any horse lame, exhausted, or treated with stimulants or sedatives was liable to elimination." [5]

Another subtle but significant rule change was enacted for the 1936 Games: The ratio of marks was altered to give more weight to the speed-and-endurance and less to the stadium jumping. In another indication of changes to come, the weight requirement was dropped entirely for the

dressage — although it remained the same for speed-and-endurance and jumping.

Despite the fact that all the rules governing speed-and-endurance day remained the same as those used in the 1928 and 1932 Olympics, only twenty-seven of the fifty horse-and-rider combinations entered finished the competition. The main culprit was the infamous water jump, as discussed in Chapter 4. [6]

Argentina, Portugal, and Brazil competed in the three-day event for the first time at the 1948 London Olympics, bringing the total number of entrants up to forty-six. There were a few new rule changes. The half-pass was added to the dressage test, although flying changes of lead were forbidden. The total distance on speed-and-endurance day dropped to thirty-three and one-half kilometers (twenty-two kilometers of roads and tracks, three and one-half kilometers of steeplechase, and eight kilometers of cross-country). [7]

Today's Olympic three-day event has changed little in the past fifty years. The dressage test now includes single flying changes; the steeplechase-course speed has been increased to 690 mpm; and the cross-country course has been shortened to a maximum of six kilometers, with thirty-two to thirty-four jumps not to exceed 1.20 meters in height and ridden at a pace of 570 mpm. Beginning with the 1996 Atlanta Olympics, the rules were modified and the requirements eased somewhat in cases of anticipated excessive heat (see Chapter 3). Minor modifications doubtless will continue to be made, but the essence of the sport remains the same.

The 1936 Olympic three-day event team and individual gold medalists Ludwig Stubbendorff and Nurmi of Germany.

The U.S. claimed the team silver in 1964, with help from Lana du Pont (left), the first female Olympic event rider.

Milestones in Olympic Eventing Competition

By the time the Army's dominance of international equestrian sport came to an end, the rules of three-day eventing were much as they are today. But the sport continued to evolve in the latter half of the 20th Century, and eventing enthusiasts recognize that it remains far from static as we look toward the 2000 Sydney Olympic Games and beyond.

Coed Eventing

Military forces the world over once were all-male, so Olympic equestrian competition automatically was a boys-only club for many years. The gender barriers largely fell after international horse sports became the property of the civilian sector in the early 1950s, but it took several years before the individual disciplines began allowing women to compete. Fears that eventing is too stressful a sport for the "weaker sex" kept women out of Olympic eventing until the 1964 Games in Tokyo, when the American Helena "Lana" du Pont (now Wright) became the first female Olympic eventer. ("Perhaps she has paved the way for future female participation," wrote the editors of *Olympic Games 1964* [8] — a terrific understatement if there ever was one.)

Aboard her Mr. Wister, du Pont tackled the cross-country course at Karuizawa, Japan, the footing of which had become slippery and treacherous because of heavy rains. It was pouring when the pair set out on course, and du Pont describes her mishap at the third fence in *The U.S. Equestrian Team Book of Riding*: "We fell hard, Wister breaking several bones in his jaw. We were badly disheveled and shaken, but Wister was nonetheless eager to continue. We fell a second time near the end of the course, tripping over another spread. When we finished, we were a collection of bruises, broken bones and mud. Anyway, we proved that a woman could get around an Olympic cross-country course, and nobody could have said that we looked feminine at the finish." [9]

The FEI and the horse world may have made much of women's entree into three-day eventing, but du Pont's Olympic teammates took the historic events in stride. "For us, it was no big deal," said three-time Olympian Michael Page, who rode on the 1964 three-day squad with du Pont. "She rode with us; she trained with us; she had a great horse; it was great to have her there. {Du Pont's making the Olympic team} might have been a big deal from a historical perspective, but it was not a big deal from a riding perspective."

Since the 1964 Games, women have gone on to achieve success records equal to — and sometimes better than — their male counterparts. In fact, the national levels of all three Olympic disciplines are female-dominated, although the elite levels are more evenly split between the sexes. It may be hard for today's women riders to imagine a time when they would have been excluded from Olympic competition, but they indeed owe a debt of gratitude to du Pont and the other pioneering women of international equestrian competition.

The Weight Rule

The FEI reduced the minimum weight event horses must carry from 165 pounds to 154 pounds for the 1996 Olympic Games, to help horses cope with the anticipated heat and humidity in Atlanta. After studies showed that extra weight affected horses' jumping and could well lead to crashes or leg injuries, the FEI abolished the weight rule altogether in 1998. Although some riders and officials continue to believe that the absence of a weight rule gives lightweight riders an unfair advantage, those same small riders — usually petite women, mounted on small horses — argue that having to comply with the weight rule by adding lead weights to their saddle pads put themselves and their mounts at a disadvantage and even in danger.

"Separate but Equal"

Prior to the 1996 Atlanta Olympics, the International Olympic Committee mandated that an athlete could not win both team and individual medals for the same effort. The decision had little effect on the dressage and show-jumping competitions, as those sports had traditionally used tests or rounds as qualifiers for a final individual championship event. But it meant big changes for the three-day event, which was already taxing to organizers in terms of funding, course building, and numbers of volunteers needed. (In the past, both team and individual three-day-eventing medals had been awarded for a singular performance.)

Fortunately for the sport, the challenge fell squarely on the capable shoulders of Kate Jackson, the secretary-general of the American Horse Shows Association, who organized the 1996 Olympic equestrian events. Jackson, herself a former event rider and an experienced organizer — she was the three-day-event director for the 1984 Los Angeles Games, and the Korean Olympic organizing committee brought her in to help with the planning for the 1988 Seoul Games — and the FEI grappled with the ruling and had to create an entirely new type of Olympic eventing competition.

The basic problem was that, unlike in show jumping or dressage, the demands of the three-day event are such that an event horse isn't physically capable of competing in back-to-back competitions. So the process of using the team competition as a qualifier for the individuals wouldn't work for eventing. That left only one possible solution: Host two more-or-less "separate but equal" events, one for the team medals

and one for the individuals. But how to stage two separate competitions with one competition's resources? How to determine which riders would compete in which divisions?

"The FEI had to try to figure out the balance: Is the team competition or the individual competition more important?" Jackson said of the issues they faced. "Are they to be exactly the same level of competition, in which case you have to build two totally different courses — clearly an impossibility — or is it better to build one course with two varying routes? The latter is what we ended up doing in Atlanta: adding a few extra jumps for this, a few extra jumps for that."

Building a cross-country course that could accommodate the two competitions was a tremendous challenge, but one that course designer Roger Haller met "brilliantly," said Jackson. "He had to design equally balanced yet different courses in the same place, meaning that he had to devise different routes over many of the same jumps. That task could be considered exciting," she added with a laugh.

"Running the two events at the end of July was incredibly challenging," Jackson said. "We had a total of six hundred volunteers just for the sports themselves, and most of those volunteers were for the three-day. So we had to ask many volunteers to commit to two three-day events. In addition, the schedule was such that the team stadium-jumping phase was followed immediately — on the same day — by the first half of the dressage competition for the individual three-day competition. We were really scrambling."

Andrew Hoy on Darien Powers, members of the 1996 gold-medal-winning Australian team.

What came out of ACOG's efforts to comply with the IOC ruling, said Jackson, was an Olympic three-day event to which many nations were able to send both team and individual riders. (The U.S. sent three individuals.) The development of the separate competitions raised yet another issue of particular importance to riders: "Would you rather compete on the team or as an individual? That's a difficult question, and one that the eventing world hasn't answered yet."

Another issue that arose was that of the scoring system. According to Jackson, the FEI, realizing that its system of tracking riders' competitive achievements at the time of the Atlanta Games was such that "a team's not finishing meant that those riders on that team who did finish didn't get credit for having completed an Olympic Games, came up with the convoluted scoring in which riders on non-finishing teams were not shown as eliminated but instead were shown with their scores plus about one thousand points — which enabled them to maintain a score in the {World Three-Day Event Rider} rankings for having completed an Olympic Games." Confusing? Yes, said Jackson, but "they're working toward resolving it."

Jackson does not have an organizing role in the Sydney Games, but she thinks the team-individual split in the three-day event will continue to pose a challenge as the rules change and evolve. One such rule change for Sydney: allowing team riders to switch to the individual competition in certain circumstances. "Let's say a rider in the team competition has completed phases A, B, and C, and two of that rider's teammates have previously been eliminated. That rider will be permitted to withdraw from the team at that point and go into the individual competition," she explained. "From an organizer's standpoint, that's a nightmare because you're running the next competition within a couple of days, but you don't know how many entries you'll have, what your schedule will be, or how long the individual competition will last, until after the team competition has finished."

Beating the Heat

The intense Spanish summer heat — well over 100 degrees Fahrenheit — produced some exhausted horses at the end of the cross-country at the 1992 Barcelona Olympics. Other international-level three-day events that had formerly been held in the hottest months had been moved to more temperate times of the year; the Rolex Kentucky event, for example, was moved from June to April to lessen the chances of horses', riders', and spectators' suffering heat-related ailments. But the equestrian community can't get the Olympic Games moved just to suit its fancy, and so the hand-wringing about the 1996 Olympic three-day event began immediately after the International Olympic Committee awarded the Games to Atlanta, Georgia. Horse lovers worried that the gallant event horses would give everything they had on cross-country and then collapse. Animal-welfare and animal-rights groups alike fretted about the perceived inevitable casualties. It would not be an exaggeration to say that the majority of people looked forward to the equestrian events at the Atlanta Games with a sense of impending doom.

Behind the scenes, however, a team of veterinarians took it upon themselves to make sure that everyone's worst fears did not materialize.

Professor Leo Jeffcott of England's University of Cambridge and American veterinarians Kent Allen and Catherine Kohn mobilized the equestrian community and conducted extensive research into the effects of heat and humidity on exercising horses (see Chapter 3). Based on their findings, they made several easy-to-follow recommendations to the FEI and the Atlanta Games organizing committee: start the cross-country in the relative cool of the early morning; shorten the distance of the cross-country course; institute an additional hold and vet check during phase C on speed-and-endurance day, the second roads and tracks; and use special misting fans to help cool the horses during the competition.

The strategy worked incredibly well, and the equestrian events of the 1996 Olympics were generally acknowledged as the best ever in terms of equine welfare, safety, and preparation. The measures were so successful that the FEI has gone on to implement or adapt them for a variety of competitions held in hot weather. Riders and horses now have the Atlanta Games to thank for providing the inspiration to research and improve the competitive experience when the sun beats down.

Legends in Olympic Eventing

Of the long and impressive roster of individuals who have made their mark on Olympic three-day-eventing history, a few names stand out as having achieved extraordinary records.

Jack Le Goff: Excellence by Example

One of the greatest coaches in three-day-eventing history, Frenchman Jack Le Goff came to the United States in 1970 to take on a formidable chal-

Extensive studies of heat and humidity's effects on horses resulted in the use of misting fans and other heat-beating measures at the 1996 Atlanta Games.

lenge: create, practically from scratch, a medal-winning U.S. three-day team. He recruited and trained a phalanx of then-unknown horses and riders and, just two years later, saw his relatively inexperienced team win silver at the 1972 Munich Olympics. But the following Games, in Montreal in 1976, was Le Goff's crowning glory: double gold medals, an achievement that has not yet been repeated in U.S. Olympic eventing history.

In many ways, the story of Jack Le Goff is the story of eventing in the 20th Century — and certainly of U.S. eventing.

The son of a French cavalry officer, Le Goff became interested in horses and riding at an early age. By the time he reached his teens, he had already competed in eventing, show jumping, and dressage and was an accomplished steeplechase jockey.

"I had a general riding education as a kid because, in those days, cavalry officers in every country did a bit of dressage, a bit of show jumping, a bit of racing," he explained. "They were all-around horsemen, and my dad was a very good one."

Le Goff's father died at age forty-one, when his son was seventeen. "When he died I kept racing, but I soon realized that there was no way I could make a career as a steeplechase jock; I was too tall," he said. "So I went to Saumur to do my military service, and I was very interested in going to the Cadre Noir, which is the French Army's riding academy. They didn't want to take me at first

Coach Jack Le Goff built the powerhouse U.S. eventing team from scratch.

because I was six feet one and I weighed something like 130 pounds." He managed to gain enough weight to earn the academy's approval and ended up staying on as a riding master for ten years.

Le Goff remembers the post-World War II years as "a tough time" for aspiring equestrians. "I could teach horses piaffe, passage, and all that stuff; I was show jumping at the international level, but I didn't have enough horses from the Army to compete just in show jumping. And," he said jestingly, "since I wasn't born with the wealth I deserved, I couldn't buy horses either. Sponsors in those years after the war had other

things to put their money into besides riders."

Financial difficulties aside, Le Goff still managed to compile an impressive record in eventing, a sport that enabled him to make use of his all-around equestrian education. ("Eventing kind of came easy," he said.) He was named French national champion in 1956 and 1964 and rode on the 1960 and 1964 French three-day Olympic teams, earning a team bronze medal in Rome at his first Games.

Le Goff himself bridged the transition between Army- and civilian-controlled equestrian competition. When the French Ministry of Sport asked him to coach the French three-day team following the 1964 Olympics, he became France's first civilian equestrian coach. Under his leadership, France earned the individual gold medal at the 1968 Olympics and also won gold medals at the 1967 and 1968 European Junior Championships. But frustrated by what he saw as bureaucratic interference in his job, he decided to move on when then-USET president Whitney Stone offered him the three-day coach's position. Le Goff accepted and reported for work on January 1, 1970.

"When I got here {to the U.S.}, I have to say, I was a little shocked," Le Goff laughed. "There was one open-intermediate horse trial on the East Coast at the time, and there was a similar competition on the West Coast. There was nothing over intermediate level. At the Team headquarters, there were no horses, no saddles, no grooms — nothing. But, actually, it was better that way, because I could build it up myself."

The new coach's first challenge was to "put my hands on some riders." He knew of only three American riders with any international eventing experience: Kevin Freeman, J. Michael Plumb, and Jim Wofford. (A fourth experienced rider, Michael Page, was at that time retired from the sport.) Le Goff brainstormed with Neil Ayer, who had just assumed the presidency of the United States Combined Training Association. "I said, 'I need to have more competitions so I can train riders,'" Le Goff recalled. "{Ayer} said, 'I need the riders to have competitions.'" Le Goff responded, "Looks like we've got something going!"

At Le Goff's request, Ayer organized East Coast and West Coast screening sessions — basically "cattle calls" for interested young riders. "I was trying to smell the talent," Goff said of his objective at those tryouts. "I had to judge them more on riding ability — a feeling that they could develop something on a horse." An eighteen-year-old Bruce Davidson was among the hopefuls — and evidently his raw talent shone through because, according to the coach, "He didn't know on which diagonal he was posting when he came to me. Two years later, he was riding in the Olympics."

Talent alone was not enough to make Le Goff's team. "I told them {the riders} that I was interested in having them come to the tryouts only if they were prepared to commit themselves for at least two or three years if they got picked. I wanted them to be available full-time, basically." The lucky riders — Davidson among them — embarked on a rigorous four-year, seven-days-a-week training schedule at the USET's headquarters in Gladstone, New Jersey.

Le Goff's training program consisted of the basics, drills, details, and no shortcuts. "I told the riders that the system is very simple. In the beginning, when you start, it's like the top of a funnel. When you come out, you're all going to be alike." Drawing on his own riding training, he built riders from the ground up — and training sessions often were far from glamorous and exciting. "They spent quite a bit of time on the longe line. The longe line is to the rider what the barre is to a ballet dancer. They learned to sit the g—damned trot by working without stirrups. Even today, in the year 2000, the only way to learn how to sit the g—damned trot is to go on the longe line without stirrups."

Le Goff said coaching eventers came easily to him because "I had the racing, dressage, and show-jumping experience, and those are the basics of eventing; plus, I competed in eventing quite a bit myself. I got exposed to all the different ingredients of making the sauce, and the sauce was eventing." So as a coach, "I knew exactly what I wanted to do."

Finding the horses proved as much of a challenge as finding the riders. The USET owned a few horses, most of which had been donated or lent to the Team and not all of which were of international caliber. A pragmatic Le Goff scouted for the equine equivalents of his riders: young, healthy individuals with talent. A prospect had to "run, jump, and move decently — and above all, be sound and sane. Bold, courageous, but not cuckoo. So I got one horse here, one there; and finally I got a team put together for 1972." The coach "made" his horses the same way he made his riders — through systematic training. "A rider should be a pilot, but he also should be a mechanic," he believes, and so he taught his pupils how to start young horses and bring them up through the levels.

As eventing coach, Le Goff had virtually complete authority over every aspect of his team: horse and rider selection, pairing of riders and mounts, training system, team selection for the Olympics and other international competitions, and barn management. "It was a one-man show," he said. "That was the only way it was possible to do it in such a short period of time." But with the power and the prestige came plenty of unglamorous duties. "I organized all the trips. I was the travel agent. I would hire the planes, make the hotel reservations, and I had no secretary, so I did the accounting for the six riders, five grooms, the horses, a vet. I'd pay the bills, do the books. I started work at seven o'clock in the morning, and I would teach all day until five. Then afterward I'd have to go to a social function, so I didn't get home until eight, nine, ten o'clock; and then I had to do the books and make my plan for the following day. I didn't sleep very much."

Le Goff's dedication, hard work, and drive paid off, beginning with the U.S. three-day team's silver medal at the 1972 Munich Olympics. Before he stepped down as USET coach after the 1984 Games, his riders had amassed an incredible record: a team silver medal at Munich, team and individual gold medals and the individual silver in 1976, and team gold and individual silver in 1984; plus team gold medals at the 1974 World Championships and the 1975 Pan American Games. To Le Goff, the 1976 Olympics in Montreal were — and still are — the highlight of his career.

"I had one goal — to coach an Olympic gold-medal team," he said. "As a rider, I had medaled, but I never had an Olympic gold medal. I have to say, I was a bit of a bulldozer (in pursuit of the gold)," he said with a laugh. "I probably was not a pussycat coach. I had to be a bit strong. But I tried to be fair."

The eventing team's victories at the Pan Am and the World Championships were satisfying, to be sure, but for Le Goff, nothing compares to Olympic gold. "Granted, the World Championships often are more difficult; but the Olympics are, to me, the top-class competition."

Over the course of the ten Olympic Games with which Le Goff has been involved, he has made many memories, some heartwarming, others chilling. He recalls the opening ceremonies at his first Games, in Rome in 1960: "In Rome, you get into the stadium through a tunnel. You're lined up there for hours. If the opening ceremony's at ten, you're there by eight. So we're all there, waiting as patiently as possible for things to happen. Finally they say okay, time for formation, and we line up by country, each one following the other. It was a bright day, bright sunshine. I walked through that tunnel and came into that stadium with, I don't know, 100,000, 120,000 people cheering. I looked at the crowd and I said, 'Oh my God, I'm in the Olympics!' It was kind of a shock — as if a tank had hit me. What went through my mind was, 'Am I ready? Can I do a good job and justify my selection?' After a couple of seconds of questions in my mind, I decided, 'Let's go for it!' "

If the Games in Rome were full of youthful excitement and optimism for Le Goff, then his memories of the 1972 Olympics in Munich — which by all rights should have been a time of great pride, as it was his young U.S. team's first shot at the big time — are forever tinged with sadness. "We were training quite a ways from the Olympic Village," he recalled, "and we had to

Jack Le Goff and his 1972 Olympic three-day team, which won the silver medal in Munich.

catch a bus at about five-thirty in the morning to get to the equestrian center. One day, the bus wasn't where it was supposed to be. I speak a little German, so I said I would find out what was going on. An official told me, 'I can't give you any details, but there is a major problem.' That was when the terrorists took the Israelis hostage." (Eight Palestinian terrorists broke into the Village, killing two Israeli athletes and taking nine others hostage. All the hostages later were killed during a battle with West German sharpshooters, as were five of the terrorists and one police officer.)

"The Olympic Village is always a happy place," Le Goff continued. "It's nice, friendly — a real atmosphere of sport. But then we came back that night after training and...all the police and all that. What was happening was next to our building, so we could see the guys on the balconies. It was very bad. There was nobody smiling.

"Everybody was sad. It was just terrible. Then we went to Montreal {for the 1976 Games} after that, and because of what had happened in Munich you had the feeling you were entering an Army camp there. There were police and machine guns everywhere. That was not very pleasant."

Mother Nature conspired to make the three-day event competition at the 1968 Mexico City Olympics a nail-biter, if not as tragic as the events of the Munich Games. "Every single day, at the same time, it poured," recalled Le Goff, who was coaching the French team at the time. "We asked if they could move the competition times forward, but they wouldn't do it because of television problems (air-time conflicts). So there really were two Olympic Games there for the three-day: one for those who went before the rains, and one for those who went after." The rains turned one water jump into a 100-feet-wide raging river, "so you gallop and you fall into it because your horse can't see it. The horses fell two or three times at that, and you had to cross the river two or three times while on course.

"A horse and rider fell at the last crossing, and they were taken by the current," said Le Goff. "Several people, including {1968 U.S. Olympic three-day team member} Kevin Freeman, jumped into the water to save the horse — he was drowning. And then one of us saw a human hand — just by luck. It was the rider, going down; he was drowning too. They grabbed him and pulled him out. They pulled out both the horse and the rider. It's true."

Le Goff, who today has homes in Pennsylvania, Arizona, and his native France, retired from the USET after the 1984 Olympics, although he continued to work with the Team as a coach for its developing-rider program. He coached the 1992 Canadian Olympic three-day team part-time, but since the early 1990s he has focused primarily on giving clinics and on his work as a member of the

Flooding made the cross-country course treacherous at the 1968 Mexico City Games.

FEI's Three-Day Event Committee. (An FEI "O", Official International, three-day-eventing judge, he may a member of the FEI Jury of Appeals at the 2000 Sydney Games.) He said he's happy to see the Americans back under the wing of a capable

coach — Britain's Captain Mark Phillips, himself an Olympic eventing team gold medalist, has been the U.S. eventing team's coach and *chef d'équipe* since 1993 — and added that "You can't imagine having a football team or a basketball team without a coach. You need to have somebody in charge." Clearly, Le Goff has passed the torch; now it's up to Phillips and his riders to make the next generation of Olympic memories.

Michael Page and the remarkable Grasshopper negotiate the drop at the 1960 Rome Olympics.

Michael Page: Sportsmanship Personified

Michael Page is another of American eventing's elder statesmen. He rode in consecutive Olympic Games in 1960, 1964, and 1968 — the latter following two years of retirement from competition — winning team silver in '64 and '68 as well as the individual bronze medal in '68. His Olympic-competition days ended for good after his third Games, but his Olympic involvement continued: Page coached the Canadian three-day team for the 1976 Montreal Olympics and then served as *chef d'équipe* of the American team for the 1988 and 1992 Games.

Page began his riding career in the hunter-seat-equitation ranks, winning the American Horse Shows Association Medal Finals in 1956 at the age of eighteen. He and his father decided that the sport of eventing offered the greatest opportunities to a budding horseman at the time, and so the younger Page sailed for England two days after his Medal win. His studies would take him to Switzerland, West Germany, and France. His trainer in Germany was dressage master Paul Stecken, whose school was in Münster, Westphalia; another of Stecken's pupils was a local young man by the name of Reiner Klimke. Eventually Page was accepted at the French Cavalry School in Saumur, where he met Jack Le Goff.

Synchronicity brought Page together with what was to become his greatest mount, the 15.1-hand Anglo-Connemara gelding Copper Coin, who was already a veteran of the 1956 Stockholm Olympics with his previous owner's son, Irishman Ian Dudgeon. Wealthy Californians Mr. and Mrs. John Galvin (whose daughter, Trish, rode the family's Rath Patrick in the 1960 and 1964 Olympic dressage competitions) bought Copper Coin after the '56 Games, rechristened the little horse Grasshopper, and offered him to the USET. At the same time, USET president Whitney Stone asked whether Page would like to return to the States to ride for the Team. Page jumped at the chance and was soon paired with Grasshopper on account of the rider's light weight. The combination finished seventeenth at the 1960 Rome Olympics — the team coached by Army Olympic team veteran Colonel Earl "Tommy" Thomson — and capped their partnership by finishing fourth individually at the 1964 Tokyo Games, leading their team to a silver medal.

"He was a special horse," Page said of Grasshopper. "He was able to maintain his soundness and his speed probably longer than any horse I've ever known. He was nerved (a pain-reduction procedure in which nerves in the feet are cut) before his third Olympics, and two weeks after the procedure he was one hundred percent sound."

Grasshopper's performance in Tokyo was even more remarkable when one considers the fact that the sixteen-year-old gelding hadn't galloped for the preceding two months so he could recover from a knee concussion from the hard clay footing at Gladstone. "{T}he course was hock-deep in mud in many places," Page wrote in *Great Horses of the United States Equestrian Team*. "On the steeplechase course he blew hard, and I wondered if I'd have to pull him up on the cross-country. I still don't know where he got the strength, but like an engine gradually getting a richer mixture of fuel, Grasshopper seemed to get stronger and faster with every stride; in the run-in, he seemed fresh and fit enough to start round all over again. I don't expect ever to see another horse like him." [10] The USCTA inducted the little horse into its Hall of Fame in 1999.

Grasshopper was retired from competition after Tokyo, but Page's Olympic career was far from over. He left eventing competition for two years but came back in 1966 to ride another Irish-bred, Foster, a half-brother to Grasshopper. The pair went on to win a team silver medal at the 1968 Mexico City Games, and Page capped his Olympic experiences by clinching the individual bronze. Foster retired from competition after those Games and became a valued schoolmaster at USET headquarters in Gladstone.

Page retired from competition a second time after Mexico City — this time for good — but remained active in the horse world, focusing on hunters and jumpers for nearly a decade. Three-day eventing beckoned again when the Canadian event team asked him to be its coach for the 1976

Olympics in Montreal.

Page described the situation he encountered with the Canadian three-day team as "chaos. Nobody was listening to anybody." Page enlisted the aid of his former coach, Lars Sederholm,

After his competitive career, Michael Page served as chef d'équipe for the three-day team.

because he had been out of eventing for enough time that he thought he needed "technical, contemporary guidance from someone who was an outstanding trainer. I hadn't galloped a horse {in preparation} for Badminton for fifteen years; that year, Sederholm had trained twelve horses for Badminton."

With Sederholm on board as "technical advisor" and Page managing the selection process, "We had a very good training program," Page said. The Canadians had two unfortunate falls at

Montreal, but "it was a very relaxed, focused team," he recalled.

Page's next Olympic involvement would come more than ten years later, when he served as *chef d'équipe* of the U.S. three-day team for the 1988 and 1992 Olympic Games. His job as *chef*, he said, was "to make selected riders, and perhaps different training programs and methods, come together as a team." He thinks a good *chef* has to have "a personality and experience that allow riders to respect your judgment and that team members need to understand that "representing their country is a responsibility and that working together creates a stronger team."

A rider's cultural background tends to influence his or her views of teamwork, Page has found. "The main reason the Germans are so successful is that, even though they're each stars in their own right, they understand that the team is stronger if they work together. As a culture, the French lose a lot of wars" because competitors fail to put their team first. The United States is somewhere in between."

Page stepped down from his position as *chef* in 1993, when the USET hired Captain Mark Phillips in the dual role of eventing-team coach and *chef*. Page refers to his own six years in the job as "a transitional phase from the coaching phase of Jack Le Goff to the *chef d'équipe* phase. {The USET} went through the arbitration (the legal proceedings that resulted in the Team's changing much of its selection procedure from a subjective to an objective process). Once that was over and done, they were ready for a new era." He has high praise for Phillips, whom he calls "the perfect person, in the right time and the right place, to move the team forward."

(Under Phillips' leadership, the three-day team has won a team silver medal at the 1996 Atlanta Olympics, among other international achievements.)

Today, Page directs the riding program at the Kent School, a private secondary school in Connecticut; judges at a handful of horse shows each year; gives clinics around the country; and speaks regularly at the annual meetings of the American Riding Instructor Certification Program, for which he is a Master Instructor. The best part of his life, though, is "the opportunity to ride horses daily."

"It's a great sport," Page said of eventing. "It's tough on the horses, but the great horses thrive on it. It's something they absolutely love to do, and the harder, the better. Those great horses have given us the opportunity to go to those places and to have our little moments in the sun. If it weren't for those horses, we never would have been there."

Michael Plumb: "Mr. Olympics"

The book *Riding for America* calls Mike Plumb "the iron man of the USET." The diehard eventer is sort of the Energizer Bunny of both his sport and the Olympic Games: Sixty years of age this year, he's still going strong at the highest levels of three-day eventing, and he's marched in more opening ceremonies than any other Olympic athlete in history. His first Games were in 1960, when Plumb was just twenty; his most recent Olympic appearance was in Barcelona in 1992, and he also competed in the "Alternate Olympics" in Fontainebleau, France, in 1980, the year the United States and many other nations boycotted the Moscow Games. He's the proud

owner of six Olympic medals: team silvers from 1964, 1968, and 1972; an individual silver from 1976; and team golds from 1976 and 1984. Atlanta Olympic organizers honored his achievements by inviting him to take part in the "100 Great Athletes" festivities in 1996.

A true "rider's rider," Plumb trains horses and teaches a select group of students at his JMP Farm in Southern Pines, North Carolina, but he eschews "the politics that are involved" in team coaching and has chosen to make most of his contributions to the eventing world from the saddle.

"Each one of my Olympic experiences probably means more to me than anything," said Plumb, although his 1977 second place at the Maryland Hunt Cup, which his race-riding father Charles had previously won, ranks right up there. "But you can't beat the Olympic Games — riding in those different countries, against the best in the world."

Plumb claims that his seven Olympic mounts made up in heart and bravery what they lacked in sheer talent. Ironically, he calls the chestnut Thoroughbred gelding Better and Better, who carried him to team gold and individual silver medals at the 1976 Montreal Games, "the least talented one. But he was a brave horse, and he would give his best and keep trying."

Plumb had to choose between Better and Better and the USET's Good Mixture — ridden by Kevin Freeman to a team silver medal in Munich in 1972 — for the Montreal Games. He picked Better and Better because of the horse's younger age and because "I had something going with him. I really had a feeling that he and I were a team. Between the two of us, where one failed, the other would take over."

Plumb called Bold Minstrel, his team-silver-medal-winning mount for the 1964 Tokyo Games, his most talented Olympic horse to date. He was slated to ride Markham, with whom he'd finished fifteenth at the 1960 Games; but the horse panicked en route to Japan and had to be humanely destroyed in midair. "There was an alternate horse on the plane, but he was not appropriate for the team," Plumb recalled. "My friend Billy Haggard (William D. Haggard III), who owned Bold

Winning the team gold in 1976: Mary Anne Tauskey, Bruce Davidson, Mike Plumb, and Tad Coffin.

Minstrel and was not selected for the team, shipped that horse over to me in Tokyo and I rode him." The duo's performance was even more remarkable when one considers the fact that Plumb had ridden Bold Minstrel "maybe a couple of times" before the Olympics. "But this was a wonderful horse, and you know what he did after that? He shares the high-jump (puissance) record at the old Madison Square Garden (the National Horse Show) with Billy Steinkraus.

"I don't think that would happen today," Plumb said of Haggard's generosity. "He was a great horseman, and he was a good friend. He

was the best man at my wedding. It was a great thing to do, and I'm not sure whether too many people know about it. It was a very sportsmanlike thing to do." Sadly, Haggard broke his neck in a riding accident in the mid-1990s and is now a paraplegic.

Plumb considers himself lucky to have learned his craft under the tutelage of USET eventing coach Jack Le Goff. "He was a disciplinarian, he was very strict, and he coached the team," he said. "I think we miss his approach. He could ride any of the horses brought to the Team, whether it was dressage or steeplechase or cross-country. I think that's important. That's the way I operate: I teach through example."

Plumb by no means considers his Olympic competition days to be over. He said he probably won't have a horse ready to go for Sydney, though. "I've got a couple of possibilities, but I want to do it right." And if there's anybody who knows how to do it right, it's Mike Plumb.

Virginia Leng: Eventing's Leading Lady

England's Virginia "Ginny" Leng (née Holgate) is the first woman ever to win an Olympic individual medal for eventing. Aboard her Priceless, she won the individual bronze medal at the 1984 Games in Los Angeles and also was a member of the silver-medal-winning British team. Four years, a marriage, and a new horse later, Leng repeated the individual bronze/team silver wins at Seoul with the relatively inexperienced Master Craftsman.

Leng, a "military brat" with a Royal Marines officer father, got little opportunity to ride until she reached her teens. A quick study, she and her first horse, Dubonnet, won a team gold medal at

the 1973 Junior European Championships. She competed at the prestigious Badminton three-day event for the first time the following year, and by 1976 she and her horse, Jason, were long-listed for the Montreal Olympics.

Mike Plumb and Adonis on course at Barcelona.

Leng had acquired a young horse by the name of Priceless during the time she was prepping Jason for Montreal, and over the next several years she and Priceless would go on to amass numerous honors, including the 1984 Olympic medals, a win at Badminton in 1985, and individual and team gold medals at the 1986 World Championships. And, like his stablemate, Master

New Zealander Mark Todd won back-to-back individual golds with the diminutive Charisma.

Craftsman won Badminton and other prestigious events in addition to his Olympic medals.

Mark Todd: The Eventer with Charisma

Mark Todd's riding "defies explanation or emulation, and that's why they call him 'the Maestro,' " the weekly U.S. horse-sport magazine *The Chronicle of the Horse* wrote in its salute to the 1984 and 1988 Olympic individual three-day-event champion in its "50 Most Influential Horsemen of the 20th Century" feature. "Todd has a 'feel' that few others have ever possessed, an ability that certainly cannot be copied." [11] "Toddy" put New Zealand on the eventing map; today, the Kiwis are arguably the world's number-one eventing powerhouse. (See "The Thunder Down Under" later in this chapter.)

Todd began Pony Clubbing at the age of nine and competed in gymkhanas (mounted competitive games, particularly for youngsters), horse trials, and jumping competitions. His first horse, Top Hunter, started as a jumper but realized his potential as an event horse, hooking his rider on eventing in the process. The pair's first international competition was the 1978 World Championships in Lexington, Kentucky, where they were eliminated on cross-country. Soon after, Todd began bringing horses from New Zealand to England to train and compete; just two years after he burst onto the international eventing scene, he and New Zealand-bred mount Southern Comfort astonished the horse world by winning the Badminton CCI****, the most prestigious and formidable three-day event in the world.

Following a series of horse-related setbacks, Todd returned to his family's dairy farm in New Zealand in 1981. He would not event again for two years. In 1983, he "catch-rode" a horse at Badminton; shortly thereafter, he returned to New Zealand to compete a "sort of small, hairy, black horse" [12] named Charisma.

The 15.3-hand, not-quite-purebred Thoroughbred gelding (he's one-sixteenth Percheron) and the six-feet-four-inch man may have appeared an unlikely match, but there was kismet between them. They won several events in New Zealand, capped off by a win at that country's Olympic trials, and then flew to England to prepare for the 1984 Games in Los Angeles. They were second that year at Badminton and then made history in L.A. by clinching the individual gold medal after American rider Karen Stives and Ben Arthur pulled a rail in stadium jumping.

The dynamic duo was good as gold again at the 1988 Olympics in Seoul, when Charisma was at the relatively advanced age of sixteen. After the Games, Todd retired the little horse back to New Zealand. He wrote a book about their partnership, titled simply *Charisma*.

Todd's eventing accomplishments have been so tremendous that some people may not realize that this gifted and versatile equestrian also has ridden on two Olympic show-jumping teams, in 1988 and 1992, both times finishing in the top twenty.

Todd has said that "I don't think I'll ever go back to dairy farming. I love the farm life, but in 1984 I had to make up my mind, farming or horses, and I think I'll always be involved with horses in some way." [13]

More recent reports have quoted the eventer as saying he plans to go back to his family farm after the 2000 Olympics. Whatever he decides, he's already put his country — and himself — on the map for good.

Bruce Davidson: Self-Made Success

An Olympic individual gold medal is the only honor that's eluded Bruce Davidson, America's perennial eventing star. The winner of consecutive World Championship titles in 1974 (aboard Irish Cap) and 1978 (Might Tango) — a feat that's never been repeated — has ridden on five Olympic teams: 1972 (Plain Sailing), 1976 (Irish Cap), 1984 (J. J. Babu), 1988 (Dr. Peaches), and 1996 (Heyday); and earned team gold medals in 1976 and 1984 and team silvers in 1972 and 1996.

Davidson, of Unionville, Pennsylvania, was the first American to win England's Badminton CCI**** (in 1995, aboard Eagle Lion), and he has won the Rolex Kentucky CCI*** five times. He has been named the USCTA's Rider of the Year with almost ho-hum regularity, earning the title fifteen times to date and holding it for an astonishing fourteen years in a row, from 1982 to 1995.

In an essay in *The U.S. Equestrian Team Book of Riding*, Davidson recalled his early years, Pony Clubbing and becoming fascinated with the highest levels of equestrian competition — interests that manifested despite his growing up the only horse-crazy member of his family. He calls U.S. eventing-team coach Jack Le Goff's invitation to train at the USET headquarters in Gladstone a "fantastic" opportunity "to really study riding with someone who could perform all phases at the highest level. To be able to do so myself became my goal, and still is." At Gladstone, an eager yet inexperienced Davidson "had to work hard, because I didn't want to be sent home and lose my chance to learn more about those things about which I was so obviously ignorant." [14]

Davidson is famous for his string of international successes on self-made horses. He bought 1976 Olympic mount Irish Cap as a five-year-old, 1984 Olympic mount J. J. Babu as a yearling, whole system right on through." [15]

The fifty-year-old Davidson is "carrying the whole system through" in another way as well: His son, Bruce Jr. ("Buck"), is a rising star in the

Bruce Davidson and Heyday at the 1996 Olympics.

1978 World Championship victor Might Tango as a two-year-old ex-racehorse, and three-time Rolex Kentucky CCI*** winner Dr. Peaches as a yearling. He breeds and trains young horses at his Chesterland Farm and says that "the ultimate in the sport is to breed, train, and win, to carry the eventing world, riding on the U.S. eventing squad at the 1999 Pan American Games. Perhaps we'll see father and son sharing the Olympic medal podium in the not-too-distant future.

The Art of Course Design

The speed-and-endurance element is the heart of three-day eventing, and the cross-country course is likewise weighted most heavily in the scoring process. The cross-country is generally considered to be the ultimate test of horse and rider fitness, endurance, agility, cleverness, and — that most important yet hard-to-define quality — heart.

Of all the people whose efforts help to produce an equestrian competition of the complexity and magnitude of a three-day event, none receives the scrutiny (and, frequently, criticism) to which the cross-country course designer is subjected. The course designer's job is to plan a series of obstacles that will be a challenging yet appropriate test of horse and rider. Ideally, the cross-country course should facilitate the superior competitors' rising to the top of the standings without posing an undue threat to the lesser combinations. It should encourage horses to gallop on and to jump boldly and confidently yet at the same time pose enough "questions" (as designers call them) to be a true test of skill and fitness at that level. It should take into account the terrain and the anticipated weather conditions so it rides true to level — neither too little of a challenge, nor too Herculean of an effort.

Many factors that govern or affect cross-country course design are specified in the rule books: ranges of course length; numbers, height, and breadth of obstacles; acceptable materials and construction methods; and pace. But these guidelines leave plenty of room for interpretation, and so course design is both a science and an art. An accomplished designer can create a course with a particular "feel" and flavor. At the highest levels of eventing competition, the designer walks a line between creating a challenge worthy of the occasion and creating a trap.

An accident on cross-country prompts the inevitable process of reconstructing the series of events that led up to the crash. Many times, the cause appears to be "pilot error." Other times, though, the fence itself is determined to be at fault: too big, too tricky, too something. In the latter case, the course designer in question comes under fire for jeopardizing competitors' welfare.

Course design is an inexact science, and its practitioners continually strive to improve their craft and their sport. Designers set trends in course design through their efforts to come up with a test that people haven't seen before, and perhaps from a natural desire to push the envelope a bit.

Although course design is a high-profile job within the eventing world, its practitioners are few in number and it's not generally the first horse-related occupation that comes to mind. Most course designers are horse enthusiasts who "fall into" their line of work through some combination of events.

Atlanta 1996 Olympic three-day event course designer Roger Haller is a good example. A self-described "frustrated architect," Haller evented and did hunters and equitation while growing up in the 1960s in New Jersey, not far from the U.S. Equestrian Team's Gladstone headquarters. While in college, having cut riding from his schedule so he could focus on his studies, he kept his hand in the horse world by judging a 1967 Pony Club rally and the 1968 Essex Horse Trials at Gladstone.

Haller began developing an interest in course design, and "Jack Le Goff (then USET's eventing coach) liked my courses and encouraged me to continue. I rode actively in the 1970s but kept on

designing, judging, and working as a technical delegate. After a time, I started doing more design work and cut back on my riding."

There were far fewer events in the United States in those days ("it was a different time — very much an amateur sport") and Haller had plenty of opportunities to work at high-profile competitions, even as a relatively inexperienced

1976 and 1977 prep events for the 1978 Worlds; and for the '78 Worlds, held at the Kentucky Horse Park in Lexington," among others, he said.

By the time organizers began planning the 1996 Games, Haller had gained a wealth of firsthand knowledge about Olympic-level eventing. He had been a spectator at the Games in 1968, 1972, 1976, and 1992 as well as at the 1980 Alternate

Cross-country obstacles are elaborately designed and ask "questions" of both horse and rider. Preceding page: Kiwi Blyth Tait and Messiah clearing the ditch en route to the water at Barcelona.

designer and a then-full-time civil engineer. "I worked on courses for the 1974 World Championships, in Burghley, England; for the

Olympics; and he had worked as a steward in Seoul in 1988. He also had served on an FEI three-day-event committee from 1988 to 1992. It was only natural that his name came up when the Atlanta Games organizing committee (ACOG) set out to find a cross-country course designer.

The job presented Haller with a unique challenge: The equine heat-stress studies had not yet been completed, and so the Olympic eventing rules were not finalized at the time ACOG hired him in 1993. "Normally, you would open the FEI rule book and have some guidelines right there. I didn't know how long any of the courses {for phases A, B, C, and D} would be when I went in." As the study results emerged, Haller adapted his designs accordingly. "We had to cre-

ate holding areas for washing down the horses to cool them down," he said. "We had to create routes with shorter loops. For example, the cross-country course was in the shape of a cloverleaf with a long stem. We designed it so that, if it got hot, we could chop off one of the loops to shorten the course; as it turned out, we didn't need to."

The Design Process

"The normal way I go about designing any cross-country course is first to look at the site," Haller explained. "I sit down with the landowners (in the case of the 1996 Olympics, representatives of the city of Conyers, Georgia) and talk about land use and where things are going to be. When Atlanta won the Olympic bid, we looked at about half a dozen potential sites and made evaluations and recommendations. We had a pretty good running start because we knew the land — it was a collection of former farms — and soon got a feeling for where things could be."

Haller said he was "very conscious of the consequences of failure" if the 1996 Olympic cross-country phase were to go poorly. "I was very much aware of the worldwide window of the Olympic Games, and I knew there was always the possibility that a tired horse could fall at a fence." He responded by trying "to come up with obstacles that tended to be safer. There were a lot more rounded fences toward the end of the course. The course didn't have a big oxer; I felt I couldn't take that chance. I created other ways of challenging riders and horses. I did receive some complaints about this, but I won't apologize. I designed the course so that riders would have to make turns before the obstacles; I do that quite often in the lower levels to help set up and balance the horses. I did that even with some relatively straightforward elements in Atlanta: They were like little speed bumps along the way, to make the riders have to ride."

Haller said his Olympic course offered less-challenging options for those competitors who wished to play it a bit safer. "There's always a competitive variation {in the level of horses' and riders' skill and experience} in the Olympics," he said.

"The scope of the Atlanta Games was bigger than anything I'd done before," Haller said. "I was also involved in designing the roads, the golf courses, and the arenas that tied into the cross-country course itself. There were times that I was juggling so many balls in the air; there were so many things going on. But I got into my routine: I would make one decision and go on to the next issue. Looking back, if I'd truly realized the magnitude of what I was doing, the job would have been overwhelming. Luckily, I had a good team of people, and they made it all possible.

"I feel fortunate that we had an exciting yet safe event," Haller concluded. "I think the eventing world gave a sigh of relief when it was successful."

Haller said he likes to design fences that require the rider to think "as opposed to fences that you just 'kick on' over. From the beginning, my courses have contained more tests of riders and their training, instead of just requiring sheer ability and big jumping efforts. I try to ensure that my obstacles offer the rider a series of choices or alternatives, perhaps through the use of the terrain. I also try to come up with variety."

The Evolution of Course Design

"In the 1930s, cross-country courses were essentially series of big, straightforward fences; and courses were much longer than they are now. The evolution of eventing as a sport is reflected in the ways course design has changed," explained Haller. "The three-day event at the 1960 Rome Olympics was the start of the trend of courses' asking 'questions' of riders by using combinations and water crossings, which required riders to think about their lines and their speed. The 1966 World Championships in Burghley brought the sport up to a truly international level: The world was seeing another top course besides the one at the Olympics.

"There were three types of three-day-event competitors in the early Olympics: those who went very fast because they were going for the medals, those who just got around, and those who got eliminated," Haller continued. "Nowadays, the field is much tighter from top to bottom because Olympic eligibility requirements have been tightened and the performance standards have risen accordingly. It used to be that all a country had to do was certify that its riders were ready to go. Today, countries have to earn the right to send participants."

Los Angeles 1984: Something from Nothing

The site itself can prove the greatest challenge for the cross-country course designer, as it did for the 1984 Olympic Games in Los Angeles. The dressage and the stadium jumping were to be

American Karen Stives and her mount Ben Arthur captured team gold and individual silver medals at the 1984 Los Angeles Games.

137

held at Santa Anita Park racetrack near Los Angeles, but the cross-country course had to be located elsewhere because of the dearth of open space in the Los Angeles area.

As he recalls in his memoirs, *Olympic Vet*, Joseph C. O'Dea, DVM, who served on the committee comprising the FEI Bureau and the L.A. Olympic organizing committee to select a site for the cross-country, had his doubts about the site favored by course designer Neil Ayer. Ayer, an experienced designer who had recently stepped down as president of the U.S. Combined Training Association (USCTA) after more than two decades, liked the Fairbanks Ranch land in Rancho Santa Fe, California, formerly owned by movie stars Douglas Fairbanks and Mary Pickford and slated for development into extravagant luxury homes and a top-flight golf course. Ayer wanted to work with Fairbanks Ranch's golf-course designer, Ted Robinson, to create a cross-country course that could be converted to a golf course after the Games.

When he toured the site with Ayer and Robinson, O'Dea wasn't so sure: "It was nothing but an almost dry river bottom of sand and tumbleweed, rocks and rattlesnakes in the middle of which stood a scrubby dome, a veritable mountain which millions of years of erosion had left undiminished." [16]

Robinson assured upstate New Yorker O'Dea that the California climate would assure swift progress and that even the mountain could be leveled quickly.

The task indeed proved quite manageable, and Ayer's four-and-one-half-mile, thirty-three-obstacle cross-country course was an unquestionable success, with a commendable forty-one of the

forty-six starters finishing. [17] To top off the 1984 Olympic experience — the first time since 1932 that the summer Games had been held in the U.S. — the USET squad of J. Michael Plumb, Torrance Watkins Fleischmann, Bruce Davidson, and Karen Stives won the team gold medal. Stives and her Ben Arthur claimed the individual silver, losing the gold by a rail in stadium to New Zealand's Mark Todd and Charisma.

The State of the Sport

Where is three-day eventing headed? Let's look at some current trends:

Too dangerous? The biggest current controversy in three-day eventing is over what has caused the recent rash of on-course rider fatalities. The FEI and the British Horse Trials Association have formed the FEI/BHTA International Eventing Safety Committee to study the issue. Committee members include international-level riders David O'Connor of the United States and Christopher Bartle of Great Britain, Irish jumper rider and trainer Gerry Mullins, German three-day-team veterinarian Dr. Gerit Matthesen, and FEI Eventing Committee representative Mike Tucker of Great Britain, among others. Meanwhile, most seasoned eventers have already formed their own ideas as to the probable causes and likely solutions.

Is the culprit course design? Jack Le Goff points out that, as eventing grows in popularity, the increase in numbers of competitors will naturally be reflected in an increased number of accidents. At the highest levels of the sport, however, course design — not speed, as some experts have suggested — may be to blame, he believes. "In ninety percent of the cases, the fatality happened because the rider fell and the horse fell on the rider," he said. "That's the only common denominator that exists — not speed, not type of fence, not level.

"In Barcelona in 1992, for example, there were

perhaps two or three hundred truly international-level event riders in the world today, probably only twenty or thirty are top-class. So you have twenty-five riders who can tackle that straight course, and

Questions and concerns long have persisted about the dangers of eventing.

really two different cross-country courses: the straight one — the shortest one — which was very difficult, and the alternate, longer route. I believe the {use of an alternate route} allowed the course designers to get out of line. They could build a very big, straight course and say, 'Well, they don't have to jump it; they can go around.' But people want to win, so they take the shorter route. And of the

everybody else is trying to do it, too, but they can't. That's how those accidents happen."

A member of the FEI Three-Day Event Committee, Le Goff said he and his fellow committee members are working on getting more restrictive qualifying criteria passed and on tightening the rules of course design so designers can't build fences that allow horses to get in too close before making the jumping effort. Many of the recent fatalities, he said, happened after the horse refused and the rider asked him to jump another part of the obstacle — say, a "long route" option set at a right angle to the direct route — from a near-standstill. He hopes that setting limits on those ultra-technical fences will reduce the likelihood of future fatalities.

Is the culprit poor riding skills? Most eventing experts agree that cross-country courses have become more technical in recent years, but some believe that the safety issue lies in rider education's not having kept up with the sport's sophistication, not in the course design itself. Explained Mike Plumb, "I don't know that our expertise in teaching people how to ride has gone hand in hand with the fact that there are more competitors and that the courses are more technical. I think that's the answer for the accidents. I don't think people spend enough time learning how to ride. {Eventing} requires a lot of basics, a lot of fundamentals, and a lot of understanding. Right now they're talking about fixing the jumps, but I think the answer is basic horsemanship. When I was a kid, I didn't start out as a three-day-event rider; I started out as a fox hunter and equitation rider, and I did the Medal and the Maclay and I learned how to ride."

Course designer Roger Haller agreed with Plumb. "You cannot make the sport bulletproof," he pointed out. "Riding a horse is a risk experience." It doesn't help, he added, that today's riders "are growing up in suburbia, riding in rings, instead of learning the ropes through fox hunting or on the trails. We need new answers: How can we better prepare a horse and rider so their educational foundation can help them make better decisions at the obstacles?"

Haller disagreed with Le Goff's view that loss of momentum and getting too close to a fence is a likely accident scenario, and he points out that cross-country course design has become safer in many aspects. "At the lower levels, the horses aren't going very fast and can lose momentum at a jump, but they have time to stop and regroup. At the higher levels, they are usually going too fast to stop and can hit and flip, and the horse lands on the rider. So we have some things to look at, but I think it's incorrect to say that it all ties in to course design.

"Courses are now much safer," Haller continued. "I remember jumping manure spreaders, cars with tires in back, very thin and flimsy fences. Now the timber is much thicker and jumps are better constructed. A difficult, scary fence is the exception now."

Is the culprit speed? Former USET veterinarian O'Dea has sent briefs to the FEI Veterinary Committee, detailing his concerns about the eventing deaths and putting forward his theories and recommendations. He believes that changes to the three-day-event scoring system (cross-country time penalties were increased from 0.4 per second to 1 per second, and the penalties for first refusals and falls were stiffened) encouraged more speed, which, in his opinion, can be deadly when combined with today's more technical courses. He worries that the increased speed may cause the unavoidable "time lag" between the rider's brain and the horse's body to get competitors into trouble: "The rider approaches the fence, sees it, decides what he's going to do and how he's going to do it. That has to take place from his eyes to his brain. Then he has to transmit from his brain, through his hands, seat, and legs, to the horse. The horse has to take that information as well as what he sees himself and process that, and then try to make his body do what this whole collation of information calls for. That process creates a time lag that we can measure. At a normal rate of speed, the horse is

Meanwhile, the FEI Three-Day Event Committee decided in the fall of 1999 to revert to the former scoring system, thereby lowering the time penalties. The reinstated scoring system

Australian gold: 1992 three-day event gold medalists Andrew Hoy, Gillian Rolton, and Matthew Ryan show their precious metals.

capable of doing it. But when you speed up to a point at which the time lag is too short for that sequence of events, the horse is in trouble."

Le Goff believes that speed is not the sole factor, pointing out that "in England, they have gone at six hundred meters per minute {on cross-country} for years and nobody thought anything of it. And all of a sudden we have all of these accidents, and the international speed today is five-seventy."

took effect January 1, 2000, and will be used for two years, during which time an ad hoc FEI Working Group will work with the FEI/BHTA International Eventing Safety Committee to review the fatalities and the possible contributing factors and, ultimately, to make recommendations for improving the safety of this exciting but inherently risky sport.

The Thunder from Down Under

Sweden and the Netherlands dominated the early days of Olympic three-day-eventing competition; the Dutch rider Charles Pahud de

Mortanges won team gold in 1924 and, aboard Marcroix, unprecedented back-to-back individual gold medals in 1928 and 1932. The British won their first team gold medal in 1956, and British teams remain a dominant force in international eventing to this day. But some of the event world's biggest stars of the past five decades have hailed from Australia or New Zealand, and the "land Down Under" is becoming as well-known for its eventing successes as it is for Vegemite and "Crocodile Dundee."

Australia started the trend when the team of Lawrence Morgan on Salad Days, Neale Lavis on Mirrabooka, and J. William Roycroft on Our Solo won that country's first Olympic team gold medal in eventing at the 1960 Rome Games. Morgan and Lavis also earned the individual gold and silver medals in Rome. The Aussies won team bronze again in 1968 and 1976 and have since returned to the top of the medal podium, claiming the team and individual gold medals at the 1992 Barcelona Olympics and the team gold at the 1996 Atlanta Games. They will, of course, have the home-court advantage at the 2000 Olympics in Sydney — always a boost to morale.

Australia cannot claim all of the Down Under honors, however: Neighboring New Zealand has rocketed to the top of the charts in recent years, particularly with the tremendous success of Mark Todd and Charisma, who won individual gold medals in 1984 and 1988 — the first time De Mortanges' back-to-back victories of the 1920s and early 1930s had been repeated in Olympic eventing history. New Zealand won team bronze in 1988, team silver in 1992, and team bronze in 1996; and Kiwi Blyth Tait won individual bronze in 1992 and captured the individual gold medal in 1996 aboard Ready Teddy.

Traditional eventing powerhouses like Great Britain, the United States, and Germany continue to claim their share of Olympic medals; but the Aussies and the Kiwis are positioned to figure prominently in the standings for a long time to come.

The Next Millennium

"I do believe that the sport will have to change in the long run; I said that thirty years ago, actually," said Jack Le Goff. "It's a public sport; we have to show it on TV and so forth. If we want to have a good sport, it has to be pleasing to the eye and not a battlefield.

"If you want to keep the sport going and attractive, you have to have horses that are still fresh to tackle the most important part of the competition, which is the cross-country. I think we should keep the steeplechase. But, as I said many years ago, nobody watches those darned roads and tracks phases; they're boring, and they take too much out of the horses: They get to the cross-country and they are half-cooked. We should keep the steeplechase and allow the same amount of time before cross-country; but instead of going on roads and tracks, we should just let the horses walk around and regroup."

Whatever direction the sport of three-day eventing takes, said Michael Page, its essence will remain. "The more it changes, the more it stays the same. You still put a leg on each side of the horse, you have to be fit, the horse has to be sound and talented, and you have to sacrifice for many years in order to achieve your goals. I don't think the fundamentals have changed whatsoever."

Official Results
Three-Day Eventing

STOCKHOLM 1912

TEAM COMPETITION

GOLD: SWEDEN

Rider	Horse	Points
• Axel Nordlander	Lady Artist	46.59
• Nils Adlercreutz	Atout	46.31
• Ernst Casparsson	Irmelin	46.16
		Total: 139.06

SILVER: GERMANY

• Friedrich von Rochow	Idealist	46.42
• Richard Graf von Schaesberg-Tannheim	Grundsee	46.16
• Eduard von Lütcken	Blue Boy	45.90
		Total: 138.48

BRONZE: UNITED STATES

• Benjamin Lear	Poppy	45.91
• John Montgomery	Deceive	45.88
• Guy Henry, Jr.	Chiswell	45.54
		Total: 137.33

INDIVIDUAL COMPETITION

GOLD	Axel Nordlander (SWE)	Lady Artist	46.59
SILVER	Friedrich von Rochow (GER)	Idealist	46.42
BRONZE	Jean Cariou (FRA)	Cocotte	46.32

ANTWERP 1920

TEAM COMPETITION

GOLD: SWEDEN

Rider	Horse	Points
• Graf Helmer Mörner	Germania	1775.00
• Åge Lundström	Yrsa	1738.75
• Georg von Braun	Diana	1543.75
		Total: 5057.50

SILVER: ITALY

• Ettore Caffaratti	Caniche	1733.75
• Garibaldi Spighi	Otello	1647.50
• Giulio Cacciandra	Facetto	1353.75
		Total: 4735.00

BRONZE: BELGIUM

• Roger Moeremans d'Emaus	Sweet Girl	1652.50
• Oswald Lints	Martha	1515.00
• Jules Bonvalet	Weppelghem	1392.50
		Total: 4560.00

INDIVIDUAL COMPETITION

GOLD	Graf Helmer Mörner (SWE)	Germania	1775.00
SILVER	Åge Lundström (SWE)	Yrsa	1738.75
BRONZE	Ettore Caffaratti (ITA)	Caniche	1733.75

PARIS 1924

TEAM COMPETITION

GOLD: HOLLAND

Rider	Horse	Points
• Adolph van der Voort van Zijp	Silver Piece	1976.00
• Charles Pahud de Mortanges	Johnny Walker	1828.00
• Gerard de Kruyff	Addio	1493.50
		Total: 5297.50

SILVER: SWEDEN

• Claës König	Bojar	1730.00
• Carl Torsten Sylvan	Amita	1678.00
• Gustaf Hagelin	Varius	1335.50
		Total: 4743.50

BRONZE: ITALY

• Alberto Lombardi	Pimplo	1572.00
• Alessandro Alvisi	Capiligio	1536.00
• Emanuele di Pralormo	Mount Felix	1404.50
		Total: 4512.50

INDIVIDUAL COMPETITION

GOLD	Adolph van der Voort van Zijp (HOL)	Silver Piece	1976.00
SILVER	Frode Kirkebjerg (DEN)	Meteor	1853.50
BRONZE	Sloan Doak (USA)	Pathfinder	1845.50

AMSTERDAM 1928

TEAM COMPETITION

GOLD: HOLLAND

Rider	Horse	Points
• Charles Pahud de Mortanges	Marcroix	1969.82
• Gerard de Kruyff	Va-t-en	1967.26
• Adolph van der Voort van Zijp	Silver Piece	1928.60
		Total: 5865.68

SILVER: NORWAY

• Bjart Ording	And Over	1912.98
• Arthur Quist	Hildalgo	1895.14
• Eugen Johansen	Baby	1587.56
		Total: 5395.68

BRONZE: POLAND

• Michal Antoniewicz	Moja Mita	1822.50
• Józef Trenkwald	Lwi Pazur	1645.20
• Karol Rómmel	Doneuse	1600.22
		Total: 5067.92

INDIVIDUAL COMPETITION

GOLD	Charles Pahud de Mortanges (HOL)	Marcroix	1969.82
SILVER	Gerard de Kruyff (HOL)	Va-t-en	1967.26
BRONZE	Bruno Neumann (GER)	Ilja	1944.42

LOS ANGELES 1932

TEAM COMPETITION

GOLD: UNITED STATES

Rider	Horse	Points
• Earl Thomson	Jenny Camp	1811.000
• Harry Chamberlin	Pleasant Smiles	1687.833
• Edwin Argo	Honolulu Tomboy	1539.250
		Total: 5038.083

SILVER: HOLLAND

• Charles Pahud de Mortanges	Marcroix	1813.833
• Karel Johan Schummelketel	Duiveltje	1614.500
• Aernout van Lennep	Henk	1260.750
		Total: 4689.083

BRONZE: NO MEDAL AWARDED

INDIVIDUAL COMPETITION

GOLD	Charles Pahud de Mortanges (HOL)	Marcroix	1813.833
SILVER	Earl Thomson (USA)	Jenny Camp	1811.000
BRONZE	Clarence von Rosen (SWE)	Sunnyside Maid	1809.416

BERLIN 1936

TEAM COMPETITION

GOLD: GERMANY

Rider	Horse	Points
• Ludwig Stubbendorff	Nurmi	-37.70
• Rudolf Lippert	Fasan	-111.60
• Konrad Freiherr von Wangenheim	Kurfürst	-527.35
		Total: -676.65

SILVER: POLAND

• Henryk Rojcewicz	Arlekin III	-253.00
• Zdzislaw Kawecki	Bambino	-300.70
• Seweryn Kulesza	Tosca	-438.00
		Total: -991.70

BRONZE: GREAT BRITAIN

• Alec Scott	Bob Clive	-117.30
• Edward Howard-Vyse	Blue Steel	-324.00
• Richard Fanshawe	Bowie Knife	-8754.20
		Total: -9195.50

INDIVIDUAL COMPETITION

GOLD	Ludwig Stubbendorff (GER)	Nurmi	-37.70
SILVER	Earl Thomson (USA)	Jenny Camp	-99.90
BRONZE	Hans Mathiesen-Lunding (DEN)	Jason	-102.20

LONDON 1948

TEAM COMPETITION

GOLD: UNITED STATES

Rider	Horse	Points
• Frank Henry	Swing Low	-21.00
• Charles Anderson	Reno Palisade	-26.50
• Earl Thomson	Reno Rhythm	-114.00
		Total: -161.50

SILVER: SWEDEN

• Robert Selfelt	Claque	-25.00
• Olof Stahre	Komet	-70.00
• Sigurd Svensson	Dust	-70.00
		Total: -165.00

BRONZE: MEXICO

• Humberto Mariles Cortés	Parral	-61.75
• Raúl Campero	Tarahumara	-120.50
• Joaquin Solano Chagoya	Malinche	-123.00
		Total: -305.25

INDIVIDUAL COMPETITION

GOLD	Bernard Chevallier (FRA)	Aiglonne	+4.00
SILVER	Frank Henry (USA)	Swing Low	-21.00
BRONZE	Robert Selfelt (SWE)	Claque	-25.00

HELSINKI 1952

TEAM COMPETITION

GOLD: SWEDEN

Rider	Horse	Points
• Hans von Blixen-Finecke, Jr.	Jubal	-28.33
• Olof Stahre	Komet	-69.41
• Karl Folke Frölén	Fair	-124.20
	Total:	**-221.94**

SILVER: GERMANY

• Wilhelm Büsing	Hubertus	-55.50
• Klaus Wagner	Dachs	-65.66
• Otto Rothe	Trux von Kamax	-114.33
	Total:	**-235.49**

BRONZE: UNITED STATES

• Charles Hough	Cassivellannus	-70.66
• Walter Staley	Craigwood Park	-168.50
• John Wofford	Benny Grimes	-348.00
	Total:	**-587.16**

INDIVIDUAL COMPETITION

GOLD	Hans von Blixen-Finecke, Jr. (SWE)	Jubal	-28.33
SILVER	Guy Lefrant (FRA)	Verdun	-54.50
BRONZE	Wilhelm Büsing (GER)	Hubertus	-55.50

STOCKHOLM 1956

TEAM COMPETITION

GOLD: GREAT BRITAIN

Rider	Horse	Points
• Francis Weldon	Kilbarry	-85.48
• A. Laurence Rook	Wild Venture	-119.64
• Albert Hill	Countryman III	-150.36
	Total:	**-355.48**

SILVER: GERMANY

• August Lütke-Westhues	Trux von Kamax	-84.87
• Otto Rothe	Sissi	-158.04
• Klaus Wagner	Prinze B	-233.00
	Total:	**-475.91**

BRONZE: CANADA

• John Rumble	Cilroy	-162.53
• James Elder	Colleen	-193.69
• Brian Herbinson	Tara	-216.50
	Total:	**-572.72**

INDIVIDUAL COMPETITION

GOLD	Petrus Kastenman (SWE)	Iluster	-66.53
SILVER	August Lütke-Westhues (GER)	Trux von Kamax	-84.87
BRONZE	Francis Weldon (GBR)	Kilbarry	-85.48

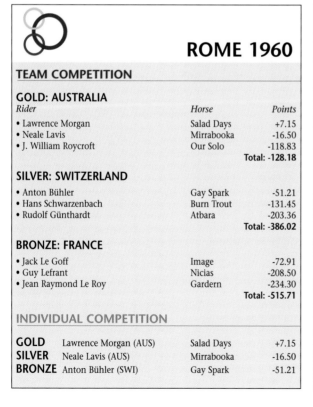

ROME 1960

TEAM COMPETITION

GOLD: AUSTRALIA

Rider	Horse	Points
• Lawrence Morgan	Salad Days	+7.15
• Neale Lavis	Mirrabooka	-16.50
• J. William Roycroft	Our Solo	-118.83
	Total:	**-128.18**

SILVER: SWITZERLAND

• Anton Bühler	Gay Spark	-51.21
• Hans Schwarzenbach	Burn Trout	-131.45
• Rudolf Günthardt	Atbara	-203.36
	Total:	**-386.02**

BRONZE: FRANCE

• Jack Le Goff	Image	-72.91
• Guy Lefrant	Nicias	-208.50
• Jean Raymond Le Roy	Gardern	-234.30
	Total:	**-515.71**

INDIVIDUAL COMPETITION

GOLD	Lawrence Morgan (AUS)	Salad Days	+7.15
SILVER	Neale Lavis (AUS)	Mirrabooka	-16.50
BRONZE	Anton Bühler (SWI)	Gay Spark	-51.21

TOKYO 1964

TEAM COMPETITION

GOLD: ITALY

Rider	Horse	Points
• Mauro Checcoli	Surbean	+64.40
• Paolo Angioni	King	+17.87
• Giuseppe Ravano	Royal Love	+3.53
	Total:	**+85.80**

SILVER: UNITED STATES

• Michael Page	Grasshopper	+47.40
• Kevin Freeman	Gallopade	+17.13
• J. Michael Plumb	Bold Minstrel	+1.33
	Total:	**+65.86**

BRONZE: WEST GERMANY/EAST GERMANY

• Fritz Ligges	Donkosak	+49.20
• Horst Karsten	Condora	+36.60
• Gerhard Schulz	Balza X	-29.07
	Total:	**+56.73**

INDIVIDUAL COMPETITION

GOLD	Mauro Checcoli (ITA)	Surbean	+64.40
SILVER	Carlos Moratorio (ARG)	Chalan	+56.40
BRONZE	Fritz Ligges (GER)	Donkosak	+49.20

MEXICO CITY 1968

TEAM COMPETITION

GOLD: GREAT BRITAIN

Rider	Horse	Points
• Derek Allhusen	Lochinvar	-41.61
• Richard Meade	Cornishman V	-64.46
• Reuben Jones	The Poacher	-69.86
	Total:	**-175.93**

SILVER: UNITED STATES

Rider	Horse	Points
• Michael Page	Foster	-52.31
• James Wofford	Kilkenny	-74.06
• J. Michael Plumb	Plain Sailing	-119.50
	Total:	**-245.87**

BRONZE: AUSTRALIA

Rider	Horse	Points
• Wayne Roycroft	Zhivago	-95.05
• Brien Cobcroft	Depeche	-108.76
• J. William Roycroft	Warrathoola	-127.55
	Total:	**-331.36**

INDIVIDUAL COMPETITION

GOLD	Jean-Jacques Guyon (FRA)	Pitou	-38.86
SILVER	Derek Allhusen (GBR)	Lochinvar	-41.61
BRONZE	Michael Page (USA)	Foster	-52.31

MUNICH 1972

TEAM COMPETITION

GOLD: GREAT BRITAIN

Rider	Horse	Points
• Richard Meade	Laurieston	+57.73
• Mary Gordon Watson	Cornishman V	+30.27
• Bridget Parker	Cornish Gold	+7.53
	Total:	**+95.53**

SILVER: UNITED STATES

Rider	Horse	Points
• Kevin Freeman	Good Mixture	+29.87
• Bruce Davidson	Plain Sailing	+24.47
• J. Michael Plumb	Free and Easy	-43.53
	Total:	**+10.81**

BRONZE: GERMANY

Rider	Horse	Points
• Harry Klugmann	Christopher Rob	+8.00
• Ludwig Goessing	Chikago	-0.40
• Karl Schultz	Pisco	-25.60
	Total:	**-18.00**

INDIVIDUAL COMPETITION

GOLD	Richard Meade (GBR)	Laurieston	+57.73
SILVER	Alessandro Argenton (ITA)	Woodland	+43.33
BRONZE	Jan Jönsson (SWE)	Sarajevo	+39.67

MONTREAL 1976

TEAM COMPETITION

GOLD: UNITED STATES

Rider	Horse	Points
• Edmund "Tad" Coffin	Bally Cor	-114.99
• J. Michael Plumb	Better and Better	-125.85
• Bruce Davidson	Irish Cap	-200.16
	Total:	**-441.00**

SILVER: GERMANY

Rider	Horse	Points
• Karl Schultz	Madrigal	-129.45
• Herbert Blöcker	Albrant	-213.15
• Helmut Rethemeier	Pauline	-242.00
	Total:	**-584.60**

BRONZE: AUSTRALIA

Rider	Horse	Points
• Wayne Roycroft	Laurenson	-178.04
• Mervyn Bennett	Regal Reign	-206.04
• J. William Roycroft	Version	-215.46
	Total:	**-599.54**

INDIVIDUAL COMPETITION

GOLD	Edmund "Tad" Coffin (USA)	Bally Cor	-114.99
SILVER	J. Michael Plumb (USA)	Better and Better	-125.85
BRONZE	Karl Schultz (GER)	Madrigal	-129.45

MOSCOW 1980

TEAM COMPETITION

GOLD: U.S.S.R.

Rider	Horse	Points
• Aleksandr Blinov	Galzun	-120.80
• Yuri Salnikov	Pintset	-151.60
• Valery Volkov	Tskheti	-184.60
	Total:	**-457.00**

SILVER: ITALY

Rider	Horse	Points
• Euro Federico Roman	Rossinan	-108.60
• Anna Casagrande	Daleye	-266.20
• Mauro Roman	Dourakine 4	-281.40
	Total:	**-656.20**

BRONZE: MEXICO

Rider	Horse	Points
• Manuel Mendivil Yocupicio	Remember	-319.75
• David Barcena Rios	Bombon	-362.50
• José Luis Perez Soto	Quelite	-490.60
	Total:	**-1172.85**

INDIVIDUAL COMPETITION

GOLD	Euro Federico Roman (ITA)	Rossinan	-108.60
SILVER	Aleksandr Binov (SOV/KYR)	Galzun	-120.80
BRONZE	Yuri Salnikov (SOV/RUS)	Pintset	-151.60

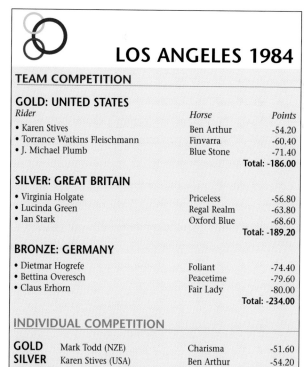

LOS ANGELES 1984

TEAM COMPETITION

GOLD: UNITED STATES

Rider	Horse	Points
• Karen Stives	Ben Arthur	-54.20
• Torrance Watkins Fleischmann	Finvarra	-60.40
• J. Michael Plumb	Blue Stone	-71.40
	Total:	**-186.00**

SILVER: GREAT BRITAIN

Rider	Horse	Points
• Virginia Holgate	Priceless	-56.80
• Lucinda Green	Regal Realm	-63.80
• Ian Stark	Oxford Blue	-68.60
	Total:	**-189.20**

BRONZE: GERMANY

Rider	Horse	Points
• Dietmar Hogrefe	Foliant	-74.40
• Bettina Overesch	Peacetime	-79.60
• Claus Erhorn	Fair Lady	-80.00
	Total:	**-234.00**

INDIVIDUAL COMPETITION

GOLD	Mark Todd (NZE)	Charisma	-51.60
SILVER	Karen Stives (USA)	Ben Arthur	-54.20
BRONZE	Virginia Holgate (GBR)	Priceless	-56.80

SEOUL 1988

TEAM COMPETITION

GOLD: GERMANY

Rider	Horse	Points
• Claus Erhorn	Justyn Thyme	-62.35
• Matthias Baumann	Shamrock	-68.80
• Thies Kaspareit	Sherry	-94.80
	Total:	**-225.96**

SILVER: GREAT BRITAIN

Rider	Horse	Points
• Ian Stark	Sir Wattie	-52.80
• Virginia Holgate Leng	Master Craftsman	-62.00
• Karen Straker	Get Smart	-142.00
	Total:	**-256.80**

BRONZE: NEW ZEALAND

Rider	Horse	Points
• Mark Todd	Charisma	-42.60
• Judith "Tinks" Pottinger	Volunteer	-65.80
• Andrew Bennie	Grayshott	-162.80
	Total:	**-271.20**

INDIVIDUAL COMPETITION

GOLD	Mark Todd (NZE)	Charisma	-42.60
SILVER	Ian Stark (GBR)	Sir Wattie	-52.80
BRONZE	Virginia Holgate Leng (GBR)	Master Craftsman	-62.00

BARCELONA 1992

TEAM COMPETITION

GOLD: AUSTRALIA

Rider	Horse	Points
• Matthew Ryan	Kibah Tic Toc	-70.00
• Andrew Hoy	Kiwi	-89.40
• Gillian Rolton	Peppermint Grove	-129.20
	Total:	**-288.60**

SILVER: NEW ZEALAND

Rider	Horse	Points
• Blyth Tait	Messiah	-87.60
• Vicky Latta	Chief	-87.80
• Andrew Nicholson	Spinning Rhombus	-115.40
	Total:	**-290.80**

BRONZE: GERMANY

Rider	Horse	Points
• Herbert Blöcker	Feine Dame	-81.30
• Ralf Ehrenbrink	Kildare	-108.40
• Cord Mysegaes	Ricardo	-110.40
	Total:	**-300.30**

INDIVIDUAL COMPETITION

GOLD	Matthew Ryan (AUS)	Kibah Tic Toc	-70.00
SILVER	Herbert Blöcker (GER)	Feine Dame	-81.30
BRONZE	Blyth Tait (NZE)	Messiah	-87.60

ATLANTA 1996

TEAM COMPETITION

GOLD: AUSTRALIA

Rider	Horse	Points
• Wendy Schaeffer	Sunburst	-61.00
• Phillip Dutton	True Blue Girdwood	-69.40
• Andrew Hoy	Darien Powers	-73.45
	Total:	**-203.85**

SILVER: UNITED STATES

Rider	Horse	Points
• Karen O'Connor	Biko	-105.60
• David O'Connor	Giltedge	-76.00
• Bruce Davidson	Heyday	-79.50
	Total:	**-261.10**

BRONZE: NEW ZEALAND

Rider	Horse	Points
• Blyth Tait	Chesterfield	-70.10
• Andrew Nicholson	Jagermeister II	-100.65
• Vaughn Jefferis	Bounce	-97.80
	Total:	**268.55**

INDIVIDUAL COMPETITION

GOLD	Blyth Tait (NZE)	Ready Teddy	-56.80
SILVER	Sally Clark (NZE)	Squirrel Hill	-60.40
BRONZE	Kerry Millikin (USA)	Out and About	-73.70

Wallechinsky, David. (1996). *The Complete Book of the Summer Olympics.* Boston: Little, Brown, pp. 368-378.

Note: Results and scores in this table do not show "drop scores" — discounted scores of lowest-scoring riders on four-rider teams.

CHAPTER SIX

Show Jumping

The most popular of the three Olympic equestrian disciplines, show jumping is also the most colorful. Even those who don't follow equestrian sports enjoy watching the eager horses and smartly attired riders race against the clock to negotiate a sea of painted poles, faux stone walls, gates, and water jumps.

The 1928 individual gold medalists Frantisek Ventura of Czechoslovakia and Eliot. Opposite: 1996 U.S. team silver medalists Leslie Burr-Howard and Extreme, on course in Atlanta.

The audience holds its collective breath during each round, letting out audible gasps or sympathetic murmurs with each fallen rail, refusal, or seemingly impossible extrication from disaster; and bursts into cheers as horse and rider sprint through the finish flags to stop the clock.

Show jumping is an easy sport for spectators to follow. There's no subjective evaluation of the fine points of equitation, and miles of trudging across hill and dale to view the action is not required. Put simply, the name of the game is: Whoever makes it around the course with the fewest faults (penalties) wins. If more than one competitor goes "clean" in the first round, they then vie for the ribbons in a "jump-off" against the clock, in which the rider with the fewest faults and fastest time wins.

At the 2000 Olympic Games in Sydney, the show-jumping competition will comprise five rounds. All entrants will ride in the first three rounds. The first round will be used as a qualifying round for the individual competition, and the second and third rounds will constitute the competition for the team medals.

Each rider's faults from rounds two and three will be totaled and added to those of his or her teammates; the score of the lowest-placing rider from each four-member team will be dropped. The three teams with the lowest total number of faults from rounds two and three will win the gold, silver, and bronze medals in the team competition (also known as the *Prix des Nations*, or Nations Cup).

Next, the top forty-five individual riders from the first three rounds will advance to round A of the two-round individual competition. The top twenty riders from round A will then compete in round B, the final round. The riders with the

three highest combined scores from rounds A and B will win the individual medals. In the event of a tie for a medal placing, a jump-off round will determine the final individual placings.

German competitors Kurt Hasse and Tora won double gold at the 1936 Berlin Olympic Games.

The rules for determining team and individual show-jumping medalists have changed somewhat over the years since the sport debuted in the modern Olympic Games in 1912. Course design has become more technical, and the fences themselves would make early-20th

Century jumper riders gawk. Today's competitors regularly jump such oddities as automobiles, Shamu the whale, beer bottles, and oversized "billboards" bearing the names and logos of the sport's many sponsors. Show jumping has largely stayed true to its roots in terms of the rules, but there are still plenty of stories to tell!

Show Jumping Through the Years

In the first half of the 20th Century, Olympic show jumpers competed over what looked more like hunter courses than the fanciful layouts of today. A course had considerably more obstacles than today's rules permit, and the earliest fences were tame compared to modern standards.

The show-jumping course at the 1912 Stockholm Olympics consisted of fifteen obstacles — about the same number you'll find on an international jumper course today — but some had to be jumped twice, bringing the total of jumping efforts up to twenty-nine. In modern course design, each fence is jumped only once. (All rules and specifications in this section are taken from *Equestrian Olympic Games: Ancient and Modern*.) [1] Obstacles could be a maximum of 1.4 meters (approximately four feet, seven inches) high; water jumps could not exceed four meters (about seven feet, three inches) in breadth. The designated speed was 400 meters per minute (mpm); completing the course under the time allowed was of no advantage. In addition to the water jump, obstacles included brush, post-and-rail, stone wall, ditch, and triple bars.

Competitors earned ten points per jump negotiated cleanly, with deductions assessed as follows: -2 for a first refusal, -4 for a second refusal or the fall of horse and rider, -6 for a third refusal or the fall of the rider only, -1 if the horse touched the fence with either hind legs or forelegs, -2 for a knockdown by the hind legs, -4 for a knockdown by the forelegs or both fore- and hind legs, -1 if the hind legs touched the demarcation line of a spread jump, -2 if the forelegs touched the demarcation line or the hind legs touched within the demarcation line, and -4 if the forelegs touched within the demarcation line. Riders lost two points for every five seconds they went over the time limit. They were eliminated for going off course, deviating from the course, or receiving third-party assistance. [2]

Participating nations were permitted to enter six riders and three alternates in the individual competition, as well as four riders and two alternates in the team competition. The teams consisted of the three highest-placed riders. Each horse had to carry a minimum of seventy-five kilograms (165 pounds). No rules governed competitors' choice of saddlery, but there was a dress code: "undress" uniform for military officers; black or "pink" (scarlet) coats with silk hats or hunt caps for civilian competitors. A total of thirty-one riders representing eight nations took part. [3]

The rules changed little for the 1920 Antwerp Olympics. The 800-meter-long show-jumping course had fourteen obstacles of 1.3 to 1.4 meters in height, with maximum water-jump spreads of four meters. The rules regarding speed, minimum weight, dress, and saddlery remained the same as in 1912. Penalties were assessed as follows: first refusal, -2; second refusal, -4; third refusal, -8; fourth refusal, elimination; fall of horse and rider, -8; fall of rider only, -4; knockdown with forelegs, -2; knockdown with hind legs, -1; going off course, -2; hind legs within the demarcation line of spread obstacles, -1; forelegs within the demarcation line, -2. Twenty-five riders from a total of six nations competed. [4]

An additional fence was added to the show-jumping course in the 1924 Paris Games; rules and penalties remained unchanged. Eleven nations were represented, for a total of thirty-four competitors. [5]

The course for the 1928 Amsterdam Olympics consisted of sixteen obstacles. The penalty for exceeding the time allowed dropped from -1 for every five seconds over to -1/4 per second over.

Penalties were assessed as follows: first refusal, -2; second refusal, -6; third refusal or disobedience, elimination; knockdown with forelegs, -4; knockdown with hind legs, -2; forelegs within the demarcation line of spread jumps, -4; hind legs within the demarcation line, -2; fall of horse and rider, -6; fall of rider only, -10; going off course, -2. Other rules remained unchanged. Sixteen nations and a total of forty-six riders competed.

The course at the 1932 Los Angeles Games consisted of eighteen obstacles with a total of twenty jumping efforts. The maximum permitted height increased from 1.4 meters to 1.6 meters (approximately five feet, three inches); the maximum breadth of the water jump also increased, from four meters to five meters (approximately sixteen feet, five inches). Time and jumping penalties remained the same as in 1928. Only eleven riders from four nations (Japan, Mexico, Sweden, and the United States) competed on account of the high cost of transporting horses overseas, made additionally burdensome in light of the worldwide post-World War I economic slump. [7]

The seventeen obstacles (twenty total jumping efforts) in the 1936 Berlin Olympic show-jumping course included a narrow gate, a wall with a roof-shaped top, a double oxer, an open ditch, and a wall topped with a garden fence. The time penalties and prescribed pace remained the same as in 1932. Jumping penalties were assessed as follows: first refusal or disobedience, -3; second refusal or disobedience, -6; third refusal or disobedience, elimination; knockdown or landing within the

Ulrich Kirchhoff of Germany and Jus de Pommes, the 1996 team and individual gold medalists.

demarcation line by either forelegs or hind legs, -4; fall of horse and rider, -6; fall of rider only, -10.

Three competitors each from eighteen nations took part. Jump-offs decided the gold and bronze medalists in the individual competition. [8]

The competition at the 1948 London Games marked the debut of several nations. Although they had taken part in previous Olympic equestrian events, Denmark and Finland had never before competed in show jumping; and it was the first time Brazil and Ireland had competed in any Olympic equestrian event. These nations' participation brought the total number of countries in show jumping to fifteen, with a total of forty-four riders vying for the medals. The rules for the London Games remained about the same as for Berlin. [9]

Olympic show-jumping team qualifying and selection procedures have seen more than their share of changes since the 1948 Games (see Chapter 2 for details on the U.S. Equestrian Team's move to a numerical selection system), but the competition itself hasn't changed much since that time. In Olympic competition, obstacles can be no more than 1.7 meters (about five feet, seven inches) high. Spread obstacles may not exceed two meters (six feet, seven inches) in breadth, except for the triple bars, which can have a spread of up to 2.2 meters (about seven feet, two inches). Water jumps can have a spread of up to 4.5 meters (fourteen feet, nine inches). The total metric length of the course cannot exceed the number of obstacles multiplied by sixty (example: 15 obstacles multiplied by 60 = 900 meters maximum course length). [10] A knockdown incurs four faults, as does putting a foot in the water or on the edge ("lathe") of a water jump. The first refusal incurs three faults, with six faults for the second refusal. A third refusal or a fall of horse or rider results in elimination. [11]

Legends in Olympic Show Jumping

Show jumping's Olympic medalists are among the most famous riders and horses in history. Often possessed of strong personalities and unique styles and "ways of going," top jumper riders and their mounts are among the highest-profile celebrities of the horse world.

The 1948 team gold medalists: Alberto Valdes, Humberto Mariles Cortés, and Ruben Uriza of Mexico.

The greatest of this group of stars, however, have done more than just bedeck magazine covers and attract gaggles of fans: They have changed and influenced the sport in countless ways. Some, like the legendary William Steinkraus, have gone on to shape the world of show jumping by heading important equestrian organizations — Steinkraus is a former U.S. Equestrian Team president and is a member of the FEI Bureau, for example — and by serving in various official capacities to help advance the sport. Others, like U.S. co-*chefs d'équipe* George Morris and Frank Chapot, put their impressive

body of competitive know-how toward helping today's (and tomorrow's) competitors achieve their goals. Whatever direction their lives have taken following their own Olympic heydays, though, these superstars have earned their place in show-jumping history.

Humberto Mariles Cortés: Man of Mystery

Legendary American trainer and coach George Morris called the Mexican general a "bigger-than-life horseman."[12] By all accounts opinionated and flamboyant, Mariles led his team to a gold medal in the 1948 London Olympics and himself claimed the individual gold — a singular accomplishment to date for Mexico — and went on to numerous wins in prestigious horse shows throughout North America before his mysterious death in 1973 at the age of sixty.

Mariles, who trained with the Italian and German show-jumping teams, displayed unusual craftiness aboard his Mexican-bred horse Arete — a remarkable animal who jumped boldly despite being blind in one eye — to clinch the win in London. Last to go, and almost certainly relishing the audience's suspense, he made his way around the course and approached the final two fences: a water jump to a wall, the distance between which had proved the other competitors' nemesis. "To the amazement of all, Arete was allowed to pop into the water, and consequently was the only horse to arrive at the wall sufficiently balanced to clear it."[13]

The events of the last years of the general's life were strange and controversial. In 1964, he shot and killed a man in an incident of "road rage" and served five years of his twenty-year prison sentence. In 1973, he was arrested for drug trafficking in Paris and was later found dead in his jail cell. Whether the cause of death was suicide or murder was never determined, and so people will keep talking about Mariles — just what he would have wanted.

Bertalan de Némethy: A Coach for All Seasons

In many ways, the 1960s, 1970s, and early 1980s were the golden age of equestrian sports in the United States. In eventing, much of the cred-

U.S. show jumping made tremendous progress under coach Bertalan de Némethy.

it goes to USET coach Jack Le Goff. Retired Swedish cavalry officer Colonel Bengt Ljungquist coached U.S. dressage squads to several international victories. And in show jumping, the Team's many competitive successes and enormous strides in riding and training techniques and in course design were direct results of the influence of coach Bertalan de Némethy.

Born in Hungary in 1911, de Némethy began riding as a child and competed in show jumping for the first time as a teenager. One of his uncles was a cavalry officer, and so the young man chose to continue his education at the military academy of Ludovica, in Budapest. After his graduation in 1932, de Némethy entered the cavalry school and, in 1937, became a riding instructor at the school. He was slated to ride on Hungary's 1940 Olympic show-jumping squad, but those Games were cancelled in the looming face of World War II.

Just as the U.S. Army occasionally sent cavalry officers abroad to study at other countries' cavalry schools, the Hungarian Army sent de Némethy to the German cavalry school. Here he trained with a number of master horsemen, including Fritz Stecken, "Bubi" Günther, and Otto Lörke; competed in jumping events; and observed firsthand the formidable "German system" of training horses and riders.

World War II had tragic consequences for untold millions of people, but it led to one positive outcome for American show jumping: de Némethy's emigration from Hungary and eventual move to the United States. Having had to leave Germany and the cavalry school there because of the impending conflict, he returned to Hungary, only to find the Russian Army closing in on Budapest. He and the military school's cavalry cadets fled the city and headed toward Denmark, trying to keep ahead of the Russians and to find enough to eat along the way. The young men made it safely to Denmark, and de Némethy would remain in Copenhagen for six years, teaching riding.

In 1952, the U.S. Embassy granted him permission to emigrate, and he settled in New Jersey, not far from Hamilton Farm in Gladstone, which in 1960 would become the headquarters of the U.S. Equestrian Team. He befriended and impressed William Steinkraus and Arthur McCashin — both members of the USET's inaugural civilian Olympic team in 1952 and winners of a team bronze medal — among others, and he also began designing show-jumping courses for a number of American shows. Steinkraus and McCashin told the USET about de Némethy's talents, and USET president Whitney Stone offered him the position of jumping-team coach in 1955. [14]

De Némethy would remain with the Team until 1980. In his twenty-five years with the Team, he helped to mold some of the greatest jumper riders in American equestrian history: Steinkraus, George Morris, Frank Chapot, Hugh Wiley, Joe Fargis, Kathy Kusner, and Michael Matz, to name just a few.

Much of his success as a coach stemmed from his insistence on solid fundamentals: an independent seat and hand, plenty of basic dressage schooling, longe-line work, and gymnastic work over cavalletti and low fences. He brought his European cavalry tradition to a country that was largely unfamiliar with dressage, and his emphasis on correct basics refined the skills of his human and equine pupils. From his methodology evolved what *The Chronicle of Horse* called "the classic American style — a light, elegant seat on horses developed physically and mentally through his system of rigorous flatwork and progressive series of gymnastic exercises." [15] (He later documented his training system in a book, *The de Némethy Method.*)

De Némethy-coached teams never did win an Olympic team gold medal, but they garnered enough other medals to prove that the American show jumpers could more than hold their own

De Némethy's 1972 silver-medal-winning team: (from left) Kathy Kusner, Frank Chapot, Neal Shapiro, and William Steinkraus.

on the world stage. In 1960, the team of William Steinkraus, Frank Chapot, and George Morris captured the team silver medal. Eight years later, in Mexico City, Steinkraus made history by winning America's first-ever equestrian individual gold medal, aboard the legendary Snowbound. At the Munich Games in 1972, Steinkraus, Neal Shapiro, Kathy Kusner, and Chapot captured another team silver; and Shapiro and his great mount Sloopy won the individual bronze. The team gold medal that eluded de Némethy during his coaching career came at the 1984 Los Angeles Olympics, held just four years after his retirement. It is a fitting testament to the coach's ongoing influence that all four riders on the 1984 team — Joe Fargis, Conrad Homfeld, Leslie Burr, and Melanie Smith — were de Némethy protégés. To top off the triumph in Los Angeles, the USET also brought home the individual gold and silver medals, thanks to outstanding performances by Fargis and the great mare Touch of Class, and by Homfeld and the Trakehner stallion Abdullah.

Ironically, despite Steinkraus's individual gold medal in Mexico City, de Némethy considered the 1968 Olympic Games to have been a "disaster," with a Nations Cup that was "almost impossible to ride." [16] With big fences, little time allowed, and difficult distances, the Nations Cup course was far more challenging than others at international competitions of the day, the result being that even team gold-medal-winning Canada had an astronomical 102 faults; thirty faults per rider was average in the competition.

"We almost had it in our hands," de Némethy said of the elusive team gold medal at the 1972 Munich Games. The last American rider to go, Steinkraus on Main Spring, put in the best individual performance of the competition, a foot in the water costing them a mere four faults. [17] The U.S. team finished a maddening three-quarters of a fault behind the German team, and so the team gold medal both team captain Steinkraus and his coach yearned for was not to be.

That the USET did not win a team gold medal during de Némethy's watch does not diminish his greatness or his influence. Steinkraus himself has pointed out that the coach's philosophies and training system have become ingrained in modern show-jumping methodology — so much so that it would be impossible to separate the two.

Hans Günter Winkler: Legendary Partnership

The seven-time Olympic medalist — only dressage rider Dr. Reiner Klimke has won more equestrian medals for Germany — Hans Günter Winkler will always be remembered for his partnership with the incredible mare Halla, who carried him to team and individual gold medals at the 1956 Stockholm Games and a second team gold four years later, at the 1960 Olympics in Rome. The mare's astonishing jumping ability caught the public's eye, and her performance in

the final round at Stockholm — which Winkler says is his foremost Olympic memory — entrenched her firmly in equestrian legend.

In the first round at Stockholm, the eleven-year-old Halla took off early for the next-to-last fence, throwing Winkler into the air and causing him to pull a groin muscle. In great pain, and knowing he had to ride in the final round or his three-member German team would be eliminated, he faced the most critical performance of his career.

"They gave me some tranquilizers," he recalled of the period between rounds. "As long as I was sitting down it was OK. But then, after two hours, I had to remount and it was a disaster." Winkler was given more medication, but soon he was faced with another problem: "{A}nything strong enough to kill the pain also dulled the brain! I managed one or two practice jumps. But then I began to feel dizzy and to have double vision, so I was given some strong black coffee. And so I entered the Olympic arena.

"Then came the miracle," Winkler said. "Halla was just like a dog: She realized that I was ill and felt that I couldn't help her. All I could do was guide her to the fences, and when she took off I could only sit back, falling onto her as she landed, and I couldn't help crying out with pain. Partly because of this and partly because of my light way of riding her on a long rein, she didn't run away with me as she would have done before, and she just helped herself. It was a big, stiff course with a lot of distance problems, but she jumped clear." [18]

Halla's behavior was even more amazing when one considers that Winkler himself called the ex-steeplechaser "almost impossible to train" when he met her in 1952. He recognized the Hessen-bred's extraordinary jumping ability as well as her "intelligence, will, and great personality" but had to spend the better part of two years teaching the mare to jump high as well as wide. After that time, though, Halla "jumped the Puissance as if she was jumping cavalletti." [19]

Winkler's Olympic medals with Halla may be the most remembered, but this veteran equestrian went on to make four additional Olympic appearances, garnering plenty of medals along the way. He won team gold again at the 1964 Games in Tokyo, aboard Fidelitas; a team bronze aboard

Hans Günter Winkler and the immortal Halla, winners of team and individual gold in 1956.

Enigk at Mexico City in 1968; his fourth team gold at Munich in 1972 aboard Torphy; and a team silver aboard Torphy at Montreal in 1976. [20] He has earned plenty of other international titles in his career — among them back-to-back World Championships with Halla in 1954 and 1955 — but he treasures his Olympic medals the most.

"Olympic successes are the highlight of any sportsman's career, no matter which sport it is; no matter who you are. World records come and go, but you remain an Olympic champion for a lifetime. Only those who have not been Olympic champions say differently! I have been both Olympic and World Champion, and the Olympic title always ranks higher than the World title. The Olympic Games are the greatest sporting event on

earth — so big, so magnificent, so unique."

At seventy-four, Winkler's competitive days are behind him, but he's as involved as ever in equestrian sports. As a member of the show-jumping committee of the German Olympic Committee for Equestrian Sports, he will help select Germany's show-jumping squad for the 2000 Games. He'll be in Sydney in his role as a consultant to United Parcel Service, which is a major sponsor of all three German Olympic teams. Winkler hasn't missed an Olympic Games since he rode on his first Olympic team in 1956, and it's plain he has no intention of missing a Games anytime soon.

William Steinkraus: A Wonderful Life

Of all the outstanding riders mentored by Bertalan de Némethy, none equals the achievements and contributions made by Bill Steinkraus, whose quiet classicism in the saddle has become a sort of equestrian holy grail and who has served horse sports in so many ways since his retirement from competition.

During his lengthy and illustrious competitive career, Steinkraus rode in five Olympic Games (his sixth Olympic appearance, in Tokyo in 1964, was quashed when mount Sinjon was injured) and earned a total of four medals: team bronze in 1952 (aboard Hollandia), team silver in 1960 (Ksar d'Esprit), individual gold in 1968 (Snowbound), and team silver in 1972 (Main Spring). He retired from international competition after the 1972 fall show season, but his involvement in the horse world was far from over: He would hold the presidency or the chairmanship of the USET for the

William Steinkraus, who rode in five Olympic Games, and Ksar d'Esprit in 1960.

next twenty years, until 1992 (he still serves on the Team's board of directors), and he continues to be an honorary member of the FEI Bureau. He has written or edited a number of important equestrian texts, including *Riding and Jumping* (1961), *The U.S. Equestrian Team Book of Riding* (1976), *The Horse in Sport* (1987), and *Reflections on Riding and Jumping* (1991).

Steinkraus was introduced to horses at the age of ten, while at summer camp. The "horse bug" bit hard, and he began taking riding lessons soon after, studying with Gordon Wright (George Morris' teacher and mentor) and well-known horse dealer Morton W. "Cappy" Smith, among others. He gained invaluable experience riding the many horses that went through Smith's sales stables, and in 1941 he won both the ASPCA Maclay Cup and the Good Hands Finals at New York's National Horse Show at Madison Square Garden. He entered Yale University the following year, but higher education got postponed when he joined the cavalry branch of the Army following his freshman year, becoming one of the last cavalrymen to go through the Army's basic train-

ing on horseback. A member of the 124th Cavalry Regiment, he served in Burma during World War II, from 1943 to 1945.

After Steinkraus returned stateside, he finished his studies at Yale and picked up his riding career where he'd left off. He graduated in 1949 as a member of the class of 1948 and, four short years later, made his Olympic debut in Helsinki.

"The Olympics rank as major highlights of my career," said Steinkraus. "Each of the Games I've ridden in had its own special character, and each was a wonderful experience in its own way. Clearly, 1968 (his individual gold medal in Mexico City) has to stand a little higher than the

The 1952 medal-winning show-jumping teams: Chile, Great Britain, and the U.S.: (left to right) John Russell, William Steinkraus, and Arthur McCashin.

others, because a gold medal changes the public perception of an athlete much more than does a bronze or a silver. Athletes know, however, that the effort you put into it is still the very best — and is not always reflected by the results."

Steinkraus was similarly diplomatic when asked to compare his Olympic mounts: Hollandia, Ksar d'Esprit, Night Owl, Riviera Wonder, Sinjon, Snowbound, and Main Spring. "All were truly dream horses, though their temperaments and talents were quite different; and I think each of them would have been capable of winning a gold medal under the right circumstances and at the right time in their careers. I couldn't single out one over the others any more than I can name a favorite son or a favorite composer."

In Steinkraus's opinion, the Olympic Games —

and the athletes themselves — have changed quite a bit from a half-century ago. "The Games that took place before commercialism, professionalism, and gigantism took over had an entirely different character from today's 'modern' Games." (One of the sport's few enduring amateurs, Steinkraus maintained a business career even during his competitive heyday — a sharp contrast to most of today's Olympic riders, who are full-time professional equestrians.)

Along with Steinkraus's retirement from competition came a variety of new experiences on the other side of the arena fence and the camera lens. He did television commentary from 1976 through 1988, but he tired of the "frustrations of doing TV because I had no control over my own product. Most of our best equestrian coverage was either cut to ribbons in editing, or it never got on the air at all." Next, at the 1992 Barcelona Games, he tried his hand at judging and found that "in a way, the same thing was true of judging {as it was of TV commentary}: You don't have much control over what others may do." He opted to make the 1996 Atlanta Olympics his first "off duty" Games, taking part in the USOC/Xerox-sponsored "100 Great Athletes" festivities for gold medalists. Eventer J. Michael Plumb also received an invitation, and Steinkraus got the opportunity to catch up with Harrison Dillard, the hurdler whose experiences had so affected his views of the team-selection process. The only problem with the trip to Atlanta, he said, was the fact that "I had to fall back on TV for much of the equestrian coverage, and that left big gaps in what I got to see."

At seventy-four, Steinkraus considers himself "basically retired, though through various honorary or emeritus roles I'm still somewhat involved with the USET and the FEI, and very occasionally may serve on an appeals committee somewhere." The accomplished violist and violinist still plays chamber music, does "a bit of writing," and also "ride{s} out on an old pensioner if the weather is nice."

Fritz Thiedemann: A Hero for the People

The multi-talented German was the only rider in Olympic history to win medals in different disciplines at the same Games. At the 1952 Olympics in Helsinki, he won the individual bronze medal in show jumping aboard his legendary Holsteiner gelding Meteor; he also won a team bronze medal in dressage riding Chronist, who belonged to the German Olympic Committee for Equestrian Sports at Warendorf, the country's national equestrian training center. Thiedemann's partnership with Meteor took him to two more Olympic Games, and the little man and the huge horse won team gold medals in 1956 and 1960, finishing fourth and seventh individually.

The son of a farmer, Thiedemann's equestrian prowess showed itself early, and he excelled in local horse shows. At the age of seventeen, he went to Berlin to study with the well-known instructor and rider Major Felix Bürkner. The young man fulfilled his military obligation at the German Cavalry School at Hanover and later led a squadron of a cavalry unit in World War II. He was captured after being hampered by an injury and was sent to a Russian prison camp, where he remained until the war's end. After his release, he returned to his family farm and worked as a farmer, horse breeder, and riding instructor at a nearby riding school. He soon found his way back to equestrian competition, and he made his historic Olympic debut in jumping and dressage in 1952.

Thiedemann and Meteor — whom his owner and rider called *den Dicken* or "the Big One" — became an immensely popular pair at horse shows throughout Europe and North and South America. Friendly, approachable, and down to earth, Thiedemann acted as a sort of German goodwill ambassador and was credited with helping to mend international relations after the war. The

Italian jumper rider Raimondo d'Inzeo (in uniform) is congratulated after his individual gold-medal win at the 1960 Rome Games.

German sporting press named him Sportsman of the Year in 1958, and the German Republic and German Federation bestowed its highest civil decorations on the unassuming hero.

Thiedemann and Meteor retired from competition after winning the Nations Cup at Aachen in 1961, but the horseman remained active, designing courses and judging.

Thiedemann died on January 8, 2000, at the age of eighty-one. In his tribute to the horseman, German FN President Dieter Count Landsberg-Velen called him an idol of all German sportsmen.

Piero and Raimondo d'Inzeo: Brotherly Love

The reign of brothers and Olympic champions

Piero and Raimondo d'Inzeo was the heyday of Italian show jumping. Older brother Piero rode on eight Olympic teams, winning individual bronze and team silver in 1956 (aboard Uruguay) and individual silver and team bronze in 1960 (The Rock). The younger Raimondo, who made seven Olympic appearances, rode with his brother on the 1956 silver-medal-winning team and, aboard Merano, also claimed the individual silver; he achieved his greatest Olympic triumph in his home country in 1960 by winning the individual gold medal — with the only clear round of the competition — as well as the team bronze medal aboard Posillipo.

(The brothers will be honored in an unusual way at the 2000 Games. The Australian city of Liverpool, which will be the host community for 120 Italian athletes and delegates before and during the Games, has built a village called Base Italia. Three streets in the village have been named after famous Italian Olympians, and one of the three is d'Inzeo Place.)

Like many horsemen of their era, the d'Inzeo brothers were born into a cavalry family. Father Carlo Constante d'Inzeo, a warrant-officer instructor, started both boys riding when they turned nine, Piero in 1932 and Raimondo in 1934. Piero entered the Italian Military Academy at Modena in 1942; four years later, he rode on the Italian equestrian team for the first time. Raimondo took a slightly different path to the world of international show-jumping competition, studying engineering in college for two years before joining the cavalry and making his debut on the Italian team in 1947 at the Nations Cup.

Both brothers are versatile horsemen. Raimondo rode on both the show jumping and three-day-event teams at his first Olympic Games, in London in 1948. He and Piero both were eliminated in the jumping, but Raimondo finished thirtieth in the three-day. Piero's turn on the three-day team came in 1952 in Helsinki, where he finished an impressive sixth aboard Pagoro. Piero also has played polo and ridden steeplechasers and is an accomplished sailor as well.

Piero summed up much of the reason for his success when he said, "Patience, dedication, hard work, and sacrifice form the basis for success, and a young rider must realize that before expecting success in competitions, he must prepare himself by achieving a sound basis of general equitation." [21]

Raimondo echoed many of his brother's sentiments when he advised the aspiring competitor "to love his horse, and to be strongly dedicated to his training, and to be humble and persevering." He lamented the loss of "real" sport in modern show jumping and decried what he called "exaggerated professionalism." [22] The ideals and accomplishments of the d'Inzeo brothers still stand as benchmarks against which riders from Italy and around the world must measure themselves.

George Morris: Teacher Extraordinaire

No 20th Century horseman has had as much impact on the worlds of jumpers and hunter-seat equitation as the legendary George H. Morris. Countless aspiring young (and older) riders pore over his "Jumping Clinic" photo-critique column in *Practical Horseman* magazine, enjoy his insights (and, occasionally, take umbrage at his opinions) in his "Between Rounds" column in *The Chronicle of the Horse*, and study dog-eared copies of his best-selling book, *Hunter Seat Equitation*, which was first published in 1971 and

George Morris and Sinjon, members of the silver-medal-winning U.S. team in 1960.

is still in print. The proponent of the crest-release jumping position and the trainer of numerous Medal and Maclay winners and finalists, Morris is the acknowledged doyen of detail in everything from toe position to braid job. He's on the road constantly, giving his always-popular clinics and striving to elevate standards of equitation and horsemanship.

This versatile horseman, who runs Hunterdon Farm in New Jersey, is also a superb rider and trainer of jumpers. Morris was a member of the team-silver-medal-winning 1960 Olympic squad, finishing fourth individually aboard Sinjon. Nearly thirty years later, in 1988, he piloted Rio to victory — and a total purse of more than a half-million dollars — in the du Maurier International at Canada's Spruce Meadows. He has coached many of America's current jumping stars, including Anne Kursinski, Conrad Homfeld, Melanie Smith-Taylor, and Leslie Burr-Howard.

Morris' ties to equitation, hunters, and

jumpers aren't surprising, considering that he was — and still remains — the youngest-ever winner of both the Medal and Maclay Finals in the same year, at the age of fourteen. He's known for his opinion that a solid education in the basics of hunter-seat equitation and hunter riding — and he includes basic dressage in his must-have list of skills — is an essential building block in a jumper rider's training.

Like Steinkraus, Morris has experienced the evolution of Olympic show-jumping course design from astronomically more difficult than other international competitions to about on par. He recalled blanching upon seeing the course for the individual finals at Rome in 1960. "I remember {coach} Bert {de Némethy} dragging my horse down the ramp. I didn't want to go," he has said. [23] But his "great American Thoroughbred horse," Walter B. Devereux's Sinjon, tackled the seemingly impossible course with his customary "bravery and confidence" and "great heart" to fare "not badly," as Morris put it modestly.

" 'Johnny's' was not an easy temperament," Morris has said of the 16.1-hand bay gelding, "but he was extraordinarily honest and brave...He had a peculiar habit common to several outstanding jumpers I have known — he crossed his hind legs in jumping."

Morris stays keenly attuned to the ever-changing Olympic scene through his role as co-*chef d'équipe* of the U.S. show-jumping squad. With colleague and fellow Olympic veteran Frank Chapot, he'll be standing at the in-gate in Sydney, watching anxiously as the U.S. team members go. He says the pressure on today's riders is lessened somewhat by the leeway allowed by the drop score, "but the stress of watching four riders go — it's all stressful!"

Ludger Beerbaum: The Struggle to Stay on Top

At age thirty-six, Germany's Ludger Beerbaum is one of today's hottest show-jumping stars. He has made three trips to the Olympics, each time returning with a gold medal: team gold in 1988 with The Freak, individual gold in 1992 with Classic Touch, and a second team gold in 1996 with Ratina Z.

Beerbaum got a lucky break at the 1988 Seoul Games when his then-employer and mentor, 1976 Olympic show-jumping veteran Paul Schockemöhle, arranged for him to ride German rider Dirk Hafemeister's reserve mount, The Freak, after Beerbaum's horse, Landlord, went lame.

George Morris, now co-chef d'équipe of the U.S. jumping team, with student and fellow Olympic veteran Anne Kursinski.

"The nicest Olympic memories I have are from Seoul," said Beerbaum. "When the lameness happened with Landlord, I thought, okay, that's it. But then I got the chance with The Freak. I felt I could not lose, and we succeeded."

If Seoul produced both anxious and tri-

Germany's Ludger Beerbaum and his 1992 partner in gold, Classic Touch.

umphant moments for Beerbaum, his nerves would really be put to the test at the 1992 Games. "At Barcelona the Nations Cup was a disaster, for the whole team but also for me personally. I was very embarrassed when Classic Touch's hackamore (bitless bridle) tore during the Nations Cup competition and we were eliminated. Winning the individual gold medal afterward was the great redemption. Fortunately, at that

time, the Nations Cup was not the qualifier for the individual final as it is today!"

All of Beerbaum's Olympic experiences thus far have followed the same pattern: the highs are incredible, and the lows are heartbreaking. The 1996 Atlanta Games were no different. "Ratina Z and I won the team gold medal and, with the only double clear round in the Nations Cup, we were the top combination to qualify for the individual final. She was in top form, and I had every chance of winning the individual gold medal again. But then she got a swollen leg and I had to retire her before the final. That was a very difficult experience for me."

Beerbaum echoes what other Olympic gold medalists have said about the achievement: "If you win a gold medal at the Olympics, you become a part of history. A gold medal is different from a championship in your own sport, which is for the most part recognized only by equestrian enthusiasts and other sports insiders. If you have been an Olympic champion, some doors open more easily." He realizes, however, that staying on top is perhaps even more difficult than attaining that first gold medal. And with his current mount, the nine-year-old chestnut Hanoverian stallion Goldfever, he hoped to make it to Sydney, doing his best to keep the gold medals coming his way.

Paul Schockemöhle: Sibling Rivalry?

Many Olympic veterans go on to make their mark outside the competition arena. Some, like Germany's Paul Schockemöhle, have worn a variety of hats: coach, horse and farm owner, and trainer, among others.

Schockemöhle, who won a team silver medal aboard Agent at the 1976 Montreal Games and a team bronze with Deister at the 1984 Los Angeles Games, is the brother of veteran show jumper Alwin Schockemöhle. Alwin, also a member of that 1976 team, won the individual gold aboard Warwick Rex; he also won team gold in 1960 (aboard Ferdi) and team bronze in 1968 (Donald Rex).

Although Paul describes his relationship with his brother today as "very good," there once was quite a rivalry in the house of Schockemöhle — particularly when Paul began achieving his own Olympic and international success. Still, according to Paul, he put his team first in Montreal and was "very glad that my brother had the success of winning the '76 Olympic gold medal. He was one of the most important riders of his era, but for a long time he had missed winning an outstanding individual title. I am happy that he was able to end his career with the title of Olympic champion. His was a tremendous performance, for he won by a great margin."

Both Schockemöhle brothers run successful horse businesses in the town of Mühlen, in Oldenburg. Alwin owns a small stable of jumpers and trotters; Paul owns a huge breeding and training facility with numerous arenas and 400 stalls. Paul breeds and sells young jumper prospects; his Performance Sales International runs an internationally respected annual auction of young horses. He also maintains a string of international-caliber jumpers and over the years has attracted the likes of Olympic gold medalists Franke Sloothaak and Ludger Beerbaum to ride them.

One of Paul's most satisfying moments came at the 1988 Seoul Olympics, when three of his rid-

ers — Sloothaak, Beerbaum, and Dirk Hafemeister — rode on the gold-medal-winning German show-jumping team. He calls the achievement "one of my greatest successes as a trainer." He has taught other respected international-level competitors and even coached two Saudi Arabian riders at the 1996 Atlanta Games.

Paul could have a hand in Germany's bid for gold at the 2000 Sydney Olympics: Sloothaak might compete Paul's Filias if Joli Coeur, his 1996 mount, is not sufficiently recovered from an injury; Beerbaum has high hopes for Paul's Goldfever; and Beerbaum's sister-in-law, Meredith Michaels-Beerbaum, also has enjoyed considerable success recently and is considered a strong team candidate. Germany is a major force in modern show-jumping competition, and Paul hopes that, with the help of his behind-the-scenes efforts, it will stay that way.

Michael Matz: Real-Life Hero

Horse people are fond of lamenting that the mainstream media don't fawn over its celebrities the way they do over the likes of Michael Jordan and Tiger Woods. But in 1989, the name and likeness of American jumper rider and Olympic veteran Michael Matz were splashed across headlines around the world.

Matz didn't attain instant fame for his equestrian achievements, however; his newsworthy actions far transcend any medal-winning clean round. He and his wife, fellow jumper rider and former USET president Dorothy "D.D." Alexander Matz, were passengers on a United

Michael Matz, captain of the U.S. jumping team, aboard Rhum IV at the 1996 Atlanta Games.

Airlines jet that crashed in Sioux City, Iowa, killing 112. The Matzes escaped the burning wreckage, and Michael returned to the aircraft to save two children. ABC News named him "Person of the Week" for his heroic efforts. [25]

Matz, of Collegeville, Pennsylvania, demonstrated the same levelheadedness in the face of disaster that he regularly does in the arena. The veteran of the 1976 and 1992 Olympic Games (riding Grande and Heisman, respectively) had won plenty of other honors but never an Olympic medal when he made the 1996 team for the Atlanta Games. Matz piloted Mr. and Mrs. F. Eugene Dixon's Rhum IV to a team silver medal in Atlanta, but his biggest thrill of those Games was yet to come: The entire U.S. Olympic contingent selected him to carry the American flag in the closing ceremonies, the first time an equestrian athlete was so honored. It was a gesture befitting a hero, and Matz is unquestionably that.

The Evolution of Course Design

Although many of the rules of show jumping have remained essentially similar to those of nearly a century ago, courses themselves have managed to undergo a substantial evolution, in much the same way that three-day eventing cross-country course design has changed.

"In 1912, there wasn't really an international standard of course design for the sport," said Linda Allen of Salinas, California. Allen, a former hunter/jumper competitor, is now a nationally and internationally accredited jumper judge and technical delegate but is best known as a course designer. She designed the show-jumping course — and the fences themselves — for the 1996 Atlanta Olympics and also designed the course for the 1992 World Cup Show Jumping Final. "From today's standpoint, the courses were very unsophisticated: You went straight, around the outside, and up the middle — that type course was very typical of that era. The main focus of the competition was not how well you navigated the course itself, but how high or wide your horse could jump the individual obstacles.

"After World War II, the sport began to progress more and course design became a lot more developed," said Allen. "From my research, it appears that the jumps became higher and wider and the Olympic show-jumping competition became a power contest: How big and difficult a course could horses and riders handle? They built courses that no one would jump today, with very heavy rails and cups. Show jumping became a survival contest. Even the winners of the 1964 Olympic team competition, for example, incurred an astronomical number of penalties; there was lots of crashing at those Games."

American show-jumping veteran and legendary hunter/jumper trainer George Morris, a member of the silver-medal-winning show-jumping squad at the 1960 Rome Olympics, attested to Allen's comments about the "intimidation factor" of the courses of those days. Morris had won the Grand Prix of Aachen (Germany) — at that time, the most prestigious jumping competition outside of the Olympic Games — earlier that same year, and so the twenty-two-year-old had already proven himself at the highest levels of international competition by the time he arrived at Rome's Piazza di Siena to walk the Olympic course. He discovered, to his great dismay, that "the course to me looked like something I couldn't do. It was bigger and

harder than anything I'd ever seen — much worse than the course at Aachen."

The trend toward "blood and guts" courses (as Morris calls them) remained through the 1976 Olympics in Montreal, which Allen termed "the end of an era. The equipment was still very heavy — the cups were very deep and the rails were heavy, so it was hard to knock a rail down — and it was difficult for competitors to complete a course."

By the 1980 alternate Olympics in Rotterdam, though, "The level of course design had become more sophisticated. There was a feeling that the Games needed to fit into the nature of the sport as an 'every week' event, not an every-four-years deal.

"From 1980 through 1996, the show-jumping competition at the Games was essentially the same as international-level competitions held over the rest of the year," said Allen. "Here's an analogy: An Olympic marathon is not longer than other top marathons, just because it's the Olympics. But in this sport, that's just what happened with the Olympics up until 1980: The jumps were not what you saw elsewhere in the sport."

As Allen pointed out, course design has experienced a major shift over the past twenty years: from rewarding pure athletic ability to rewarding cleverness. Today's horse has to be as talented a jumper as his predecessors, to be sure; but he also has to be gymnastic, elastic, and infinitely adjustable. And today's rider spends more time walking the course, pacing off the distances, and planning how to ride practically every footfall than riders did some years ago.

American Greg Best and Gem Twist jump to double silver medals at the 1988 Seoul Olympics.

That's because modern jump courses incorporate so-called related distances, meaning that the correctness of the striding to the first obstacle of a line or a combination fence directly affects how smoothly riders meet the subsequent obstacles in that line or combination. If a rider meets the first element of a tight, tricky combination badly, he or she will have a difficult time adjusting the horse's stride to make the elements that follow "flow" as they should.

Along with the advent of increasingly technical courses have come trends in fence-building itself: away from those deep jump cups and heavy, hard-to-dislodge rails to very flat, shallow cups and almost flimsy poles that topple at the slightest brush. As a result, competitors can no longer get by with a so-so distance and a hard "rub" (a solid thunk with the legs that yesterday's fences likely would have stood up to). As Allen put it, in show-jumping competitions of yore, "The best horses were sheer power horses; power and bravery were what you wanted in a jumper. Carefulness, ridability, trainability — these played much less of a role. As course design changed, much more emphasis was placed on the overall harmony and communication between horse and rider and on the horse's education. The horse now had to learn his craft over a number of years: It goes without saying that a good jumper has to be able to jump; but to put in a clear round over today's Grand Prix courses, he also needs the training — as well as an inclination to be careful. And a careful horse is more inclined than a "power horse" to lose confidence if he's unsuccessful and hits a fence, so the rider has to work to help him cope with that."

Allen had two mentors who served as influential models of brilliant course design. She heralded British course designer Pamela Carruthers as "really the first designer" — explaining that "I started competing in the days when there was no such thing as a course designer" — and that she "questioned Carruthers a lot when I was riding." Carruthers designed courses for shows in Europe, the United Kingdom, Canada, and the United States; Allen competed over Carruthers-designed courses and later worked as the designer's assistant. Said Allen, "She was really good at building an extremely challenging but good course."

Allen's other mentor was former USET show-jumping coach Bertalan de Némethy, who designed the course for the 1984 Los Angeles Olympics. "He did a brilliant job of combining the technical with the aesthetic. His courses were challenging, yet at the same time they showcased the beauty of the sport."

Allen's experience as a rider and a competitor, combined with her work with Carruthers and de Némethy, led to the development of her own philosophies and approach to course design. "I try to build balanced courses that don't have one particular emphasis. I don't like a 'bogey' fence or line. My goal is to create a course such that every horse and rider in the class can jump ninety percent of the obstacles without any great problem, but also that will highlight a pair's weaknesses on that day. But I'm very concerned about safety; I think every course designer is."

Show jumping has become a year-long sport, and Allen takes the near-constant competition schedule into account when planning courses. "Every four years for the Olympics and not much else — those days are over. Now there are major competitions pretty much all year, and you have to be careful not to overdo it in any one competition. You can challenge riders mentally every week and they only get better, but to challenge the horses similarly in a physical manner is counterproductive to the sport. No one competition should take too much out of a horse; the show has to fit into the season."

The Chronicle of the Horse called Allen's handiwork for the 1996 Olympic Games perhaps "the best Olympic course ever." The fences were "appealing to the human eye and encouraging to the equine eye. And the best indication of the influence each fence exerted was that every single fence in the Nations Cup had faults, even though FEI (Fédération Equestre Internationale) rules do not allow course designers to build fences as big as {Bertalan} de Némethy built {for the Los Angeles Olympics} in 1984," the magazine wrote.

Each of Allen's Olympic courses had a different theme. The course for the individual qualifier was a nod to the Olympic host city, with architectural themes of the South and native flora. (FEI-licensed course designer and amateur horticulturist Richard Jeffery, who had decorated the 1984 and 1988 Olympic courses, added the final polish to Allen's designs with his tasteful use of flowers and plants.) Each fence in the Nations Cup course echoed a piece of Americana, and the course for the individual final had an Olympic theme, beginning with a "Barcelona Vertical" and ending — in the charming and now-established custom of looking forward to the next Olympiad — with the "Sydney 2000 Vertical."

De Némethy's course for the 1984 Los Angeles Olympics was widely hailed as a masterpiece for the way in which it allowed the best horses and riders to shine while not jettisoning lesser com-

petitors. De Némethy believes that appropriately designed and constructed fences greatly reduce the chances of a pair's getting injured in the event of a mishap, and that a designer must

Californian Linda Allen designed the show-jumping courses for the 1996 Games. Next page: Olaf Petersen's handiwork at the 1988 Seoul Games.

supervise such details as cup type, rail size and heft, and angle of solid obstacles to make courses as safe as possible.

Preferring to remain as close as possible to show jumping's classical roots, de Némethy eschews the use of bright colors and wildly unnatural elements and forms in the courses he designs. His 1984 Olympic course was arguably more of a "trainer's course" than a "designer's course" in that it stressed ridability over looks. After the 1984 Games, he explained, "My

GAMES OF
THE XXIVTH OLYMPIAD
SEOUL 1988
(E Q J E S T R I A N)
SEPT.19-OCT.2

approach is not like most course designers. I cannot forget that I was always a trainer and, because of that, I know a little bit more. I definitely know what is difficult, and I know what is dangerous." [26]

In decided contrast to de Némethy's understated style, German jumper-course designer Olaf Petersen created what *The Chronicle of the Horse* called "an elaborate masterpiece of fences" [27] for the 1988 Seoul Olympics. "I thought the fences should correspond to the country — that they should contain colors and forms taken from the Korean way of life, and from Korean history and culture," said Petersen.

"It is my opinion that we have jumped for long enough over walls, planks, and bars painted in the same colors and...that it is time to bring new ideas to the presentation of our sport. Of course we have to keep the traditional elements, but...show jumping must not stay set in old ways but must use new ideas to stay young. Seoul gave me the chance to translate my ideas for building new fences into action." [28]

Nearly all of Petersen's fences in Seoul had distinctly Asian themes: from the colorful "Dragon Jump" and the sweeping "Korean Fan" to the "Bridge in the Emperor's Palace" and the "Korean Garden House." With his "Barcelona Jump," which depicted the classic Spanish fictional character Don Quixote "tilting against windmills," Petersen began the custom of designing the final fence as a nod to the host city of the next Olympiad.

The State of the Sport

High-profile, with ever-increasing sponsor dollars, the sport of show jumping has in large part become the business of show jumping. Trends influencing the sport today include a universal style, more "power nations," an increasing number of competitions, and debate over sport vs. entertainment.

Universal style. Unlike the days of old, when the flowing Italian jumping style differed from the disciplined German, elegant French, and classical American styles, the techniques in the international show-jumping arena have become more homogenized, said George Morris. "It's all neutralized, which is probably to the betterment of riding and training. Everything's come to the common denominator of excellence and continued improvement. But it's not quite as interesting to me."

More "power nations." Western European countries dominated show jumping for much of the 20th Century, but their stranglehold on the medals has loosened, said Morris. "The Germans, the Italians, the French, and the English were once the ones to beat. The Italians are not so strong today, but you can add the Swiss, the Dutch, and the Brazilians to the list of gold-medal contenders." All those nations, plus the United States, consistently field strong teams, so the 2000 Sydney Games are shaping up to be what could become the fiercest battle in Olympic equestrian history.

Competition-of-the-week syndrome? There are so many Grand Prix jumping competitions today — especially in Europe, said course designer Linda Allen — that courses have become "a touch plain vanilla" in appearance, with fences of similar types and designs. "To me, it's taken a little of the variety out of the sport."

German Olympic veteran Franke Sloothaak

Brazil has emerged as a competitive force in show jumping, winning team bronze in 1996.

worries that the plethora of shows will lead to overexposure for the riders and the sport, resulting in a gradual loss of interest by sponsors and spectators. "When we go to forty shows a year, it is too much. We must make ourselves more rare so that the spectators are really longing to see us. The spectators, especially those who watch jumping on TV, see us too much."

Ludger Beerbaum, Sloothaak's 1988 and 1996 Olympic teammate, shares the concerns about oversaturation. "I do not know if so much TV coverage in Germany is good for the equestrian sports. In soccer, we already have the problem that people are not going to the stadiums anymore; they watch the games on TV."

(American show jumpers wish they had that problem. Unlike Europe, American television seldom broadcasts show-jumping competitions. Olympic show jumping is the rare exception.)

The jam-packed show schedule means that jumpers today compete far more often than did their predecessors. Increasingly rare is the rider who is in a position to "save" his or her mount for the most important competitions. Those who do pick and choose, including U.S. Olympians Michael Matz and Anne Kursinski, are universally lauded by their peers for their willingness to put horsemanship over prize money.

Sport vs. entertainment. Corporate sponsorship is both a blessing and a curse. It has enabled competitions to offer generous prize money and talented riders to compete on horses they themselves would not have been able to afford to buy, but unchecked it can lead to purse-chasing at the expense of equine longevity and, potentially, to riders' feeling incapable of saying no to their sponsors' competitive wishes.

Sponsors naturally want lots of spectators to see their banners and wares, and so horse shows have begun to include other types of attractions (terrier races and antique-auto shows, for example) to get people in the gate. Equestrian and entrepreneur Paul Schockemöhle commented, "Due to the trends in sponsorship, horse shows have to serve as a place for businessmen to exchange opinions and to spend an enjoyable time together."

Unlike other venues, Olympic Games competition arenas are not festooned with sponsor and advertising banners; still, the International Olympic Committee and the organizing committee of the host city have invested significant funds in staging the Games and they'd like to see a positive return on their investment. Some of that revenue, of course, comes from ticket sales, and that's why the Barcelona Games organizing committee was displeased at a turn of events that took place during the show-jumping competition in 1992.

According to Kate Jackson, who organized the equestrian events for the 1996 Atlanta Olympics, the FEI set up the team and individual show-jumping competitions differently for Atlanta than it had for the 1992 Barcelona Games. In Barcelona, instead of incorporating the team competition into the qualifying system for the individual finals, "They had the team competition, and then they had what was called the third qualifying round. As a result, many riders didn't bother with the third round. If they'd done very well, they already knew they were qualified for the individuals; if they'd done very badly, they knew they didn't have a chance. The third round wasn't mandatory, so they didn't bother. So we had a whole stadium full of people who had paid for tickets to watch this competition, which basically didn't take place because there were so few competitors. Some of the top riders were coerced into going in, and they jumped two fences, tipped their hats, and they were out of there. Lightbulb: This is not right!" she laughed ruefully. "So in Atlanta, there was a first qualifying competition, then the two team competitions (rounds). Everybody had to go; it was mandatory." The structure worked well in Atlanta and will be repeated at the 2000 Sydney Olympics, she added.

Top riders and trainers agree that horsemanship and the sport of show jumping should not take a back seat to the horse show-as-entertainment trend. They struggle with the issue of how to preserve equine welfare and sporting traditions while continuing to grow the sport. It is a balancing act to which there are no easy answers.

Official Results
Show Jumping

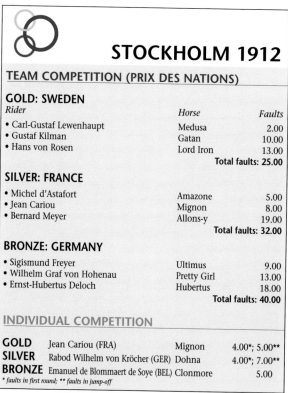

STOCKHOLM 1912

TEAM COMPETITION (PRIX DES NATIONS)

GOLD: SWEDEN

Rider	Horse	Faults
• Carl-Gustaf Lewenhaupt	Medusa	2.00
• Gustaf Kilman	Gatan	10.00
• Hans von Rosen	Lord Iron	13.00
	Total faults:	**25.00**

SILVER: FRANCE

• Michel d'Astafort	Amazone	5.00
• Jean Cariou	Mignon	8.00
• Bernard Meyer	Allons-y	19.00
	Total faults:	**32.00**

BRONZE: GERMANY

• Sigismund Freyer	Ultimus	9.00
• Wilhelm Graf von Hohenau	Pretty Girl	13.00
• Ernst-Hubertus Deloch	Hubertus	18.00
	Total faults:	**40.00**

INDIVIDUAL COMPETITION

GOLD	Jean Cariou (FRA)	Mignon	4.00*; 5.00**
SILVER	Rabod Wilhelm von Kröcher (GER)	Dohna	4.00*; 7.00**
BRONZE	Emanuel de Blommaert de Soye (BEL)	Clonmore	5.00

* faults in first round; ** faults in jump-off

PARIS 1900

INDIVIDUAL COMPETITION

	Rider	Horse	Time
GOLD	Aimé Haegeman (BEL)	Benton II	2:16.0
SILVER	Georges van de Poele (BEL)	Windsor Squire	2:17.6
BRONZE	Louis de Champsavin (FRA)	Terpsichore	2:26.0

ANTWERP 1920

TEAM COMPETITION (PRIX DES NATIONS)

GOLD: SWEDEN

Rider	Horse	Faults
• Claes König	Tresor	2.00
• Daniel Norling	Eros II	6.00
• Hans von Rosen	Poor Boy	6.00
	Total faults:	**14.00**

SILVER: BELGIUM

• Henri Laame	Biscuit	2.75
• André Coumans	Lisette	5.25
• Herman de Gaiffier d'Herstroy	Miss	8.25
	Total faults:	**16.25**

BRONZE: ITALY

• Ettore Caffaratti	Tradittore	1.50
• Alessandro Alvisi	Raggio di Sole	6.25
• Giulio Cacciandra	Fortunello	11.00
	Total faults:	**18.75**

INDIVIDUAL COMPETITION

GOLD	Tommaso Lequio di Assaba (ITA)	Trebecco	2.00
SILVER	Alessandro Valerio (ITA)	Cento	3.00
BRONZE	Carl-Gustaf Lewenhaupt (SWE)	Mon Coeur	4.00

PARIS 1924

TEAM COMPETITION (PRIX DES NATIONS)

GOLD: SWEDEN

Rider	Horse	Faults
• Åke Thelning	Loke	12.00
• Axel Ståhle	Cecil	12.25
• Åge Lundström	Anvers	18.00
	Total faults:	**42.25**

SILVER: SWITZERLAND

• Alphonse Gemuseus	Lucette	6.00
• Werner Stüber	Girandole	20.00
• Hans Bühler	Sailor Boy	24.00
	Total faults:	**50.00**

BRONZE: PORTUGAL

• Antonio Borges de Almeida	Reginald	12.00
• Hélder de Souza Martins	Avro	19.00
• José Mousinho de Albuquerque	Hetrugo	22.00
	Total faults:	**53.00**

INDIVIDUAL COMPETITION

GOLD	Alphonse Gemuseus (SWI)	Lucette	6.00
SILVER	Tommaso Lequio di Assaba (ITA)	Trebecco	8.75
BRONZE	Adam Królikiewicz (POL)	Picador	10.00

AMSTERDAM 1928

TEAM COMPETITION (PRIX DES NATIONS)

GOLD: SPAIN

Rider	Horse	Faults
• José Navarro Morenés	Zapatazo	0.00
• José Alvarez de las Asturias Bohorques y Goyeneche (de los Trujilos)	Zalamero	2.00
• Julio Garcia Fernández	Revistada	2.00
	Total faults:	4.00

SILVER: POLAND

• Kazimierz Gzowski	Mylord	0.00
• Kazimierz Szosland	Ali	2.00
• Michal Antoniewicz	Readgleadt	6.00
	Total faults:	8.00

BRONZE: SWEDEN

• Karl Hansen	Gerold	0.00
• Carl Björnstierna	Kornett	2.00
• Ernst Hallberg	Loke	8.00
	Total faults:	10.00

INDIVIDUAL COMPETITION

GOLD	Frantisek Ventura (CZE/SLV)	Eliot	0.00
SILVER	Pierre Bertran de Balanda (FRA)	Papillon	2.00*
BRONZE	Charley Kuhn (SWI)	Pepita	4.00*

in second jump-off

LOS ANGELES 1932

TEAM COMPETITION (PRIX DES NATIONS)

NO TEAM MEDALS AWARDED BECAUSE NO TEAM OF THREE RIDERS COMPLETED THE COURSE

INDIVIDUAL COMPETITION

GOLD	Takeichi Nishi (JPN)	Uranus	8.00
SILVER	Harry Chamberlin (USA)	Show Girl	12.00
BRONZE	Clarence von Rosen, Jr. (SWE)	Empire	16.00

BERLIN 1936

TEAM COMPETITION (PRIX DES NATIONS)

GOLD: GERMANY

Rider	Horse	Faults
• Kurt Hasse	Tora	4.00
• Marten von Barnekow	Nordland	20.00
• Heinz Brandt	Alchimist	20.00
	Total faults:	44.00

SILVER: HOLLAND

• Johan Jacob Greter	Ernica	12.00
• Jan Adrianus de Bruine	Trixie	15.00
• Henri Louis van Schaik	Santa Bell	24.50
	Total faults:	51.50

BRONZE: PORTUGAL

• José Beltrão	Biscuit	12.00
• Luis Marquez do Funchal	Merle Blanc	20.00
• Luiz Mena e Silva	Faussette	24.00
	Total faults:	56.00

INDIVIDUAL COMPETITION

GOLD	Kurt Hasse (GER)	Tora	4.00*; 4.00** (:59.2)
SILVER	Henri Rang (ROM)	Delfis	4.00*; 4.00** (1:12.8)
BRONZE	József Platthy (HUN)	Sello	8.00*; 0.00** (1:02.6)

*faults in first round; **faults in jump-off (time in parentheses)*

LONDON 1948

TEAM COMPETITION (PRIX DES NATIONS)

GOLD: MEXICO

Rider	Horse	Faults
• Humberto Mariles Cortés	Arete	6.25
• Rubén Uriza	Harvey	8.00
• Alberto Valdes	Chihuchoc	20.00
	Total faults:	34.25

SILVER: SPAIN

• Jaime Garcia Cruz	Bizarro	12.00
• José Navarro Morenés	Quorum	20.00
• Marcelino Gavilán y Ponce de León	Forajido	24.50
	Total faults:	56.50

BRONZE: GREAT BRITAIN

• Henry Llewellyn	Foxhunter	16.00
• Henry Nicoll	Kilgeddin	16.00
• Arthur Carr	Monty	35.00
	Total faults:	67.00

INDIVIDUAL COMPETITION

GOLD	Humberto Mariles Cortés (MEX)	Arete	6.25*; 0.00**
SILVER	Rubén Uriza (MEX)	Harvey	8.00*; 0.00**
BRONZE	Jean François d'Orgeix (FRA)	Sucre de Pomme	8.00*; 4.00** (:38.9)

*faults in first round; **faults in jump-off (time in parentheses)*

HELSINKI 1952

TEAM COMPETITION (PRIX DES NATIONS)

GOLD: GREAT BRITAIN

Rider	Horse	Faults
• Wilfred White	Nizefella	8.00
• Douglas Stewart	Aherlow	16.00
• Henry Llewellyn	Foxhunter	16.75
	Total faults:	**40.75**

SILVER: CHILE

• Oscar Cristi	Bambi	8.00
• Cesar Mendoza	Pillan	12.00
• Ricardo Echeverria	Lindo Peal	25.75
	Total faults:	**45.75**

BRONZE: UNITED STATES

• William Steinkraus	Hollandia	13.25
• Arthur McCashin	Miss Budweiser	16.00
• John Russell	Democrat	23.00
	Total faults:	**52.25**

INDIVIDUAL COMPETITION

GOLD	Pierre Jonquères d'Oriola (FRA)	Ali Baba	8.00*; 0.00**
SILVER	Oscar Cristi (CHI)	Bambi	8.00*; 4.00**
BRONZE	Fritz Thiedemann (GER)	Meteor	8.00*; 8.00** (:38.5)

*faults in first round; ** faults in jump-off (time in parentheses)*

STOCKHOLM 1956

TEAM COMPETITION (PRIX DES NATIONS)

GOLD: GERMANY

Rider	Horse	Faults
• Hans Günter Winkler	Halla	4.00
• Fritz Thiedemann	Meteor	12.00
• Alfons Lütke-Westhues	Ala	24.00
	Total faults:	**40.00**

SILVER: ITALY

• Raimondo d'Inzeo	Merano	8.00
• Piero d'Inzeo	Uruguay	11.00
• Salvatore Oppes	Pagoro	47.00
	Total faults:	**66.00**

BRONZE: GREAT BRITAIN

• Wilfred White	Nizefella	12.00
• Patricia Smythe	Flanagan	21.00
• Peter Robeson	Scorchin	36.00
	Total faults:	**69.00**

INDIVIDUAL COMPETITION

GOLD	Hans Günter Winkler (GER)	Halla	4.00
SILVER	Raimondo d'Inzeo (ITA)	Merano	8.00
BRONZE	Piero d'Inzeo (ITA)	Uruguay	11.00

ROME 1960

TEAM COMPETITION (PRIX DES NATIONS)

GOLD: GERMANY

Rider	Horse	Faults
• Hans Günter Winkler	Halla	13.25
• Fritz Thiedemann	Meteor	16.00
• Alwin Schockemöhle	Ferdl	17.25
	Total faults:	**46.50**

SILVER: UNITED STATES

• Frank Chapot	Trail Guide	20.00
• William Steinkraus	Ksar d'Esprit	21.50
• George Morris	Sinjon	24.50
	Total faults:	**66.00**

BRONZE: ITALY

• Raimondo d'Inzeo	Posillipo	8.00
• Piero d'Inzeo	The Rock	32.00
• Antonio Oppes	The Scholar	40.50
	Total faults:	**80.50**

INDIVIDUAL COMPETITION

GOLD	Raimondo d'Inzeo (ITA)	Posillipo	12.00
SILVER	Piero d'Inzeo (ITA)	The Rock	16.00
BRONZE	David Broome (GBR)	Sunslave	23.00

TOKYO 1964

TEAM COMPETITION (PRIX DES NATIONS)

GOLD: GERMANY

Rider	Horse	Faults
• Hermann Schridde	Dozent	13.75
• Kurt Jarasinski	Torro	22.25
• Hans Günter Winkler	Fidelitas	32.50
	Total faults:	**68.50**

SILVER: FRANCE

• Pierre Jonquères d'Oriola	Lutteur	9.00
• Janou Lefebvre	Kenavo D	32.00
• Guy Lefrant	Monsieur de Littry	36.75
	Total faults:	**77.75**

BRONZE: ITALY

• Piero d'Inzeo	Sunbeam	24.50
• Raimondo d'Inzeo	Posillipo	28.00
• Graziano Mancinelli	Rockette	36.00
	Total faults:	**88.50**

INDIVIDUAL COMPETITION

GOLD	Pierre Jonquères d'Oriola (FRA)	Lutteur	9.00
SILVER	Hermann Schridde (GER)	Dozent	13.75
BRONZE	Peter Robeson (GBR)	Firecrest	16.00*; 0.00**

*faults in first round; ** faults in jump-off*

MEXICO CITY 1968

TEAM COMPETITION (PRIX DES NATIONS)

GOLD: CANADA

Rider	Horse	Faults
• James Elder	The Immigrant	27.25
• James Day	Canadian Club	36.00
• Thomas Gayford	Big Dee	39.50
	Total faults:	102.75

SILVER: FRANCE

Rider	Horse	Faults
• Janou Lefebvre	Rocket	29.75
• Marcel Rozier	Quo Vadis	33.50
• Pierre Jonquères d'Oriola	Nagir	47.25
	Total faults:	110.50

BRONZE: GERMANY

Rider	Horse	Faults
• Alwin Schockemöhle	Donald Rex	18.75
• Hans Günter Winkler	Enigk	28.25
• Hermann Schridde	Dozent	70.25
	Total faults:	117.25

INDIVIDUAL COMPETITION

GOLD	William Steinkraus (USA)	Snowbound	4.00
SILVER	Marion Coakes (GBR)	Stroller	8.00
BRONZE	David Broome (GBR)	Mister Softee	12.00*
			0.00** (:35.3)

*faults in first round; ** faults in jump-off (time in parentheses)*

MUNICH 1972

TEAM COMPETITION (PRIX DES NATIONS)

GOLD: GERMANY

Rider	Horse	Faults
• Fritz Ligges	Robin	8.00
• Gerhard Wiltfang	Askan	12.00
• Hartwig Steenken	Simona	12.00
• Hans Günter Winkler	Torphy	16.00
	Total faults:	32.00

SILVER: UNITED STATES

Rider	Horse	Faults
• William Steinkraus	Main Spring	4.00
• Neal Shapiro	Sloopy	8.25
• Kathryn Kusner	Fleet Apple	32.00
• Frank Chapot	White Lightning	36.00
	Total faults:	32.25

BRONZE: ITALY

Rider	Horse	Faults
• Vittorio Orlandi	Fulmer Feather	8.00
• Raimondo d'Inzeo	Fiorello II	12.00
• Graziano Mancinelli	Ambassador	28.00
• Piero d'Inzeo	Easter Light	135.25
	Total faults:	48.00

INDIVIDUAL COMPETITION

GOLD	Graziano Mancinelli (ITA)	Ambassador	8.00*; 0.00**
SILVER	Ann Moore (GBR)	Psalm	8.00*; 3.00**
BRONZE	Neal Shapiro (USA)	Sloopy	8.00*; 8.00**

*faults in first round; ** faults in jump-off*

MONTREAL 1976

TEAM COMPETITION (PRIX DES NATIONS)

GOLD: FRANCE

Rider	Horse	Faults
• Hubert Parot	Rivage	12.00
• Marcel Rozier	Bayard de Maupas	12.00
• Marc Roguet	Belle de Mars	24.00
• Michel Roche	Un Espoir	32.00
	Total faults:	40.00

SILVER: GERMANY

Rider	Horse	Faults
• Alwin Schockemöhle	Warwick Rex	12.00
• Hans Günter Winkler	Torphy	16.00
• Sönke Sönksen	Kwepe	20.00
• Paul Schockemöhle	Agent	24.00
	Total faults:	44.00

BRONZE: BELGIUM

Rider	Horse	Faults
• Eric Wauters	Gute Sitte	15.00
• François Mathy	Gai Luron	20.00
• Edgar Gupper	Le Champion	28.00
• Stanny van Paeschen	Porsche	36.00
	Total faults:	63.00

INDIVIDUAL COMPETITION

GOLD	Alwin Schockemöhle (GER)	Warwick Rex	0.00
SILVER	Michel Vaillancourt (CAN)	Branch County	12.00*; 4.00**
BRONZE	François Mathy (BEL)	Gai Luron	12.00*; 8.00**

*faults in first round; ** faults in jump-off*

MOSCOW 1980

TEAM COMPETITION (PRIX DES NATIONS)

GOLD: U.S.S.R.

Rider	Horse	Faults
• Vyacheslav Chukanov	Gepatit	4.00
• Viktor Pohanovsky	Topky	8.25
• Viktor Asmayev	Reis	11.25
• Nikolai Korolkov	Espadron	12.00
	Total faults:	20.25

SILVER: POLAND

Rider	Horse	Faults
• Jan Kowalczyk	Artemor	12.00
• Wieslaw Hartman	Norton	24.00
• Marian Kozicki	Bremen	37.50
• Janusz Bobik	Szampan	40.00
	Total faults:	56.00

BRONZE: MEXICO

Rider	Horse	Faults
• Joaquin Perez Heras	Alymony	12.00
• Alberto Valdes Lacarra	Lady Mirka	20.75
• Gerardo Tazzer Valencia	Caribe	31.75
• Jesus Gomez Portugal	Massacre	35.25
	Total faults:	59.75

INDIVIDUAL COMPETITION

GOLD	Jan Kowalczyk (POL)	Artemor	8.00
SILVER	Nikolai Korolkov (SOV/RUS)	Espadron	9.50
BRONZE	Joaquin Perez Heras (MEX)	Alymony	12.00*; 4.00** (:43.23)

*faults in first round; ** faults in jump-off (time in parentheses)*

LOS ANGELES 1984

TEAM COMPETITION (PRIX DES NATIONS)

GOLD: UNITED STATES

Rider	Horse	Faults
• Joe Fargis	Touch of Class	0.00
• Conrad Homfeld	Abdullah	8.00
• Leslie Burr	Albany	12.00
• Melanie Smith	Calypso	(withdrawn)
	Total faults:	**12.00**

SILVER: GREAT BRITAIN

Rider	Horse	Faults
• Michael Whitaker	Overton Amanda	8.00
• John Whitaker	Ryans Son	20.75
• Steven Smith	Shining Example	27.00
• Timothy Grubb	Linky	28.25
	Total faults:	**36.75**

BRONZE: GERMANY

Rider	Horse	Faults
• Paul Schockemöhle	Deister	8.00
• Peter Luther	Livius	12.00
• Franke Sloothaak	Farmer	19.25
• Fritz Ligges	Ramzes	29.00
	Total faults:	**39.25**

INDIVIDUAL COMPETITION

GOLD	Joe Fargis (USA)	Touch of Class	4.00*; 0.00**
SILVER	Conrad Homfeld (USA)	Abdullah	4.00*; 8.00**
BRONZE	Heidi Robbiani (SWI)	Jessica V	8.00*; 0.00**

* faults in first round; ** faults in jump-off

SEOUL 1988

TEAM COMPETITION (PRIX DES NATIONS)

GOLD: GERMANY

Rider	Horse	Faults
• Ludger Beerbaum	The Freak	4.25
• Wolfgang Brinkmann	Pedro	10.00
• Dirk Hafemeister	Orchidee	12.00
• Franke Sloothaak	Walzerkönig	(withdrawn)
	Total faults:	**17.25**

SILVER: UNITED STATES

Rider	Horse	Faults
• Joe Fargis	Mill Pearl	4.25
• Greg Best	Gem Twist	8.00
• Lisa Jacquin	For the Moment	8.25
• Anne Kursinski	Starman	16.00
	Total faults:	**20.50**

BRONZE: FRANCE

Rider	Horse	Faults
• Pierre Durand	Jappeloup	5.00
• Michel Robert	Pequignet la Fayette	10.00
• Frédéric Cottier	Flambeau	16.00
• Hubert Bourdy	Morgat	16.50
	Total faults:	**27.50**

INDIVIDUAL COMPETITION

GOLD	Pierre Durand (FRA)	Jappeloup	1.25
SILVER	Greg Best (USA)	Gem Twist	4.00*; 4.00** (:45.70)
BRONZE	Karsten Huck (GER)	Nepomuk	4.00*; 4.00** (:54.75)

* faults in first round; ** faults in jump-off (time in parentheses)

BARCELONA 1992

TEAM COMPETITION (PRIX DES NATIONS)

GOLD: THE NETHERLANDS

Rider	Horse	Faults
• Jos Lansink	Egano	0.00
• Piet Raymakers	Ratina Z	4.00
• Jan Tops	Top Gun	8.00
• Bert Romp	Waldo E	40.25
	Total faults:	**12.00**

SILVER: AUSTRIA

Rider	Horse	Faults
• Thomas Frühmann	Genius	0.00
• Hugo Simon	Apricot D	4.00
• Jörg Münzner	Graf Grande	12.75
• Boris Boor	Love Me Tender (withdrawn)	
	Total faults:	**16.75**

BRONZE: FRANCE

Rider	Horse	Faults
• Hervé Godignon	Quidam de Revel	4.75
• Hubert Bourdy	Razzia du P	12.00
• Eric Navet	Quito de Baussy	16.00
• Michel Robert	Nonix	20.25
	Total faults:	**24.75**

INDIVIDUAL COMPETITION

GOLD	Ludger Beerbaum (GER)	Classic Touch	0.00
SILVER	Piet Raymakers (NED)	Ratina Z	0.25
BRONZE	Norman Dello Joio (USA)	Irish	4.75

ATLANTA 1996

TEAM COMPETITION (PRIX DES NATIONS)

GOLD: GERMANY

Rider	Horse	Faults
• Franke Sloothaak	Joli Coeur	60.25
• Ludger Beerbaum	Ratina Z	0.25
• Ulrich Kirchhoff	Jus de Pommes	1.50
• Lars Neiberg	For Pleasure	12.00
	Total faults:	**1.75**

SILVER: UNITED STATES

Rider	Horse	Faults
• Leslie Burr-Howard	Extreme	14.00
• Peter Leone	Legato	4.00
• Michael Matz	Rhum IV	8.00
• Anne Kursinski	Eros	8.00
	Total faults:	**12.00**

BRONZE: BRAZIL

Rider	Horse	Faults
• Rodrigo Pessoa	Tomboy	0.75
• Luiz Felipe Azevedo	Cassiana	12.00
• Alvaro Miranda Neto	Aspen	8.25
• Andre Johannpeter	Calei	12.25
	Total faults:	**17.25**

INDIVIDUAL COMPETITION

GOLD	Ulrich Kirchhoff (GER)	Jus de Pommes	1.00
SILVER	Willi Melliger (SWI)	Calvaro	4.00*; 0.00** (:38.07)
BRONZE	Alexandra Ledermann (FRA)	Rochet M	4.00*; 0.00** (:41.46)

* faults in first round; ** faults in jump-off (time in parentheses)

Wallechinsky, David. (1996). *The Complete Book of the Summer Olympics.* Boston: Little, Brown, pp. 368-378.

Note: In team results, total team faults do not reflect "drop scores" included in individual rider totals.

Dressage

Some of the Olympic sports that attract the most controversy have little of the heart-pounding, edge-of-the-envelope excitement of other high-action events. In figure skating, for example, the sedate ice-dancing competition, not the more spectacular singles and pairs events, draws the most heated criticism over judging and placings. In the Olympic equestrian disciplines, jumping and eventing draw their share of scrutiny and criticism; but dressage seems to take most of the heat, with accusations of biased judging, insufficient spectator draw, and even unworthiness of Olympic inclusion.

Dressage itself is a paradox. Some devotees rank it firmly in the category of athletic pursuit; others regard it as an art that should remain untainted by subjection to competition and ribbons. The majority of people who don't follow horse sports don't understand what it is — and get bored too quickly to try to figure out its nuances. (Even mainstream sporting publications don't attempt to hide their disdain for dressage: In his *Complete Book of the Summer Olympics*, *Sports Illustrated* writer David Wallechinsky states that "Until knitting is added to the Olympic program, dressage will remain the least action-packed of Olympic events.") [1]

In truth, there's nothing mysterious about dressage (the word is French for "training"): It's simply the gymnastic development of the horse. Anyone who's ridden a horse in circles, or moved him away from one leg, or asked him to "give" his poll and jaw, has used elements of classical horsemanship that have been practiced for hundreds of years. Jumper riders use dressage when they ask their horses to shorten or lengthen stride before takeoff, and event riders use dressage when they ask their horses to "come back" at the end of a steep downhill so they'll be balanced for that fence at the bottom. The recognition of dressage as a useful tool in any horse's training has spurred its popularity in equestrian circles, and more than a few riders have abandoned their previous disciplines when they discovered the sport's uniquely addictive quality.

Olympic dressage competition showcases a horse's gymnastic development at the highest levels regularly practiced today. Some of the *haute école* (high school) movements seen in the courts of 17th and 18th Century European royalty, such as the courbette and the levade, are not widely practiced today (although they are kept alive in the famed Spanish Riding School of Vienna) and are not included in the dressage "tests" (prescribed patterns of movements to be judged in competition). Today, an Olympic-level dressage horse's repertoire includes the passage, a cadenced and elevated trot; the piaffe, essentially a trot in place; the canter pirouette, in which the horse's hindquarters remain "on the spot" while his front legs prescribe a small circle and he maintains the three-beat canter rhythm with all four legs; and the flying changes

Michelle Gibson and Peron led the U.S. dressage team to a bronze-medal win in 1996.

of lead at the canter, which are executed in a certain number and sequence — up to fifteen in a row at every stride, making him look as if he is skipping.

As with three-day eventing and show jumping, the story of dressage in the Olympic Games is largely one of rule changes and externally imposed trends, while the underlying sport-slash-art remains unchanged. As a number of great horsemen have pointed out, horses haven't changed much over the centuries, and so the principles of classical riding haven't changed much either.

Olympic Dressage Through the Years

When dressage competition was added to the roster of the modern Olympic Games, at Stockholm in 1912, the required movements were simple compared to what's asked of Olympic dressage horses today — but with one significant twist: Dressage horses also had to jump! (All historical information in this section is taken from *Equestrian Olympic Games: Ancient and Modern*.) [2] The dressage arena itself was the size of today's "small arena" — forty meters long x twenty meters wide; the modern "standard arena," used in most dressage competition, is

sixty meters long x twenty meters wide. Competitors had ten minutes to execute the test, which consisted of walk, trot, and canter on both reins (in both directions); a "slow trot," a "slow" and extended canter; turns on the haunches and small circles at the slow trot, a figure-of-eight of eight-meter circles at the canter with and without changes of lead; and at least four flying changes on a straight line. Piaffe, passage, and other *haute école* movements were strictly forbidden. Riders could get extra points for taking the reins in one hand — and the most extra credit for doing so at the canter. As in modern dressage

competition, the panel of judges in Stockholm awarded each movement a numerical score out of a scale of zero to ten. (The adjectives used to describe what each number signifies may have changed over the years; today, zero means "not performed" and ten means "excellent.")

Next, the dressage horses at Stockholm had to jump four fences of up to 1.1 meter in height, plus one spread obstacle three meters across. Finally, the judges conducted an "obedience test," in which riders had to walk their horses past or between objects at which they had shied.

Horses had to be exhibited in double bridles without martingales or bearing reins of any kind; the rules specified no particular type of saddle. Military officers had to wear "undress uniform"; civilian competitors wore black or "pink" coats and silk hats. A total of twenty-one riders from Belgium, Denmark, France, Germany, Norway, Russia, Sweden, and the United States took part. Only individual medals were awarded in the 1912 Games, and the same would be true of the 1920 and 1924 Olympics; team dressage competition was not introduced until 1928.

The dressage test was more complex by the time of the 1920 Antwerp Olympics, and the arena dimensions had increased to fifty meters x twenty meters. Rules specified that the test must be ridden from memory. The word "collected" replaced "slow," and competitors had to demonstrate the collected walk, trot, and canter. Riders had to alternate between the extended trot rising (posting) and the collected trot sitting. New movements included a five-loop canter serpen-

The dressage arena at the 1920 Antwerp Games was much plainer than the floral-decorated venues of today.

tine with flying changes on the center line, followed by a five-loop serpentine on the counter ("wrong") lead; counter-changes of hand in the canter with flying changes (half-pass "zigzags"); and flying changes of lead every four, three, and two strides, culminating with changes at every stride (four-, three-, two-, and one-tempi changes). Riders walked into the final halt and salute to the judge. Seventeen riders from five nations competed. [3]

The 1936 individual gold medalists, Heinz Pollay of Germany and Kronos. The pair also was part of the gold-medal-winning team.

The dimensions of the dressage arena had reached their present proportions by the time of the 1924 Paris Olympics. The test was almost identical to that used in 1920. Twenty-four riders representing nine nations competed. [4]

The time factor was the only significant change in the dressage competition at the 1928 Amsterdam Games. The time limit was extended from ten minutes to thirteen minutes, with riders losing two points for every second they went over the allotted time. A total of twenty-nine riders from twelve nations competed. [5]

The dressage competition at the 1932 Los

Angeles Olympics was significant because the passage and the piaffe were included in the test for the first time in Olympic competition. Just ten riders from four nations competed — presumably because of the worldwide economic slump and the difficulties in transporting horses to the U.S., not because riders were deterred by the test's increased difficulty. [6]

The dressage test continued to increase in both length and complexity, as evidenced by the competition at the 1936 Berlin Olympics. In Berlin, the time limit had been increased to seventeen minutes — astonishingly long by today's standards; the modern Grand Prix test takes about ten minutes. The test included the following movements: reins in one hand at the trot, extended and "ordinary" trot rising, halt for eight seconds, half-turns on the haunches in the walk, canter serpentine of five eight-meter loops, canter pirouettes, tempi changes (from fours to ones), piaffe, and passage. Interestingly, the highest coefficient movements (the movements that were weighted the most heavily) were bending on two tracks (lines of movement) at the collected trot and the collected canter. Twenty-nine riders from eleven nations competed. The team and individual gold medalists, Germany's Lieutenant Heinz Pollay and Kronos, gave an exhibition ride immediately before the closing ceremonies. [7]

The most famous director in the history of the Spanish Riding School of Vienna, Colonel Alois Podhajsky, won the individual bronze medal at the 1936 Olympic Games. His Austrian team finished fourth. In 1939, Podhajsky, who had trained at the School for two years before the Berlin Games, assumed the directorship at the famed institution. He wrote several books about his philosophies and his beloved Lipizzaners, including *The White Stallions of Vienna* and *My Horses, My Teachers*.

The dressage test of the 1948 London Olympics was an anomaly: For the first and only time since their introduction at the 1932 Games, piaffe and passage were dropped from the test. As the legendary rider and trainer Vladimir S. Littauer explains in his book, *The Development of Modern Riding*, "This was due to the fact that there had not been sufficient time to prepare horses during the rather short interval since the end of the war. The programs in the next three Olympic Games, although differing somewhat from one another, were all at least of the standard of the Berlin test." [8] The 1948 test was shorter as a result of the omitted piaffe and passage and included half-pass, renvers (haunches-out), canter pirouettes, and tempi changes. The one-tempi changes had the highest coefficient. Nineteen riders from nine nations competed. [9]

The renvers is no longer part of the Grand Prix and the Grand Prix Special tests, but the level of difficulty of Olympic-level dressage has changed little since the piaffe and the passage were reinstated in the early 1950s. What has changed are judges' preferences, which have influenced everything from riding styles to dominant horse breeds. Sport-horse breeding has become big business, and few dressage horses of yesteryear had the enormous movement exhibited by the warmbloods who now dominate the international dressage arena. Despite the changes, though, dressage's principles and goals remain as unchanged — some would say elusive — as ever.

Judging: The Perpetual Controversy

Why is dressage judging so fraught with debate? As Vladimir Littauer explains in *The Development of Modern Riding*, "High School, as any art, is a matter of taste — in this case, national rather than personal taste. This taste is largely the product of economic and geographic conditions and historical factors; no two nations can see quite alike. Thus, for instance, the two major Dressage schools of today, the French and the German, are bound to appreciate different things, and therefore to strive for different results." [10] With its heavier, more phlegmatic horses, the German school traditionally produced a more mechanical style of riding, with stronger and more obvious aids. French horses were typically more refined and sensitive, enabling their riders to use a more delicate touch, with the resulting emphasis being on "lightness" and nearly invisible aids.

Nationalism in Judging?

Over the years, international-level dressage judges have been accused of favoring riders from their home countries, or of feeling obligated to give the nod to riders from the "dressage power" nations — usually Germany. Even as recently as the 1998 World Equestrian Games, the judges drew audience and press criticism when Germany's Isabell Werth and Nissan Gigolo FRH won the individual gold medal over the Netherlands' Anky van Grunsven and Gestion Olympic Bonfire. Werth and Van Grunsven are the sport's hottest rivals, and insiders have speculated that the judges still favor Germany over relative upstart the Netherlands.

At least these two ladies are arguably today's top two performers; in the past, the judging has at times appeared substantially more skewed. Three-time Olympian Jessica Ransehousen of Unionville, Pennsylvania, whose competitive career has spanned five decades (and counting), relates a dramatic example. "At the 1959 Pan American Games in Chicago, the FEI chief of the jury was Chilean. Before the competition got under way, representatives of another nation saw that judge riding a Chilean horse (a judge's schooling a horse entered in the competition is forbidden under FEI rules). They called up the FEI and told them what they'd seen, and the judge was automatically removed from the jury. But for whatever reason, he was reinstated before the competition started.

"The Chilean horse and rider entered the competition area and were going around the outside of the arena to warm up before the bell rang. General {Guy V.} Henry, the American judge on the jury, kept waiting for the chief of the jury to ring the horse out of the arena because he was lame. He didn't, and with his score the Chilean horse won the gold medal. We were fit to be tied. That judge should have been brought up in front of a hearing committee; he should have been taken off the jury. When you see things like that time after time, you don't have the greatest respect for international competition."

The "Halo Effect"

Another judging phenomenon is the so-called halo effect, in which top riders tend to keep winning, even for what may be lesser performances. Ransehousen explained that "because dressage competition is subjective, there is a lot of political influence, and a lot of pressure placed on the judges that's hard to put into perspective. We {dressage enthusiasts} would like to think that, on any given day, the best ride will win. Based on what I've seen over the years, though, I have to

are recognized in the top five or six." At the most recent Werth-Van Grunsven meeting, the 1999 FEI Dressage World Cup, the Dutch competitor bested her German rival for the first time. Just

say that's not exactly true. There have been times when I've been sitting in the audience at a competition with all the riders and a lot of interested and knowledgeable people, and {in our collective opinion} that {premise that the best performance will always win} wasn't quite correct."

There has been progress, said Ransehousen. "At least now those people {who put in the best rides}

Olympic dressage judging often is fraught with controversy.

one year before, at the World Equestrian Games in Rome, Werth had scored an unpopular victory over Van Grunsven. "For me, and for most of the people who were watching, Anky was the World Champion," said Ransehousen. "At least some of the judges thought so, too. Years ago, they probably wouldn't have felt the strength to put her first and have the German rider second. I feel that the judging is much more honest now and has been since the time of the 1988 Seoul Olympics (Ransehousen's most recent Olympic competitive experience). There's been a big improvement. Nineteen eighty-eight was probably the last of the pretty mediocre judging."

All dressage judging draws its share of critics, but tensions ran particularly high in Seoul, said Ransehousen. "Most of us felt very strongly that {the individual silver medalists, French rider Margit Otto-Crepin and her mount} Corlandus should have been placed higher. Corlandus showed not only wonderful piaffe and passage, but he was also trained more correctly. {The gold medalist, Germany's} Nicole Uphoff was young and attractive; she and Rembrandt were very attractive. But the horse was very difficult at that point in his career; he did several things in the test that nowadays might have prevented her from winning the gold medal. For one thing, he did not show a proper walk. He did not pace, but he was definitely not in the same rhythm in front as he was behind. For another, he was very unsteady — and actually halted at the end of a canter extension — and was not really on the aids.

"{The incident with Corlandus} put everybody in a very bad mood — that and the fact that the chief of the jury was very high on a Swiss horse," Ransehousen said frankly. "The horse and rider cantered down the center line, halted, and saluted; and the horse piaffed the whole time. He never made a halt in the entire test, and he just ran across the diagonal instead of showing the proper rhythm in his trot extensions. His score from the Swiss judge was so high that it seemed to put the other judges totally off balance. I think they thought, 'My standard can't be right.' We had an international riders' meeting (a meeting of the International Dressage Riders Club) in Korea after the Grand Prix, and everybody was just furious. The riders rightly felt injured; it was a long way to go to compete and a very expensive trip for all the nations. Then to have bad judging — you felt, 'What in the world am I here for?' " (The U.S. squad — Ransehousen on Orpheus, Robert Dover on Federleicht, Belinda Baudin on Christopher, and Lendon Gray on Later On — finished sixth in Seoul. Dover, the highest-placed American rider, finished thirteenth individually.)

Dover, who is the most decorated competitor in the history of American dressage, concurs with Ransehousen's sentiments regarding judging. "The judging has always been a source of major conflict," he said. "It probably will continue to be, unless something completely changes within the minds of those who rule our sport. In order to change the situation, what one would have to do is to remind everyone within our sport that, just because somebody is a wonderful rider and they've had one wonderful horse, it does not mean that same person on another horse cannot have a bad day — or maybe the other horse is not as good. As long as the judges believe that this wonderful rider ought to have a score that's perhaps far above what the performance really deserves, regardless of the horse, we're going to have this problem."

The European Perspective

Are Ransehousen, Dover, and others just sour-graping because they're the American under-

Jessica Ransehousen, pictured here with George Morris, has ridden for the U.S. and currently serves as dressage chef d'équipe.

dogs? Actually, no. Dutch superstar Anky van Grunsven herself said of dressage judging, "I do not think that much has changed over the years. The judging is still a matter of personal taste. Of course, we all try to get this improved and more objective, but it is a difficult matter."

Judges on Judging

So are all judges swayed by blind patriotism and adulation of celebrity riders? Fortunately, no. In fact, some of the best-known judges say they continually strive not to allow such prejudices to creep into their marks.

In the book *Riding for America*, the late Colonel Donald W. Thackeray, an FEI "O" (Official) dressage judge, observed that "Judging is not an exact science and it should not be. Other sports also have judging troubles. Why do baseball managers rush out to the mound and jaw with the umpire? Why do we have the instant replay in football? {I}n Europe…the judges get to know the horses and riders. Their placings evolve into the judges' scores being partially based on observations that the horse is doing either better or worse than, for example, last winter at Aachen. Therefore, when European judges come to America, they have no comparison basis and tend to mark lower (on the safe side)." [11]

FEI "O" judge Eric Lette of Sweden, who chairs

the FEI Dressage Committee and who will serve as chief of the ground jury at the 2000 Sydney Olympics, has said: "If riders, trainers, and spectators are to respect our sport, it is of great importance that the judging be good." He affirms that judging has changed for the better. "I remember years ago, when I still competed, that judging was all about spotting mistakes and punishing them. My number one criterion is to look for quality. Once I have a mark for quality I will step up or down the scale depending on the technical correctness of the movement." Furthermore, he said, good judges do not award marks with the final placings in mind. "We don't allow ourselves to give a leeway for a better mark simply because we know that a top competitor is scheduled to ride two hours after another favorite. We just mark what we see." [12]

The Dressage Evolution

As experts such as Lette and Thackeray have pointed out, dressage judges are only human, and so the element of subjectivity cannot be eradicated completely from judging. Over the years, judges' preferences have shaped everything from dressage-horse breeding to training

For much of the 20th Century, warmblood sport horses generally were heavy-bodied.

methods. Let's take a look at some of the ways competitors have altered their approach in an attempt to please the VIP at "C."

Breeds and Types

Most of the horses that enter at "A" in today's dressage competitions — particularly at the Olympic level — are quite different from their predecessors. In the 16th and 17th Centuries, European aristocrats enjoyed displaying their equestrian skills (and their wealth) by putting their Spanish horses (Andalusians, Lusitanos, and the like) through displays of *haute école* movements. Piaffe, passage, and the "airs above the ground" tend to come easily to the small but sturdy baroque horses, with their powerful hindquarters and high action.

In the 17th Century, the cavalry was a substantial force in western Europe, and the breeding of suitable mounts took on increased importance. France and Germany in particular began developing various "types" of horses by crossing native stock with Spanish breeds. At the same time, the Thoroughbred — stemming from three Arabian foundation sires — and Cleveland Bay breeds were being established in England. The "hot-blooded" Thoroughbred was rangy in type, with great speed; the stockier Cleveland Bay was an excellent carriage horse.

As the cavalry's influence continued in the 18th and 19th Centuries, horse breeding became more sophisticated, and western Europe gradually developed various "warmblood" types — so called because they were crosses between "hot bloods" and "cold bloods" — all of which had good endurance and free forward movement. Horses at the time also were used for farm work,

so the products of the states' breeding programs were on the brawny side.

World War II brought mass mechanization, and the use of horses in agriculture largely died

Grunox, ridden by Monica Theodorescu and a member of the 1996 German gold-medal team, represents a continuing evolution of "type."

along with the cavalry. Horses were transformed into luxury items, and the latter half of the 20th Century saw a dramatic upswing in horse sports. The focus of warmblood-breeding programs shifted accordingly, from producing horses for cavalry and transportation to producing excellent all-around sport horses for dressage and jumping competition. [13] In an ongoing process, Thoroughbred blood has been infused to refine the heavy warmbloods. The result, as FEI "C" (Candidate) judge and well-known author Charles de Kunffy has put it, is "horses that {are} more versatile than the baroque Iberians — that {can} both execute dressage movements and gal-

lop and jump cross-country." The implications of this versatility for dressage competition are that " 'the keyboard' of the dressage-competition piano has been extended from one octave (the range of dressage horses of yesteryear) to perhaps four (the range of today's warmbloods) — from the highest degree of collection to the greatest extension," he adds. [14]

As photographs from the past century of Olympic dressage competition attest, there has been a continuing evolution in the type of horse used. European sport-horse-type warmbloods were practically nonexistent in the U.S. during the Army-team days, and so the cavalrymen rode primarily Thoroughbreds or Thoroughbred crosses. After the cavalry's demise, American dressage enthusiasts began importing sport horses, and eventually Americans began breeding their own, with U.S. branches of warmblood breed registries established. Plenty of non-sport-horse breeds can be found in dressage arenas nationwide, and "other" breeds can and do excel at Grand Prix dressage — Hilda Gurney's legendary Thoroughbred Keen, who won a team bronze medal at the 1976 Montreal Olympics, immediately comes to mind — but the majority of the dressage horses at today's Olympic Games are warmblood sport horses, regardless of their riders' nationality.

Many of the warmblood sport horses in competition in the 1970s and 1980s were still quite heavy in type, requiring an assertive riding style with strong seat and legs — hallmarks of the so-called German school. The pendulum began to

Hilda Gurney and Keen helped put American dressage on the map at the 1976 Montreal Olympics.

swing the other way in the 1990s, and many of today's top dressage riders prefer a lighter, smaller, more sensitive mount. (Not surprisingly, many of today's top dressage riders are women.)

German dressage star Klaus Balkenhol, who won team gold and individual bronze medals at the 1992 Barcelona Olympics and another team gold at the 1996 Games in Atlanta and who now coaches the German dressage team, said of the evolution, "The horses do have more Thoroughbred blood today. Half-bred or even three-quarter-bred Thoroughbreds are more responsive. It is easier to deal with blood-horses. They have a lot of engagement, and they want to be ridden in a more sensitive way. I guess the future will bring normal-sized to quite big horses, but they must move light-footed and elastically. It must look easy in the ring — like a game, not like work."

Trends aside, most of today's top riders, trainers, and breeders agree that warmblood-breeding standards have improved, leading to a much larger pool of horses of excellent quality. "The quality of the horses has risen immensely," said Anky van Grunsven. "Their movement has gotten better, and there are a lot of good horses today. Until some years ago, there were only a few really good horses, but this has changed. The introduction of the freestyle has helped to attract more sponsors, and this has also led to our having better horses at our disposal. Today there are more people willing to spend quite an amount of money to buy a horse. This raises the level of the sport."

Training and Riding Methods

With the improvement in breeding programs and dressage's increased popularity has come an elevation of standards of excellence. The sport has grown increasingly competitive, and the difference between winning and losing an Olympic medal now rests on the most subtle distinctions.

"Back in 1936 and in the 1940s, the horses went without using their backs; they tended to be very short and high in the neck and hollow in the back," explained Jessica Ransehousen. "If your horse was hollow but he had a fancy trot, that was considered OK. But by the time the 1960s rolled around, judges didn't want to see that any more. They wanted to see horses longer in the frame, with necks rounder and noses deeper — not so hollow in the back. It's an ongoing evolutionary process.

"In those days," Ransehousen said of her early years of international competition, "the overall balance of the {Grand Prix} test was more toward the horse's basic training and a little less toward his ability to piaffe and passage, so a well-trained horse could have not such a wonderful piaffe and passage and still do very well.

"By the time of the 1990 World Championships in Stockholm, when the Russians did so well, we were seeing more 'tricky' riding. A lot of those horses — and this trend held over until the 1988 Olympics in Seoul — were very clever at piaffe and passage and scored very highly; they couldn't canter worth a darn and they couldn't walk very well, but they didn't have so many points taken off for that {lack of basics}.

"Now there's more of a balance between the correct basics and an ability to do the collected movements really well, and I think that's the prettiest, nicest look."

"I have competed in three Olympics, the first time in eighty-eight," mused Anky van Grunsven.

"I believe that riders and horses have become much better over this period of time. In eighty-eight, I became Dutch Champion aboard Prisco with quite a low score compared with what is needed to win today. Today, with my 1988 winning percentage of sixty-three or sixty-four, I would not be among the top twelve in Holland."

(In comparison, today's Olympic standard is seventy percent or higher, and scores of eighty-plus are not unheard of in the freestyle. Germany's Isabell Werth won the Grand Prix and the Grand Prix Freestyle at the 1996 Olympics with scores of 76.6 and 83.0 percent, respectively.)

"The dressage sport is going in the direction of a more and more refined riding style," said Klaus Balkenhol. "The rider who wants to get high scores must suit the ideal of beauty and create a picture of harmony." That picture, he said, is created through classical riding and training: by using a system of gymnastic exercises to develop the horse's movement naturally, not through the use of "tricks" or "circus-like" methods. "Today riders take care that the horses are trained with more sensibility," he said. "There are still some riders who ride with much power, but there are fewer and fewer of them. Dressage riding is going more in the direction of riders like {German stars} Nicole Uphoff, Isabell Werth, Ulla Salzgeber, and Nadine Capellmann."

The Fine Points

Many dressage enthusiasts can (and do) debate ad infinitum about the minutiae of the sport. A few recent notable controversies, by way of example: whether the shoulder-in should be executed on two tracks or three (a "track" being a line of movement); whether the horse's poll must always be the highest point; and whether the piaffe does, indeed, lack a moment of suspension. Even if a rider isn't inclined to haggle a point with her cronies, she may concern herself with the judge's views and preferences if she intends to compete.

Jessica Ransehousen illustrates how judging preferences can affect dressage riding: "The standard for the half-pass has changed. In those days (the 1950s and 1960s), you were not to ride the half-pass parallel; you had to ride the shoulders ahead of the hindquarters. If you rode it parallel {as many competitors ride it today}, you had

Dressage judges' preferences have evolved over the years. The 1952 Olympic champions, Henri St. Cyr and Master Rufus, might not win today.

points taken off."

Today, leading dressage riders and trainers spot a number of trends in horses' "way of going." Some they regard as positive developments; others give them cause for concern.

"The judges should take more care that the horses are in front of the vertical," opined former German team coach Harry Boldt. "Nicole Uphoff's 1988 and 1992 Olympic gold-medal-winning partner Rembrandt was always a bit short in the neck, but there was nobody else doing better piaffe and passage and the two-tempis as accurate. Also, Anky van Grunsven's Bonfire had a time when he was quite short in the neck, but this has become better. This does not mean that I want it condemned if a horse is

a bit behind the vertical; it should have some impact in the scoring, but perhaps only a point or two should be subtracted."

Swiss dressage rider Christine Stückelberger, who won team silver and individual gold medals at the 1976 Olympics, team silver in 1984, and team silver and individual bronze in 1988, agreed. "We must be very careful that, with all the piaffe and passage in today's Grand Prix-level tests, we do not lose the classical principles," she said. "Today you see the horses pulled together. We see many horses going with high croups and the riders having one hundred kilograms in their hands. We must not have piaffes and passages executed under tension, and 'fidget' piaffes."

One current trend, largely attributed to the "extreme stretching" used by Nicole Uphoff to supple and loosen her high-strung Rembrandt, is to ride horses "deep" by encouraging them to stretch their necks far forward and down, thereby stretching the back muscles. Klaus Balkenhol doesn't mind the use of deep work but cautions that "most riders do not try to get their horses with the forehead before the vertical again. The judges should penalize when a horse is tense and goes always behind the vertical. But I have the feeling that we are on the way to getting horses to go more before the vertical again."

Women Dressage Riders Pave the Way

The first women who were allowed to ride in Olympic Games competition were dressage riders — presumably because that sport was considered the least physically strenuous of the three Olympic equestrian disciplines. (The FEI allowed women to compete in show jumping as of the 1956 Olympics, but it was not until the 1964 Tokyo Games that American rider Lana du Pont broke the final gender barrier by becoming the first female three-day event rider in Olympic history.) One of those ground-breaking women, Denmark's Lis Hartel, put to rest any speculations that female riders were less competitive or capable by winning the individual silver medal at the 1952 Helsinki Games. (Hartel's remarkable story is discussed later in this chapter.)

Horse people take pride in pointing out the fact that the equestrian disciplines are among the very few Olympic sports in which men and women compete against one another. In fact, women riders have amassed an impressive record in the Olympics and other international competitions. At the 1972 Games in Munich, German dressage rider Liselott Linsenhoff became the first female equestrian to win an Olympic gold medal. At the 1988 Seoul Olympics, for the first time, all three individual medalists in an equestrian event — dressage riders Nicole Uphoff, Margit Otto-Crepin, and Christine Stückelberger — were women.

Kür Comes to the Olympics

The sport of figure skating was once a lesser light of Olympic competition. It was difficult to interest spectators in the "figures" segment of the competition, which consisted of skaters' painstakingly tracing figures-of-eight and other patterns on the ice. In 1991, the International Skating Union (skating's equivalent of the FEI) decided to drop the figures from competition and to focus instead on the routines to music: in singles and pairs competition, for instance, a

The aptly named Piaff partnered Germany's Liselott Linsenhoff at the 1968 and 1972 Olympics, winning a total of three medals.

"short program" and a "free skate," both of skaters' own design and choice of music. The result: a huge jump in popularity for the sport, which now fills seats at the winter Olympics as well as at performances by skating's biggest stars on numerous exhibition tours. [15]

The sport of dressage took a big step toward following in figure skating's footsteps at the 1996 Olympic Games in Atlanta, with the FEI's decision to add a musical-freestyle competition (or "Kür," as it is increasingly becoming known). For the first time, Olympic dressage competition consisted of three "rounds" instead of the traditional two. In past Olympics, the Grand Prix test determined the team medalists and was the qualifier for the Grand Prix Special (a slightly shorter test of greater intensity, with more emphasis placed on the piaffe and the passage); and the Special alone decided the individual medalists. In Atlanta, the Grand Prix determined the team medalists. The top twenty-five finishers from the Grand Prix went on to compete in the Special. Competitors' combined scores from the Grand Prix and the Special determined the qualifiers for the freestyle. In Atlanta, the riders with the top thirteen combined scores went on to the freestyle, and the cumulative scores from all three competitions determined the individual medalists.

The Kür is similar to figure skating's free skate. Competitors choreograph their own routines and choose their own music. They must include certain required elements, while other movements are prohibited. Routines must be within a certain time length. Judges award two scores: one for technical merit and another for artistic impression. A Kür starts and finishes with the traditional halt and salute to the judges, but what happens in between ideally looks more like a dance than a dressage test. Riders and their choreographers strive to create patterns and sequences that are not "test-like," and to find music that matches their horses' rhythm and tempo so that the effect is truly that of a dance. (Some competitors, such as Anky van Grunsven, even have had music custom-composed and -performed to ensure an exact fit with their horses' gaits. The Dutch star rode her 1996 Olympic freestyle to "Bonfire's Symphony," named for the horse for which it was written.)

The Kür is a crowd pleaser, but dressage riders and other insiders have varying opinions on its effects on the sport. Klaus Balkenhol and Christine Stückelberger are among many experts who recognize that the freestyle has given dressage a popularity boost with the public, but they caution against relaxing the rules so much that the competition becomes "circus-like," stressing spectacular tricks over solid, classical basics. Harry Boldt worries that some competitors choreograph their freestyle routines to conceal their horses' weak points, but he takes comfort in the fact that Olympic dressage competition includes the Grand Prix and the Special as well as the Kür — not just the Grand Prix and the Kür, as was originally proposed.

"Two years before the Atlanta Olympics, we had a meeting of the International Dressage Trainers Club," Boldt said. "Until that time, the discussion was to choose between either the Kür or the Special. I proposed, Why not have all three tests and count them together? That the basic program

Holland's Anky van Grunsven and Olympic Bonfire wow the crowd in Atlanta with their freestyle to "Bonfire's Symphony."

has to be done first is a blessing. If this ever changes, dressage standards will go downhill."

It should come as no surprise that the judging of freestyles has sparked controversy. Of concern to Balkenhol, among others, is that "many judges still have no understanding of music and choreography," an observation that begs the question of how musically naïve judges can be

Lis Hartel of Denmark (right) overcame polio to win the individual dressage silver medal at the 1952 Helsinki Games.

expected to award valid scores for artistic impression. But "O" judge and freestyle advocate Eric Lette believes that, if the performance is technically superior, the artistic issue takes care of itself. It was Lette and his predecessor at the FEI Dressage Committee, now-retired Swiss "O" judge Wolfgang Niggli, who campaigned to have

the Kür added to the Olympic and championships roster. Lette recognizes riders' and trainers' concern that the Kür "could turn into a circus act. However, we always had the dressage rules firmly in mind and kept them alive for the Kür. {T}oday we have the proof that the riders who win the Kür are the ones who show exceptional performances in the Grand Prix and the Special. When judging the Kür, we put a lot of emphasis on the correctness of the movements. If the technical marks are not high, the artistic ones won't be either. If a combination is not technically up to it, they cannot be artistic!" [16]

U.S. Olympic veteran Robert Dover, who is also equestrian-sports' representative to the U.S. Olympic Committee, goes so far as to say that the freestyle has saved the sport. "{Dressage competition in the Olympics} has been saved by the freestyle; we would be off the Olympic slate were it not for the freestyle," he stated emphatically. "The freestyle captured the imagination of the IOC (International Olympic Committee) and the general public and kept us in there." Adding the freestyle has had other advantages, too, he said: "With this system of having the freestyle on the last day of dressage competition, you lower the number of competitors in the individual finals" — a plus in the eyes of time-squeezed television broadcasters — and the music makes the finals "much more entertaining and interesting to the public."

Legends in Olympic Dressage

The dressage world has produced its share of riders and horses whose accomplishments and contributions made headlines during and after their Olympic performances. While show jumping and three-day eventing's legends gave the horse world thrilling and unforgettable moments of courage and athletic prowess, the enduring images from Olympic dressage competition are of beauty, majesty, and unsurpassed harmony between horse and rider. They are quietly magnificent, and those who were in the audience feel privileged to have seen them.

Lis Hartel: Triumph Over Tragedy

The Danish rider exhibited so much courage and determination on her way to winning two individual silver medals that she is the only equestrian featured in the book *Glory and the Games: Overcoming Adversity in Pursuit of Olympic Excellence.* [17] Hartel began riding at an early age and had become a champion in her country by her early twenties. In 1944, the twenty-three-year-old Hartel was the mother of a two-year-old, was happily pregnant with her second child, and had a lifetime of riding and competition to look forward to. But her dreams all but died when, one morning that September, she woke up with a stiff neck. Within a week, she was paralyzed, her body ravaged by polio. She spent the next four months in a hospital, not knowing whether she and her unborn baby would survive.

Survive they did, and the baby was born healthy, but Hartel remained almost completely paralyzed. Doctors told her that all she could hope for was eventually to regain enough strength and mobility to walk with two canes — and that she would never ride again. Hartel was determined, however, and a mere eight months after the polio attack she was supporting her weight on the canes. Although she never regained full use of her upper legs and her lower legs were permanently paralyzed from the knees down, she insisted on being hoisted aboard her horse, Jubilee, and began trying to ride again, despite repeated falls. Eventually she learned how to balance in the saddle without using her legs and to aid Jubilee with subtle shifts of weight instead of leg and spur. By 1947 she was competing again in Denmark, and in 1952 she was among the first women riders to compete in the Olympic Games.

Hartel's silver-medal-winning ride and medal ceremony in Helsinki were among the most moving and memorable moments in Olympic history. Still unable to use her legs, she had to be lowered into the saddle. The audience watched spellbound as she and Jubilee gave a performance worthy of any able-bodied rider. There was likely not a dry eye in the stands when the individual gold medalist, Henri Saint Cyr of Sweden, helped Hartel onto the medal podium.

Hartel and Jubilee went on to win a second individual silver medal at the following Games, in Stockholm in 1956. The Danish rider became an inspiration to polio sufferers around the world, and memories of her accomplishments continue to awe and humble all riders.

Bengt Ljungquist: Importing Excellence

The late Colonel Bengt Ljungquist played an important role in bringing dressage, then a relatively unknown commodity, to the United States. An officer in the Swedish cavalry and an outstanding all-around athlete, he competed in two very different Olympic events: fencing and dressage. By the time he rode in the Games for the first time, in Tokyo in 1964, he had already made four previous Olympic appearances and had won two medals for fencing.

Ljungquist, who also earned the Swedish

national dressage-championship title several times during his competitive career, immigrated to the U.S. in 1970 after his retirement from the service. He settled in Maryland and became the

that the U.S. Equestrian Team asked him to coach its 1974 World Championship squad. The following year, he coached the U.S. Pan American Games team to a gold-medal victory. His U.S.

Bengt Ljungquist (left) and fellow officials Jack Burton, Jack Le Goff, and Jack Fritz in 1976.

resident trainer at Idlewilde Farm in Davidsonville, home of U.S. dressage rider and trainer (and, later, 1996 Olympic dressage judge) Linda Zang. Soon a number of up-and-coming riders, including former USDF president Kay Meredith and four-time Olympian Robert Dover, were making regular treks to Idlewilde to work with the Swedish master.

Ljungquist's methods were so well-received

career highlight came in 1976 when the team of Hilda Gurney on Keen, Dorothy Morkis on Monaco, and Edith Master on Dahlwitz won the bronze medal at the Montreal Olympic Games — the first U.S. Olympic dressage medal since 1948.

Ljungquist continued to coach the U.S. dressage team until 1979, when he stepped down to focus on teaching privately at Idlewilde and at Virginia's Morven Park International Equestrian Institute. He died that July of a heart attack while on vacation in Sweden, having recently decided to move back there permanently. He was sixty-seven.

Fortunately for the dressage world, Ljungquist had set down many of his methods and philosophies in his book *Practical Dressage Manual*, which was published three years before his death. But the dressage community mourned his passing as a great loss for the sport, and the Potomac Valley Dressage Association established the annual Colonel Bengt Ljungquist Memorial Dressage Championships, a regional championship competition now in its eighteenth year, in honor of the man who did so much to further dressage education in America.

Ljungquist wrote an essay entitled "The American Dressage Outlook," published in the 1976 collection entitled *The U.S. Equestrian Team Book of Riding*. Almost a quarter-century later, his observations still bear consideration.

I believe that finding and using good instructors is essential to the future of the sport. {W}e must spread the knowledge of sound basic schooling throughout the equestrian community. The recipe that turns good fundamentals into international-level riders is very simple, but we have not yet developed a sure mechanism for locating the talented rider and horses and bringing them together for training. I believe that, ultimately, the dressage community must establish its own permanent training center to bridge the gap between the private individual working alone and the rider who is sufficiently advanced to work with the USET. [18]

Harry Boldt: Trainer of Champions

Harry Boldt has won four Olympic medals — team gold and individual silver at both the 1964 and 1976 Games — but it is as a trainer and coach that he has exerted the greatest influence. The German dressage-team coach from 1981 through 1996 played an important role in keeping his country the sport's superpower. He coached Nicole Uphoff from 1988 through 1995, during the zenith of her meteoric rise in the dressage ranks. The twenty-one-year-old woman became the youngest-ever equestrian Olympic gold medalist at the 1988 Games in Seoul, and she and her horse Rembrandt repeated their double-gold wins at the 1992 Barcelona Olympics, securing them and their coach a permanent niche in Olympic dressage history.

Uphoff and "Remmi" may be among the most celebrated dressage pairs of recent times, but they have also been among the most criticized for their somewhat unconventional training methods. Uphoff and fellow German dressage star Isabell Werth are two of the most famous proponents of using "extreme stretching" and a very "deep" frame to supple and soften their mounts. During their competitive career, Uphoff was noted for keeping her notoriously high-strung Westphalian gelding deep and behind the vertical until the moment they entered the arena. Boldt has explained that the method keeps the horses soft and ridable for the young women, and that the riders' exquisite timing and "feel" prevent the deep frame from becoming a straitjacket — but that lesser riders ought not to attempt to copy the technique. "Isabell and Nicole are expert in being soft in the hand at the right moment," he has said. "In the wrong hands, the neck shortens and breaks in front of the withers. Anyone other than an expert in this technique should concentrate on learning and

riding in the purely classical way." [19]

Boldt has plenty of classical education to draw from. The son of a riding instructor, he was introduced to horses at an early age and rode show jumpers for several years before he made the switch to dressage. He studied with such notables as former German team trainers "Bubi" Günther, Fritz Stecken, and Willi Schultheis, the latter of whom was Boldt's immediate predecessor at Warendorf.

Boldt made his Olympic debut at the 1964 Tokyo Games. Aboard Remus, he won a team gold medal and the individual silver. Twelve years later, in Montreal, he repeated his medal wins aboard Woyceck, whom he has called the best horse of his career.

Like many riders, Boldt calls his Olympic experiences "the most important events in my equestrian career. Because of the extraordinary amount of attention paid to the Olympics, they are the greatest and cannot be replaced by World and European or any other international championships." He has fond memories of the hero's welcome he received after the 1964 Games: "My whole hometown of Iserlohn got crazy. They held a parade for me, and all these people were on the sidewalks and on their balconies. It was fantastic."

Now seventy and married to an Australian dressage rider, Boldt makes his home Down Under and trains four Aussie Olympic hopefuls. (Wife Margo is out of contention with a bone chip in her knee.) He doesn't hesitate to weigh in on current issues in the sport of dressage, and

Dr. Reiner Klimke, shown winning the gold in 1984 on Ahlerich, was a great competitor and teacher.

states emphatically that he is against the new short Grand Prix test being used at the indoor shows in Europe ("it is much too easy"), but he seems to be content in the knowledge that his days in the spotlight are behind him.

"What happens after the Sydney Olympics does not touch me any more," said Boldt. "The younger generation must step in now."

Dr. Reiner Klimke: 20th Century Master

Like that of former U.S. dressage-team coach Colonel Bengt Ljungquist, the life of legendary German dressage competitor and trainer Dr. Reiner Klimke was cut tragically short by a heart attack. When Klimke died in 1999, in his sixty-fourth year, he left a huge void in the dressage community; but he also left a legacy of unmatched competitive success and efforts to further dressage education worldwide.

No German athlete in any sport has yet matched Klimke's record of eight Olympic medal wins — ten, if you count the two he won at the 1980 alternate Olympics. He won team gold aboard his Hanoverian gelding Dux at the 1964 Tokyo Games; team gold and individual bronze in Mexico City in 1968, also with Dux; team gold and individual bronze at the 1976 Montreal Olympics, this time with his Hanoverian gelding Mehmed; team gold and individual bronze at the 1980 alternate Olympics with his greatest partner, the Westphalian gelding Ahlerich; team and individual gold medals with Ahlerich at the 1984 Los Angeles Games; and a final team gold in Seoul in 1988, also with Ahlerich.

Klimke's individual gold-medal-winning tests with Ahlerich at the 1984 Los Angeles Olympics stand out as the performances of the dressage master's lifetime. He described his experiences at those Games in his book, *Ahlerich: The Making of a Dressage World Champion.*

Klimke sensed that his horse was "peaking" for the Olympics, and so he "decided to introduce

Klimke called his individual gold-medal win "the most beautiful moment of his life."

Ahlerich to the world in Los Angeles as a horse who would win because of his expression and impulsion." He recalled the attention and applause from spectators at all of their schooling sessions, and then, "On the day of the team dres-

sage, he performed a Grand Prix with impulsion and expression that many experts described as the best Grand Prix of his life." The next day was the Grand Prix Special — the individual final competition. Klimke recalled having to push the tired Ahlerich more that day, and the horse came through. "I know we cannot talk to horses," he wrote, "but I believe that Ahlerich knew what was going on that day. He outdid himself."

Klimke called the announcement of their individual gold medal "the most beautiful moment of my life." He wrote of Ahlerich, "I cannot find the words to describe the thanks I owe him." [20] Ahlerich was retired after the 1988 Seoul Olympics and died in 1992 of colic at the age of twenty-two.

Klimke was fortunate to grow up in the town of Münster, in Westphalia, where he was able to train with brothers and dressage masters Paul and Albert Stecken and, later, at the nearby German national training center in Warendorf with such experts as Herta Rau. Former German champion rider Käthe Franke later served as a coach and mentor, and Klimke also was a member of the German dressage team under the expert direction of coach Harry Boldt.

Dressage enthusiasts might not know that Klimke made a brief yet successful career switch to eventing, competing on Germany's three-day squad at the 1960 Olympic Games — his first Olympics. Aboard his first horse, a Westphalian mare named Winzerin, he finished eighteenth individually. Prior to the 1960 Games, he had won other eventing honors, most notably a team silver medal at the 1957 European Championships (on the ex-show-jumper Lausbub) and the 1959 European Team Championship title (Fortunat).

A practicing attorney and a father of three, Klimke somehow found time not only to ride before work and on his lunch breaks, but also to travel the world giving clinics and seminars. His appearances were much heralded and attracted large audiences, and several sessions were made into instructional videotapes. Klimke made several video series and wrote a number of dressage texts in addition to *Ahlerich*, including the classic *Cavalletti* (1960) and *Basic Training of the Young Horse* (1980). He was active on behalf of international dressage competition, serving on the FEI's Dressage Committee from 1998 until his death.

Reigning Olympic champion Isabell Werth, who like Klimke is studying law and hopes to combine a career with international dressage competition, feels the loss of her role model keenly. "For me, he was the person to approach when I wanted to know or discuss something regarding the sport," she said. "He was the person to go forward for the interests of our sport.

"It is often said that Reiner Klimke would never have found the right moment to quit the active sport," Werth said. "I think it was just a part of his nature and his life. It was unbelievable what he managed to do: the performance sport, his profession as a lawyer, his political activities (Klimke was a member of the Northrhine-Westphalia state Parliament and was a notary public), many honorary functions in sports, his books and videos, his clinics. He influenced sports immensely, and not just equestrian sports. He trained and brought out a lot of very different horses — horses with which other riders would not have been so successful. He has really written dressage history."

Jessica Ransehousen: America's Grande Dame

When Jessica Ransehousen (then Jessica Newberry) first rose to the top of the American dressage ranks in the 1950s, the sport was the also-ran of the U.S. Equestrian Team's three disciplines. By 1988, when Ransehousen rode in her third Olympic Games in Seoul, Korea, dressage was the fastest-growing English equestrian sport in America and star riders like Robert Dover regularly graced horse-magazine covers. Still an active trainer and competitor, Ransehousen now also serves as *chef d'équipe* of the U.S. dressage team (see Chapter 2 for more on her *chef*-ing activities) and has seen the sport continue to swell in popularity.

An outspoken advocate for her sport, Ransehousen campaigns tirelessly on behalf of dressage and dressage riders. A combination of doting den mother and no-nonsense official, she's a tough cookie with a soft center, alternately cooing over her human, equine, and canine charges and matter-of-factly letting people know what's what. It's a formula she's developed at least in part as a result of her own early Olympic experiences, at which the dressage and eventing contingencies played a distinct second fiddle to the show jumpers.

Ransehousen said her arrival in Rome for the 1960 Olympic Games didn't bode well for things to come. "{Fellow dressage-team member} Trish {Galvin} and I arrived at the Olympic Village and we had no rooms," she recalled. "We were not told in advance that we didn't; we just arrived and we didn't have any." Luckily for the riders, the track-and-field coach had some of her athletes double up so Galvin and Ransehousen could have a place to sleep.

A logistical mix-up in Rome almost cost Ransehousen the chance to compete when her horse, Forstrat, was vanned to the wrong venue. She arrived at the Piazza di Siena, the site of the dressage competition, to find her horse missing.

"In Rome, the horse area is very large; they had the stables in one area, and the horses had to be vanned to the various warm-up and competition sites. The day of the competition, my horse was taken to a racetrack that we used for schooling instead of to the Piazza di Siena. So instead of having an hour's warm-up before the Grand Prix, I had about twenty-five minutes. I was only twenty-two. That was pretty hard to take."

The stallion, unsettled by the last-minute journey, made some mistakes yet still finished a respectable twelfth. Four years later, the pair finished fourteenth at the Tokyo Games and helped the U.S. dressage team garner a fourth-place finish.

As a competitor, Ransehousen felt quite on her own before and during her first two Olympic Games. Neither the U.S. Olympic Committee nor the U.S. Equestrian Team provided much in the way of support for the dressage team, she said, and it didn't help matters that the two organizations were squabbling over the division of the equestrian teams' expenses. "The whole feeling in those days {as a dressage or an event rider} was that, if you happened to make the team, you were on your own," she said ruefully. The dressage and event riders looked on enviously, she said, as the jumper riders were given better-quality equipment and the services of a team manager; "The other teams had to work so hard just to survive."

Marriage and motherhood took Ransehousen out of the competition arena for some years fol-

lowing the 1964 Olympics, and during that time the popularity and status of dressage and eventing in the United States made great strides. The mother of two (her younger child, daughter Missy, is a well-known event rider and trainer) began judging and serving on various USET and American Horse Shows Association committees, all activities in which she's continued to participate. She returned to competition in the 1970s, and she and her children moved to Germany so she could train with Reiner Klimke and compete in Europe. The family returned to the U.S. in 1980 and settled in their current home of Unionville, Pennsylvania. In 1986, she organized a sixteen-member syndicate to buy what was to become her next Olympic mount: the Dutch Warmblood stallion Orpheus. Just two years later, "Orphy" and his rider made the team for Seoul.

Their team test at the 1988 Olympics was the best of Orphy's career, said Ransehousen. Despite what could politely be called an electric atmosphere, with restless Korean schoolchildren playing in the stands and flags snapping in a strong wind, "My horse, who was sensitive to sounds and who could be difficult, really tried his best. {German dressage veteran} Gabby {Grillo} came up to me afterward and said, 'You can be really happy because yours was a really classical ride.' " They placed seventeenth individually, with the second-highest U.S. score; the team was sixth.

One suspects that Ransehousen is as proud (or more) of having been named leading foreign lady rider at the 1959 Aachen Horse Show in Germany than she ever would be of a medal — but she takes a quiet satisfaction in her team participation and accomplishments as a pioneering force in American dressage. "I think that those of

us who spent time in Europe and did a lot of international competition paved the way for the United States to do better in dressage over time," she said. "We had to get out there and batten down the walls and achieve some good scores to be able to make that happen.

"Having been on a team is very nice for your résumé, for whatever you plan throughout your life," she continued. "It said that you achieved one of the biggest goals a rider could want: being on a Pan American Games team or an Olympic Games team. But as far as my best riding experiences go, I would say I have been the most satis-

Jessica Ransehousen calls Orpheus' 1988 Olympic team dressage test "the best of his career."

fied in some training sessions than I have ever been in an actual competition."

Christine Stückelberger: Giving to the Game

Germany may have dominated dressage competition for decades, but fifty-three-year-old Christine Stückelberger has helped Switzerland give the Germans a run for their money. In a competitive career that spans decades and is still going strong, she competed in the 1968 and 1972

Olympic Games (the former as the reserve rider); achieved her Olympic career highlight to date with an individual gold medal and a team silver medal with her great Holsteiner gelding Granat at the 1976 Montreal Games; won another team silver medal in 1984 aboard Tansanit; and captured a third team silver medal and an individual bronze in 1988 with the Swedish Warmblood stallion Gauguin de Lully. She competed with her current equine partner, STC Aquamarin, at the 1996 Atlanta Games and is hoping for a repeat Olympic appearance with either the Westphalian stallion or her other mount, the fourteen-year-old Hanoverian stallion Bolino, at the 2000 Sydney Olympics.

Much of Stückelberger's success is attributed to her enduring partnership with trainer Georg Wahl, with whom she has studied since she was eleven. With coaching from the former Spanish Riding School chief rider, she trained Granat from a good-moving but ugly-necked four-year-old to one of the most successful dressage horses in history — a feat made more impressive by the fact that the gelding was blind in one eye and was therefore inclined to be spooky.

Stückelberger and Granat were favored to win their second individual gold medal in 1980, before Switzerland and most other western nations boycotted the Moscow Olympics because of the Soviet Union's invasion of Afghanistan. They competed instead in one of the three equestrian festivals that comprised the so-called alternate Olympics: Goodwood, England (dressage); Rotterdam, the Netherlands (show jumping); and

Christine Stückelberger with Granat, with whom she won the individual gold in 1976.

Fontainebleau, France (three-day eventing). At Goodwood, the petite woman and her big horse did not let their supporters down, winning the individual gold medal with a brilliant performance in the Grand Prix Special.

Stückelberger said she does not mind not having competed in the 1980 Olympics; in truth, she is glad she did not. "My gold medal at the alternate Olympics had the same importance to me as my gold medal in Montreal," she said. "The important thing was Granat's performance; everything else is just statistics." Furthermore, she said, she was one of the first riders to demand the boycott of the Moscow Games. "I would not have enjoyed competing in Moscow under those circumstances. I do not know if it helped much, but it was the only way I could show solidarity with the people of Afghanistan. For me it was the right decision, and I would do it again today. With the current Russian war against Chechnya, I would not compete in Moscow if the 2000 Olympic Games were being held there."

A former head of the International Dressage Riders Club and member of the board of the Swiss Equestrian Federation, Stückelberger now focuses on her riding and also enjoys giving clinics in Europe and the United States, as well as teaching students at home. She is thankful to be able to continue to ride, for in 1989 a young stallion bucked and threw her against the wall of her indoor arena, breaking her back badly and forcing her to undergo a grueling seven-hour surgery. Amazingly, she recovered quickly enough to be a member of the Swiss team at the 1990 World Equestrian Games in Stockholm.

"I could not live without riding," Stückelberger said of her determination.

CHAPTER SEVEN

Gifted: American Hero

To many dressage enthusiasts — and even to many people who otherwise knew nothing about dressage — Gifted was American dressage. The supersized 17.3-hand, 1,900-pound bay Hanoverian gelding with the big blaze and bold splashes of stockings literally and figuratively dominated his U.S. rivals for the entire course of his twelve-year competitive career.

Vermont-based rider and trainer Carol Lavell found and purchased Gifted as a four-year-old in Germany, and Lavell would own the gelding for the rest of his life. With the assistance of her coach and mentor, Olympic veteran Michael Poulin, she brought Gifted up through the levels, winning year-end championships and horse-of-the-year honors as they went.

Gifted became the first U.S. dressage horse in years to earn genuine respect on the tough European competitive scene. Lavell turned down seven-figure offers from European riders for her horse. And at the 1992 Olympic Games in Barcelona, the American dressage community became even more grateful that Lavell didn't sell, when Gifted earned the highest score of the U.S. horses to clinch the team bronze medal.

Of their outstanding performance in the Grand Prix Special at Barcelona, Lavell has said, "If I had one wish in my whole life, I'd like to go back now and ride my test over so I could remember what it was really like. There was just so much pressure and so many things going wrong on the way to the Olympics that it all seems rather clouded. I look at the press cuttings and wonder what it must have felt like." [21]

Gifted's size made the collected work challenging, and yet the huge horse could execute an excellent piaffe and a magnificent, cloud-scudding passage. The sheer size and scope of his gaits was jaw-dropping.

Lavell called her most famous partner, who was humanely destroyed in January 1997 after contracting a mysterious and medically unresponsive neurological ailment, "a volunteer, with a cooperative spirit that keeps on giving." [22]

Robert Dover: Olympic Spirit

Robert Dover loves to talk about the Olympics. It's not just that he's been to four of them (1984, aboard Romantico; 1988, with Federleicht; 1992, with Lectron; and 1996, with Metallic) and won team bronze medals at the two most recent Games; it's that underneath his cool, competitive exterior beats the heart of an unabashedly patriotic American who never tires of the thrill of representing his country at the biggest sporting event in the world.

"When you look at my career, some of the worst competitions I've had in terms of personal achievement have been my Olympic competitions. But the overall experiences have been just so incredibly great," he said. And his favorite Olympics to date? Los Angeles in 1984, hands down. "It had to do with the fact that it was here in our own country. The American athletes were all treated so fantastically. I remember marching along the street from one stadium to the other with all the competitors. The sides of the street were lined something like twenty deep with people who wanted to touch us. It was just incredible. And I remember being in my room at

Gifted, Carol Lavell's beloved partner, clinched the team bronze for the U.S. in 1992.

218

Robert Dover's masterful ride on Lectron kept the American dressage team in the medal hunt in Barcelona.

the University of Southern California, watching the same competitors on television who were right underneath the room, in the pool. So we could not only watch them win but also see them get up on the podium to receive their medals. It was on national television, and it was right out our window! We were so psyched; we were just wild with national pride and excitement."

Dover was already a seasoned competitor at the time of his first Olympics, but the Grand Prix in Los Angeles was still nerve-racking. "I remember getting all the way up to the arena on Romantico, and just before I went in I said, 'Georg {Theodorescu, his coach for those Games}, we never did any piaffe or passage." Unperturbed, Theodorescu had them piaffe — but no passage — while on deck, tapping the horse with his whip a few times to encourage him to lift his hind legs. In the ring, Dover came to his first piaffe-passage transition, "put my legs on to go forward, and he just piaffed higher — because that's what he'd just been trained to do." It took an un-elegant kick to get Romantico out of the piaffe, and the scenario was repeated several more times during the test, to Dover's chagrin.

"I can remember finishing my Grand Prix and being whisked up to the media room, where everybody asked me how I thought I'd done," Dover said of that ride. "I remember not having a

Robert Dover aboard his 1996 Olympic mount, Metallic.

clue. I kept thinking, 'What just happened? What just happened?' I played it over and over in my mind that night, trying to figure out what I'd done wrong — because I'd thought I was going to win the thing. I had no international experience whatsoever, and I had no sense of the reality of my sport."

Dover called his second Games, in Seoul in 1988, his personal best; he and Federleicht were the highest-placed American combination, finishing eleventh in the team competition and thirteenth in the individual rankings. "Yet I have the fewest memories of Korea," he mused. He does remember one strange phenomenon. "They sprayed to kill the bugs that were possible harborers of disease, and it created a complete void

of birds. So we had these sort of L.A.-looking days — sunny, blue skies — but no birds whatsoever in the sky." He also found the ultramodern architecture and facilities of Seoul, while "meticulously done," to be somewhat sterile in atmosphere.

"But Barcelona was just beautiful!" Dover enthused about the 1992 Olympic host city. "Barcelona had all the excitement, flair, and personality that L.A. gave off."

Unfortunately, mount Lectron put his tongue over the bit as they cantered into the arena, forcing Dover to ride with practically no rein contact for fear of causing the stallion to toss his

221

head or stop altogether from the discomfort. His masterful handling of the crisis helped the U.S. team to a bronze medal.

Dover said he has fewer memories of the host city of the 1996 Games, but he relishes the fact that he "had something to do with everybody" on the U.S. dressage team. "I had trained Peron {Michelle Gibson's mount} along with Kenn Acebal, his rider at the time; Guenter Seidel's mount, Graf George, had been in my barn for three years and I had sold him to Guenter and trained Guenter with him; I had been training Steffen {Peters} for a long time as well. I was so proud of all of them; that was a fantastic team to field," he said.

In an eleventh-hour crisis of the type that's dogged Dover's Olympic appearances, the green-at-Grand Prix Metallic put in a solid first test in Atlanta but then fell apart in the Special, apparently succumbing to the pressures of having reached Olympic level in a very short time. (In a late-in-the-game development, Dover had lost the ride on his likely Olympic mount, and then-American Horse Shows Association president Jane Clark leased the Dutch gelding from owner and rider Anne Gribbons to ensure that Dover would have a horse for Atlanta.)

A perennial optimist, Dover has his sights set on Sydney. He said that his experienced Grand Prix horse, Everest, has "a very strong shot" and that his "younger but incredibly talented" nine-year-old, Ranier, also could be a contender. Even if the U.S. team medals, he said, "The medals themselves aren't the important thing. My mem-

German-born Steffen Peters rode longtime partner Udon for the U.S. at the 1996 Games.

ories of the Games and of the entire Olympic experience are, to me, everything."

Steffen Peters: Yankee Pride

German-born dressage rider Steffen Peters, who has called the U.S. home since the 1980s, may well have made the 1992 U.S. Olympic dressage squad had it not been for a technicality. Peters was about a month shy of fulfilling the res-

idency requirement for gaining U.S. citizenship at the time of that year's Olympic trials, and pleas to the U.S. Immigration and Naturalization Service and media coverage in his hometown of San Diego were to no avail.

Four years later, the U.S. citizen finally made the Olympic team. Aboard Lila and Bob Kommerstad's then-eighteen-year-old Dutch gelding Udon, Peters helped his country secure a team bronze medal in Atlanta. In one of those Games' enduring moments, an exhilarated Peters pulled a tiny American flag from the pocket of his shadbelly and waved it to the cheering crowd after a masterful performance in the Grand Prix Special.

Asked what it was like to compete in Atlanta, Peters replied, "It was such an incredible experience, getting the opportunity to compete in the Olympics in my home country."

Atlanta Games individual medalists Anky von Grunsven (silver), Isabell Werth (gold), and Sven Rothenberger (bronze).

The State of the Sport

Diversity appears to be the watchword for modern dressage. Sport-horse-type warmbloods still have a lock on most of the competition in the Olympic arena, but Spain's Ignacio Rambla and the majestic gray Andalusian stallion Evento made a splash at the 1996 Atlanta Games, finishing twelfth individually and thrilling the crowd with their dramatic freestyle to (what else?) Spanish music.

The Isabell-and-Anky rivalry continues to make headlines, and with the continued strong female presence in the competitive arena has emerged a trend away from the ultra-heavy warmbloods and toward lighter, more sensitive types. There is a lot of Thoroughbred blood dancing around dressage arenas nowadays, and perhaps we'll see another full-blooded specimen in the medals in the future.

A number of nations are challenging Germany's stranglehold on the medals. Robert Dover points to Denmark as one country that should field a particularly strong team for Sydney. Anky van Grunsven has led the Netherlands to a fairly secure spot on the medal podium, and the United States has established itself as one of the top four dressage superpowers as well. The new millennium looks to welcome excellent riders and horses from around the world into the Olympic dressage arena, and you can bet they'll be dancing to the sounds of music.

Official Results
Dressage

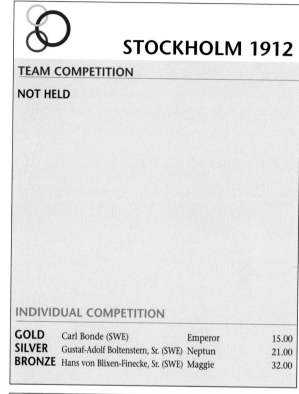

STOCKHOLM 1912

TEAM COMPETITION

NOT HELD

INDIVIDUAL COMPETITION

GOLD	Carl Bonde (SWE)	Emperor	15.00
SILVER	Gustaf-Adolf Boltenstern, Sr. (SWE)	Neptun	21.00
BRONZE	Hans von Blixen-Finecke, Sr. (SWE)	Maggie	32.00

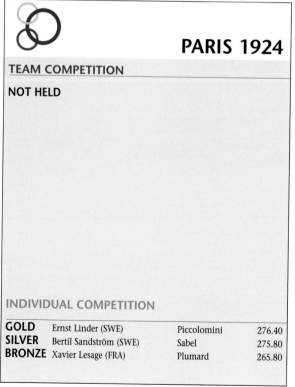

ANTWERP 1920

TEAM COMPETITION

NOT HELD

INDIVIDUAL COMPETITION

GOLD	Janne Lundblad (SWE)	Uno	27.9375
SILVER	Bertil Sandström (SWE)	Sabel	26.3125
BRONZE	Hans von Rosen (SWE)	Running Sister	25.125

Note: Col. Gustaf-Adolf Boltenstern, Sr. (SWE) and Iron placed third with a score of 26.1875 but were disqualified for practicing in the arena before the competition commenced.

PARIS 1924

TEAM COMPETITION

NOT HELD

INDIVIDUAL COMPETITION

GOLD	Ernst Linder (SWE)	Piccolomini	276.40
SILVER	Bertil Sandström (SWE)	Sabel	275.80
BRONZE	Xavier Lesage (FRA)	Plumard	265.80

AMSTERDAM 1928

TEAM COMPETITION

GOLD: GERMANY

Rider	Horse	Points
• Carl Friedrich Freiherr von Langen-Parow	Draufgänger	237.42
• Hermann Linkenbach	Gimpel	224.26
• Eugen Freiherr von Lotzbeck	Caracalla	208.04
	Total points:	669.72

SILVER: SWEDEN

• Ragnar Ohlson	Gunstling	229.78
• Janne Lundblad	Blackmar	226.70
• Carl Bonde	Ingo	194.38
	Total points:	650.86

BRONZE: HOLLAND

• Jan van Reede	Hans	220.70
• Pierre Versteegh	His Excellence	216.44
• Gérard Le Heux	Valerine	205.82
	Total points:	642.96

INDIVIDUAL COMPETITION

GOLD	Carl Friedrich Freiherr von Langen-Parow (GER)	Draufgänger	237.42
SILVER	Charles Marion (FRA)	Linon	231.00
BRONZE	Ragnar Ohlson (SWE)	Gunstling	229.78

LOS ANGELES 1932

TEAM COMPETITION

GOLD: FRANCE

Rider	Horse	Points
• Xavier Lesage	Taine	1031.25
• Charles Marion	Linon	916.25
• André Jousseaume	Sorelta	871.25
	Total points:	2818.75

SILVER: SWEDEN

• Bertil Sandström	Kreta	964.00
• Thomas Byström	Gulliver	880.50
• Gustaf-Adolf Boltenstern, Jr.	Ingo	833.50
	Total points:	2678.00

BRONZE: UNITED STATES

• Hiram Tuttle	Olympic	901.50
• Isaac Kitts	American Lady	846.25
• Alvin Moore	Water Pat	829.00
	Total points:	2576.75

INDIVIDUAL COMPETITION

GOLD	Xavier Lesage (FRA)	Taine	343.75; ordinals: 6
SILVER	Charles Marion (FRA)	Linon	305.42; ordinals: 14
BRONZE	Hiram Tuttle (USA)	Olympic	300.50; ordinals: 14

BERLIN 1936

TEAM COMPETITION

GOLD: GERMANY

Rider	Horse	Points
• Heinz Pollay	Kronos	1760.00
• Friedrich Gerhard	Absinth	1745.50
• Hermann von Oppeln-Bronikowski	Gimpel	1568.50
	Total points:	5074.00

SILVER: FRANCE

• André Jousseaume	Favorite	1642.50
• Gerard de Ballore	Debaucheur	1634.00
• Daniel Gillois	Nicolas	1569.50
	Total points:	4846.00

BRONZE: SWEDEN

• Gregor Adlercreutz	Teresina	1675.00
• Sven Colliander	Kal	1530.50
• Folke Sandström	Pergoia	1455.00
	Total points:	4660.50

INDIVIDUAL COMPETITION

GOLD	Heinz Pollay (GER)	Kronos	1760.00
SILVER	Friedrich Gerhard (GER)	Absinth	1745.50
BRONZE	Alois Podhajsky (AUT)	Nero	1721.50

LONDON 1948

TEAM COMPETITION

GOLD: FRANCE

Rider	Horse	Points
• André Jousseaume	Harpagon	480.00
• Jean Saint Fort Paillard	Sous les Ceps	439.50
• Maurice Buret	Saint Ouen	349.50
	Total points:	1269.00

SILVER: UNITED STATES

• Robert Borg	Klingsor	473.50
• Earl Thomson	Pancraft	421.00
• Frank Henry	Reno Overdo	361.50
	Total points:	1256.00

BRONZE: PORTUGAL

• Fernando Pais da Silva	Matamas	411.00
• Francisco Valadas	Feitico	405.00
• Luiz Mena e Silva	Fascinante	366.00
	Total points:	1182.00

Note: The Swedish dressage team of Gustav-Adolf Boltenstern, Jr./Trumf (477.50), Henri Saint Cyr/Dijimm (444.50), and Gehnäll Persson/unknown mount (444.40) originally was awarded the gold medal with a total score of 1366.00 but was later stripped of the award because Persson, a sergeant, had falsely been entered as an officer. (FEI rules barred all but commissioned military officers from Olympic competition through the 1948 Games.) Persson also was disqualified from the individual dressage competition, in which he placed sixth with a score of 444.00.

INDIVIDUAL COMPETITION

GOLD	Hans Moser (SWI)	Hummer	492.50
SILVER	André Jousseaume (FRA)	Harpagon	480.00
BRONZE	Gustaf-Adolf Boltenstern, Jr. (SWE)	Trumf	477.50

HELSINKI 1952

TEAM COMPETITION

GOLD: SWEDEN

Rider	Horse	Points
• Henri Saint Cyr	Master Rufus	561.00
• Gustaf-Adolf Boltenstern, Jr.	Krest	531.00
• Gehnäll Persson	Knaust	505.50
	Total points:	**1597.50**

SILVER: SWITZERLAND

• Gottfried Trachsel	Krusus	531.00
• Henri Chammartin	Wohler	529.50
• Gustav Fischer	Solimon	518.50
	Total points:	**1579.00**

BRONZE: GERMANY

• Heinz Pollay	Adular	518.50
• Ida von Nagel	Afrika	503.00
• Fritz Thiedemann	Chronist	479.50
	Total points:	**1501.00**

INDIVIDUAL COMPETITION

GOLD	Henri Saint Cyr (SWE)	Master Rufus	561.00
SILVER	Lis Hartel (DEN)	Jubilee	541.50
BRONZE	André Jousseaume (FRA)	Harpagon	541.00

ROME 1960

TEAM COMPETITION

NOT HELD

INDIVIDUAL COMPETITION

GOLD	Sergei Filatov (SOV/RUS)	Absent	2144.00
SILVER	Gustav Fischer (SWI)	Wald	2087.00
BRONZE	Josef Neckermann (GER)	Asbach	2082.00

STOCKHOLM 1956

TEAM COMPETITION

GOLD: SWEDEN

Rider	Horse	Points
• Henri Saint Cyr	Juli	860.00
• Gehnall Persson	Knaust	821.00
• Gustaf-Adolf Boltenstern, Jr.	Krest	794.00
	Total points:	**2475.00**

SILVER: GERMANY

• Liselott Linsenhoff	Adular	832.00
• Hannelore Weygand	Perkunos	785.00
• Anneliese Küppers	Afrika	729.00
	Total points:	**2346.00**

BRONZE: SWITZERLAND

• Gottfried Trachsel	Kursus	807.00
• Henri Chammartin	Wohler	789.00
• Gustav Fischer	Vasello	750.00
	Total points:	**2346.00**

INDIVIDUAL COMPETITION

GOLD	Henri Saint Cyr (SWE)	Juli	860.00
SILVER	Lis Hartel (DEN)	Jubilee	850.00
BRONZE	Liselott Linsenhoff (GER)	Adular	832.00

TOKYO 1964

TEAM COMPETITION

GOLD: GERMANY

Rider	Horse	Points
• Harry Boldt	Remus	889.00
• Reiner Klimke	Dux	837.00
• Josef Neckermann	Antoinette	832.00
	Total points:	**2558.00**

SILVER: SWITZERLAND

• Henri Chammartin	Woermann	870.00
• Gustav Fischer	Wald	854.00
• Marianne Gossweiler	Stephan	802.00
	Total points:	**2526.00**

BRONZE: U.S.S.R.

• Sergei Filatov	Absent	847.00
• Ivan Kizimov	Ikhor	758.00
• Ivan Kalita	Moar	706.00
	Total points:	**2311.00**

INDIVIDUAL COMPETITION

GOLD	Henri Chammartin (SWI)	Woermann	1504.00
SILVER	Harry Boldt (GER)	Remus	1503.00
BRONZE	Sergei Filatov (SOV/RUS)	Absent	1486.00

MEXICO CITY 1968

TEAM COMPETITION

GOLD: GERMANY

Rider	Horse	Points
• Josef Neckermann	Mariano	948.00
• Reiner Klimke	Dux	896.00
• Liselott Linsenhoff	Piaff	855.00
	Total points:	2699.00

SILVER: U.S.S.R.

• Ivan Kizimov	Ikhor	908.00
• Ivan Kalita	Absent	879.00
• Yelena Petushkova	Pepel	870.00
	Total points:	2657.00

BRONZE: SWITZERLAND

• Gustav Fischer	Wald	866.00
• Henri Chammartin	Wolfdietrich	845.00
• Marianne Gossweiler	Stephan	836.00
	Total points:	2547.00

INDIVIDUAL COMPETITION

GOLD	Ivan Kizimov (SOV/RUS)	Ikhor	1572.00
SILVER	Josef Neckermann (GER)	Mariano	1546.00
BRONZE	Reiner Klimke (GER)	Dux	1537.00

MUNICH 1972

TEAM COMPETITION

GOLD: U.S.S.R.

Rider	Horse	Points
• Yelena Petushkova	Pepel	1747.00
• Ivan Kizimov	Ikhor	1701.00
• Ivan Kalita	Tarif	1647.00
	Total points:	5095.00

SILVER: GERMANY

• Liselott Linsenhoff	Piaff	1763.00
• Josef Neckermann	Venetia	1706.00
• Karin Schlüter	Lisotro	1614.00
	Total points:	5083.00

BRONZE: SWEDEN

• Ulla Håkansson	Ajax	1649.00
• Ninna Swaab	Casanova	1622.00
• Maud von Rosen	Lucky Boy	1578.00
	Total points:	4849.00

INDIVIDUAL COMPETITION

GOLD	Liselott Linsenhoff (GER)	Piaff	1229.00
SILVER	Yelena Petushkova (SOV/RUS)	Pepel	1185.00
BRONZE	Josef Neckermann (GER)	Venetia	1177.00

MONTREAL 1976

TEAM COMPETITION

GOLD: GERMANY

Rider	Horse	Points
• Harry Boldt	Woyceck	1863.00
• Reiner Klimke	Mehmed	1751.00
• Gabriela Grillo	Ultimo	1541.00
	Total points:	5155.00

SILVER: SWITZERLAND

• Christine Stückelberger	Granat	1869.00
• Ulrich Lehmann	Widin	1425.00
• Doris Ramseier	Roch	1390.00
	Total points:	4684.00

BRONZE: UNITED STATES

• Hilda Gurney	Keen	1607.00
• Dorothy Morkis	Monaco	1559.00
• Edith Master	Dahlwitz	1481.00
	Total points:	4647.00

INDIVIDUAL COMPETITION

GOLD	Christine Stückelberger (SWI)	Granat	1486.00
SILVER	Harry Boldt (GER)	Woyceck	1435.00
BRONZE	Reiner Klimke (GER)	Mehmed	1395.00

MOSCOW 1980

TEAM COMPETITION

GOLD: U.S.S.R.

Rider	Horse	Points
• Yuri Kovshov	Igrok	1588.00
• Viktor Ugryumov	Shkval	1541.00
• Vira Misevych	Plot	1254.00
	Total points:	4383.00

SILVER: BULGARIA

• Peter Mandazhiev	Stchibor	1244.00
• Svetoslav Ivanov	Aleko	1190.00
• Georgi Gadjev	Vnimatelen	1146.00
	Total points:	3580.00

BRONZE: ROMANIA

• Anghelache Donescu	Dor	1255.00
• Dumitru Veliku	Decebal	1076.00
• Petre Rosca	Derbist	1015.00
	Total points:	3346.00

INDIVIDUAL COMPETITION

GOLD	Elisabeth Theurer (AUT)	Mon Cherie	1370.00
SILVER	Yuri Kovshov (SOV/UZB)	Igrok	1300.00
BRONZE	Viktor Ugryumov (SOV/BLR)	Shkval	1234.00

LOS ANGELES 1984

TEAM COMPETITION

GOLD: GERMANY

Rider	Horse	Points
• Reiner Klimke	Ahlerich	1797.00
• Uwe Sauer	Montevideo	1582.00
• Herbert Krug	Muscadeur	1576.00
	Total points:	**4955.00**

SILVER: SWITZERLAND

• Otto Hofer	Limandus	1609.00
• Christine Stückelberger	Tansanit	1606.00
• Amy-Cathérine de Bary	Aintree	1458.00
	Total points:	**4673.00**

BRONZE: SWEDEN

• Ulla Håkanson	Flamingo	1589.00
• Ingamay Bylund	Aleks	1582.00
• Louise Nathhorst	Inferno	1459.00
	Total points:	**4630.00**

INDIVIDUAL COMPETITION

GOLD	Reiner Klimke (GER)	Ahlerich	1504.00
SILVER	Anne-Grethe Jensen (DEN)	Marzog	1442.00
BRONZE	Otto Hofer (SWI)	Limandus	1364.00

SEOUL 1988

TEAM COMPETITION

GOLD: GERMANY

Rider	Horse	Points
• Nicole Uphoff	Rembrandt	1458.00
• Monica Theodorescu	Ganimedes	1433.00
• Ann-Kathrin Linsenhoff	Courage	1411.00
	Total points:	**4302.00**

SILVER: SWITZERLAND

• Christine Stückelberger	Gauguin de Lully	1430.00
• Otto Hofer	Andiamo	1392.00
• Daniel Ramseier	Random	1342.00
	Total points:	**4164.00**

BRONZE: CANADA

• Cynthia Ishoy	Dynasty	1363.00
• Ashley Nicoll	Reipo	1308.00
• Gina Smith	Malte	1298.00
	Total points:	**3969.00**

INDIVIDUAL COMPETITION

GOLD	Nicole Uphoff (GER)	Rembrandt	1521.00
SILVER	Margit Otto-Crepin (FRA)	Corlandus	1462.00
BRONZE	Christine Stückelberger (SWI)	Gauguin de Lully	1417.00

BARCELONA 1992

TEAM COMPETITION

GOLD: GERMANY

Rider	Horse	Points
• Nicole Uphoff	Rembrandt	1768.00
• Isabell Werth	Gigolo	1762.00
• Nikolaus "Klaus" Balkenhol	Goldstern	1694.00
	Total points:	**5224.00**

SILVER: THE NETHERLANDS

• Anky van Grunsven	Olympic Bonfire	1631.00
• Ellen Bontje	Olympic Larius	1577.00
• Tineke Bartels de Vries	Olympic Courage	1534.00
	Total points:	**4742.00**

BRONZE: UNITED STATES

• Carol Lavell	Gifted	1629.00
• Charlotte Bredahl	Monsieur	1507.00
• Robert Dover	Lectron	1507.00
	Total points:	**4643.00**

INDIVIDUAL COMPETITION

GOLD	Nicole Uphoff (GER)	Rembrandt	1626.00
SILVER	Isabell Werth (GER)	Gigolo	1551.00
BRONZE	Nikolaus "Klaus" Balkenhol (GER)	Goldstern	1515.00

ATLANTA 1996

TEAM COMPETITION

GOLD: GERMANY

Rider	Horse	Points
• Isabell Werth	Gigolo	1915.00
• Monica Theodorescu	Grunox	1845.00
• Klaus Balkenhol	Goldstern	1793.00
• Martin Schaudt	Durgo	1781.00
	Total points:	**5553.00**

SILVER: THE NETHERLANDS

• Anky van Grunsven	Olympic Bonfire	1893.00
• Sven Rothenberger	Weyden	1854.00
• Tineke Bartels-de Vries	Olympic Barbria	1690.00
• Gonnelien Rothenberger	Olympic Dondolo	1673.00
	Total points:	**5437.00**

BRONZE: UNITED STATES

• Michelle Gibson	Peron	1880.00
• Guenter Seidel	Graf George	1734.00
• Steffen Peters	Udon	1695.00
• Robert Dover	Metallic	1649.00
	Total points:	**5309.00**

INDIVIDUAL COMPETITION

GOLD	Isabell Werth (GER)	Gigolo	235.09
SILVER	Anky van Grunsven (NED)	Olympic Bonfire	233.02
BRONZE	Sven Rothenberger (NED)	Weyden	224.94

Wallechinsky, David. (1996). *The Complete Book of the Summer Olympics*. Boston: Little, Brown, pp. 368-378.

Note: Results and scores in this table do not show "drop scores" — discounted scores of lowest-scoring riders on four-rider teams.

The Millennium Games

So what can equestrian enthusiasts expect from the first Olympic Games of the new millennium? In a nutshell: a beautiful facility, an intimate setting, most likely good weather (nobody's bracing for Barcelona- or Atlanta-like heat), and a really cool place to visit in Sydney, Australia (that is, after you recover from the marathon flight).

It's probably tomorrow in Sydney as you read this. Located literally half a world away, the best-known city in the massive island continent of Australia is a full fifteen hours' worth of time zones ahead of the East Coast of the United States. Australia's Southern Hemisphere location means that its seasons are the opposite of ours — our winter is the Aussies' summer — which is why the Sydney Olympic Games will commence later in the year than usual, in September, when it will be spring in Australia.

Sydney 2000: The Host City

The city of Sydney is situated in the state of New South Wales on the western edge of Australia and is surrounded by water on three sides. The Parramatta River runs west to east along the northern border of the city, and it empties into the famed Sydney Harbor, along the edge of which is perched the spectacular and much-photographed Sydney Opera House (actually used for a variety of cultural events), with its sail-shaped exterior expanses. The harbor feeds into the Tasman Sea, which itself conjoins the Pacific Ocean.

The Olympic Stadium, the Olympic Village, and most other Olympic facilities and attractions are located at Homebush Bay, on the banks of the Parramatta River, about nine miles west of the city center (about a fifteen-minute commute by the newly built rail line, according to a Sydney-

The Sydney Opera House is one of Australia's most recognized landmarks.

SYDNEY BY THE NUMBERS

You know the Olympics are a big production, but did you know just how big? The following statistics will give you a better idea of the scope of the 2000 Games.

- 10,200 athletes
- 5,100 officials
- 200 participating nations
- 28 sports
- 15,000 media representatives
- 5.5 million tickets (the equestrian events are sold out)
- 3.5 billion expected TV viewers worldwide
- $2.288 billion (Aus) SOCOG budget
- $43 million (Aus) spent to construct the Sydney International Equestrian Centre
- 100 equestrian technical officials
- 600 equestrian volunteers
- 60 team three-day-event horse/rider combinations
- 36 individual three-day-event horse/rider combinations
- 79 show-jumping horse/rider combinations
- 50 dressage horse/rider combinations
- 41 reserve horse/rider combinations (15 for three-day, 16 for jumping, and 10 for dressage)

(From www.olympics.com — official Web site of the Sydney 2000 Olympic Games)

The Sydney International Equestrian Centre was constructed for the 2000 Games.

based journalist). [1] The stadium, which can seat 110,000, is the largest ever used in an Olympic Games. As one might expect with the city's oceanfront location, there are beaches aplenty; one of Sydney's most famous, Bondi Beach, will be the site of the beach-volleyball competition. Sydney uses its waters for both work and play: The city is a working port, the many ferries are a popular means of mass transportation, and recreational boating and water sports are favorite pastimes.

A colorful, multicultural city, Sydney offers nearly limitless kinds of cuisine (seafood, naturally, is a specialty), and the city has its own Chinatown and Little Italy, plus a number of other ethnic sections. The city is justifiably proud of its Sydney Symphony Orchestra, Australian Chamber Orchestra, Sydney Dance Company, New South Wales Art Gallery, and Taronga Zoo. Mountains, rain forests, bushlands, and the well-known Hunter Valley wine country are within a few hours' drive away.

The Equestrian Facilities

As in Atlanta in 1996, the open-space requirements of horse sports dictate that the equestrian events in Sydney will be held some distance from the city center and the other Olympic events and happenings. The Sydney Organizing Committee for the Olympic Games (SOCOG) constructed a brand-new equestrian center, the Sydney International Equestrian Centre, in the appropriately named Horsley Park, forty-two kilometers (twenty-six miles) west of Sydney proper. The Centre occupies about 222 acres of bushland in the Western Sydney Regional Park; and the designers of the complex, the firm Equus 2000, took pains to preserve the native flora and fauna.

The facility features plenty of amenities for horses and humans alike. There are an indoor arena with permanent seating for 800, which will be used for training before the Games; an 80-meter x 120-meter main outdoor arena (site of the show-jumping and dressage competitions) with permanent seating for 2,000 (temporary grandstands will increase the seating capacity to 20,000 during the Games); a 7.2-kilometer (4.5-

mile) cross-country course; a galloping track, and additional schooling areas and longeing rings; 224 stalls (stabling capacity will be increased to 340 for the Olympics); a fully equipped veteri-

event" held in September 1999 as a dress rehearsal for the facilities and personnel, daytime temperatures reached the upper seventies (Fahrenheit). Rainy days are uncommon in

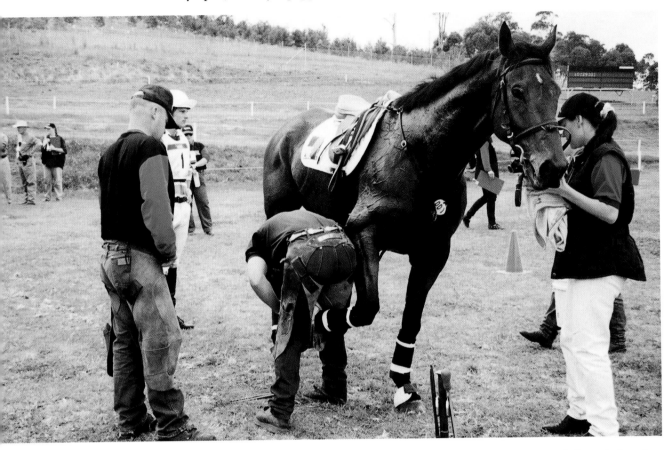

The Sydney International Three-Day Event was held in September of 1999 as a "dress rehearsal."

nary facility; temporary accommodations for 260 grooms and support personnel; and an athletes' lounge and shower and changing areas.

Because Sydney in September is usually temperate, officials do not anticipate having to take the same precautionary measures to ensure horses' welfare at these Games that they did in Barcelona and Atlanta. During the Sydney International Three-Day Event, a two-star "test

September, although the possibility of thunderstorms exists, according to Jennie Hodgson, DVM, an Australian veterinarian and director of laboratory services for the University of Sydney, who will help manage the laboratory services before and during the Games. [2]

Meet the Organizer

Masterminding the entire equestrian competition in Sydney is the German-born Franz-Josef Venhaus, who grew up near the German national equestrian training center in Warendorf but who did not start riding until he met his Australian-born wife, Toni. He has worked in human-resource management and industrial relations for various Australian companies and began getting involved with Australian horse sports about two decades ago. He assisted in the early strategic-planning phase of the Equestrian Federation of Australia (similar to the American Horse Shows Association), of which he is a director. He has been the event director of the Sydney CDI*** for the past nine years, and he directed the inaugural Australasian Volvo World Cup Dressage and Jumping Finals in 1997.

As Olympic equestrian manager, Venhaus is one of SOCOG's 1,000 employees. He supervises the three full-time and six part-time or contract staffers who comprise SOCOG's Equestrian Department. "The complexity of the operation is enormous, with almost fifty separate departments (Accreditation, Accommodation, Catering, Ceremonies, Cleaning and Waste, Finance, Ticketing, Transport, and so on) doing 'their' planning in conjunction with the sports and venues," he said of SOCOG.

Venhaus works closely with the International Olympic Committee and the Fédération Equestre Internationale. In preparing for the equestrian competition, he also interacts with:

- *Olympic Coordination Authority*, the builders and managers of the Olympic venues
- *Olympic Roads and Transport Authority*, which is responsible for getting spectators, officials, and volunteers where they need to be
- *Sydney Olympic Broadcasting Organisation*, which handles television-broadcasting arrangements
- *Australian Quarantine and Inspection Service*

(AQIS), the government agency that establishes animal and plant importation restrictions and policies for all of Australia and that has set the quarantine procedures for the Olympic horses, and

- *National Parks and Wildlife Service*, whose goal

SYDNEY 2000: OLYMPIC OFFICIALS

Here are the FEI-appointed officials who will supervise the equestrian competition and decide the medals in Sydney.

THREE-DAY EVENT

Technical delegate: Jennifer Millar (NZL)

Ground jury, team competition: Frederick Obel (DEN), Brian Schrapel (AUS), Jean Scott Mitchell (IRL)

Ground jury, individual competition: Frederick Obel (DEN), Brian Schrapel (AUS), Brian Ross (USA)

Course designer: Michael Etherington-Smith (GBR)

SHOW JUMPING

Technical delegate: Prof. Arno Gego (GER)

Ground jury: Jan Willem Koerner (NED), Leonidas Georgopoulos (GRE), Graham John Davey (AUS), Peter Herchel (SVK)

Course designers: Leopoldo Palacios (VEN), John Vallance (AUS — co-designer)

DRESSAGE

Ground jury: Eric Lette (SWE), Dr. Volker Moritz (GER), Jan Peeters (NED), Col. Axel Steiner (USA), Mary Seefried (AUS), Mariette Withages (BEL — reserve judge and foreign technical consultant)

VETERINARY COMMISSION

President: Prof. Leo Jeffcott (GBR)

Foreign veterinary delegate: Dr. Kent Allen (USA)

Associates: Dr. Julian Willmore (AUS), Dr. Brett Jones (AUS)

APPEAL COMMITTEE

President: Freddy Serpieri (GRE)

Vice-president: Barry Roycroft (AUS)

Three-day event: (Chair of FEI Three-Day Event Committee — TBA) or Jack Le Goff (USA)

Show jumping: Olaf Petersen Sr. (GER)

Dressage: Ernst Holtz (RSA)

(courtesy of Franz-Josef Venhaus, Sydney: SOCOG)

is to ensure that the Olympic equestrian events do not sully the regional parkland on which the Sydney International Equestrian Centre is located.

"The complicating factor for Sydney is, I suppose, the freighting of horses (at SOCOG's expense) to Sydney and back and the quarantine conditions, and what flows on from it," said Venhaus. "Management, both here and overseas; design of the site and the stables; feed management and importation (AQIS won't permit most foreign feed and hay to enter Australia); and the fact that all 225 competition horses and forty-one reserve horses will be on site. In Atlanta, the horses came and went" and generally were on site only for the duration of their own competitions, he pointed out. (For more on the quarantine issues, see Chapter 3.)

If You Go

Tickets are scarce for the equestrian events. According to the U.S. Olympic Committee, eighty percent of the available Olympic tickets were reserved for sale in Australia; and according to Professor Leo Jeffcott, president of the FEI Veterinary Commission for the Games, the Aussies have already snapped up their allotment of equestrian tickets. That leaves twenty percent of the remaining tickets to be distributed among the national federations. To inquire about ticket availability in the U.S., contact Cartan Tours, Inc., the USOC-designated official ticket and travel agent for the Sydney Games, at (800) 818-1998 or at www.cartan.com.

Available lodging is scarce, as are plane tickets to and from Sydney at the time of the Games. Your travel agent may be able to help you secure reservations; here are some sources you can try on your own.

- *The Official Sydney Olympic Games Web site* (www.olympics.com) contains information about practically all aspects of the Games, from sports and venues to tickets and souvenirs. Click on "Sydney" for more information about the host city and lots of travel and tourism links.
- *The Sydney Visitor Centre* (http://sydney.city-search.com.au) is a good source of information on travel, accommodations, dining, shopping, and other tourist concerns.
- Ditto for the *Tourism New South Wales* site (www.tourism.nsw.gov.au/tsnw), except that the site encompasses a broader region, as its name suggests.

A few essential facts about traveling to Sydney:

Climate. Expect spring-like weather in September and October, with cool nights and warm days, so dress in layers and bring jackets as well as your shorts and T-shirts. The sun is strong in the Southern Hemisphere, so pack high-octane sunscreen and bring your hat and sunglasses.

Customs. AQIS maintains strict policies regarding the importation of certain plants, animals, and foodstuffs. Visitors must declare any foods, plants, and medications when going through customs, and items are subject to quarantine control. And don't forget your passport!

Health considerations. Tourists from the United States and most other Western countries do not need to have additional vaccinations before entering Australia. Visitors from nations that harbor yellow fever must be vaccinated against the disease before they travel to Australia. Tourists may bring in "reasonable amounts" of

Australia prevailed at the 1999 test event at the Sydney International Equestrian Centre.

prescription drugs. Be aware that Australian pharmacies fill only prescriptions written by Australian-registered doctors, so bring a sufficient supply to last the duration of your stay if you take prescription medication.

Currency. The favorable conversion rate might help make up for the steep air fares (but probably not entirely). When we checked, one American dollar was worth about $1.55 Australian dollars. Exchange rates vary daily, so check the current rate before you go.

If you don't want to have to exchange lots of cash, bring travelers' checks or credit cards; most major credit cards are welcome in Australia.

Can't Get to Sydney?

With the vast time difference, high cost of air fare, and ticket shortage, most Americans — and probably many Europeans as well — won't be attending the Sydney Olympics in person. The time difference is such that, by the time you see an event broadcast on TV, it'll probably be old news by at least a day. Fortunately, these Games are taking place at a time when unprecedented amounts of practically instantaneous information are a just mouse-click away.

Online news sources. The Sydney Olympics will almost certainly be the most Internet-dependent Games in history. Fans will have access to results, photos, video, and commentary via mainstream-media as well as sport-specific Web sites. Equestrian enthusiasts may want to bookmark the following sites for reference

JESSICA RANSEHOUSEN: MY TRIP TO SYDNEY

In November 1999, U.S. dressage-team *chef d'équipe* Jessica Ransehousen made a get-acquainted, fact-finding trip to Sydney along with more than 100 American sports representatives. The U.S. Olympic Committee sponsored the trip, the first of its kind, to help the various national sports federations prepare for the 2000 Olympics.

Ransehousen accompanied U.S. Equestrian Team show-jumping discipline director Sally Ike and eventing discipline director Jim Wolf on the trip. The three inspected and selected accommodations for the U.S. equestrian-sport officials, athletes, horse owners, and other VIPs (after clocking the drive from each prospective hotel to the horse park); toured the Sydney International Equestrian Centre and the Olympic Village; attended receptions and meetings with SOCOG, Equestrian Federation of Australia, and USOC representatives; and even sampled the fare in various restaurants in order to recommend the best places to eat.

As for the equestrian venue, Ransehousen said, "The three-day-event course is nice. The stadium is nice and small; it's not like in Atlanta, where it was so huge."

One day, the sports representatives took part in USOC-organized round table discussions. "The USOC put their organizational people at different tables," she explained. "So we went to housing, to grants, to finance, to transportation, to accreditation, to uniforms, and so on, and gave each one our information. We found out what channels to go through if we want to transport extra equipment; they've acquired a warehouse so the various sports can send some equipment ahead of time."

Ransehousen and her associates were impressed with the trip. "They're getting more and more organized," she said of the USOC. She and her colleagues hope that their efforts will help to make American athletes' Olympic experience in Sydney glitch-free and allow them to focus on what's most important: their performance.

before, during, and after the Games.

- The *International Olympic Committee (IOC):* www.olympic.org
- *U.S. Olympic Committee:* www.olympic-usa.org
- *Fédération Equestre Internationale* (FEI): www.horsesport.org
- *Sydney Equestrian Events* (competition manager Franz Venhaus' site, with links to other pertinent organizations): www.zeta.org.au/~venhaus
- *U.S. Equestrian Team:* www.uset.org
- *The Chronicle of the Horse Online:* www.chronofhorse.com
- *Australian Quarantine and Inspection Service* (AQIS): www.aqis.gov.au
- *Cyberhorse* (Australian horse news): www.cyberhorse.net.au
- *Equestrian Federation of Australia:* www.ausport.gov.au/equest
- *The Equestrian Times* (U.K.-based international equestrian news network): www.horse-news.com
- *Worldsport* (international sporting news): www.worldsport.com
- *DressageDaily:* www.dressagedaily.com
- *HorsesDaily:* www.horsesdaily.com

Television. In the United States, NBC has the exclusive television-broadcast rights to the 2000 Olympic Games, as it did for the 1996 Atlanta Games. When this book went to press, NBC had not released its Games coverage schedule, but it does post information about its broadcasts of Olympic lead-up events — as well as other Olympic news, interviews, and information — on its Web site: www.NBCOlympics.com. NBC's cable-TV affiliate, CNBC, airs a weekly half-hour

Olympic newsmagazine called "The Olympic Show." Check your local listings.

Print media. Many of the horse magazines that cover the Olympic disciplines devote a special issue to Olympic coverage. For a soup-to-nuts primer on the horses and riders from most participating nations, it's tough to beat *The Chronicle of the Horse*'s Olympic Preview Issue — followed, of course, by complete coverage and results in its Olympic Results Issue. The only drawback to the *Chronicle* is the absence of color photography; for those luscious full-color images of the Games as well as additional coverage, look to the various equine association and commercial horse magazines, such as *USCTA News*, the AHSA's *Horse Show*, *USDF Connection*, *Practical Horseman*, *Dressage Today*, and *The Horse*. (Many Web sites also feature photos, of course.)

There won't be any shortage of Olympic Games news and information. Just don't expect too much in the way of horse sports when you turn on the TV; the networks are notorious for devoting very little airtime to the equestrian competitions. Better bet: Get Internet access if you haven't already, and peruse the magazine selection at your favorite tack shop.

Focus on Sydney: Team Selection

As the FEI's Catrin Norinder explained in Chapter 2, each sport's international federation must create an approved Olympic Games qualification system that meets the International Olympic Committee's (IOC) athlete quota. In the equestrian disciplines, as in all Olympic sports, nations must qualify to send teams of athletes. Here's an overview of the process by which nations are being selected to field teams — or individual athletes —

for participation in the 2000 Sydney Games.

Three-Day Eventing

Fifteen nations may send teams to compete in the 2000 Olympic team three-day event. The criteria:

A. Nation 1: As the host nation, Australia is automatically qualified to field a team for all three equestrian disciplines.

B. Nations 2-7: The next six nations to qualify are the six highest-placing teams at the 1998 Three-Day Event World Championship, excluding Australia.

C. Nation 8: The highest-placing team at the 1999 Pan American Games from either FEI "Olympic Qualification Group D" (North America) or "Group E" (South America), excluding the above-qualified teams.

D. Nation 9: The highest-placing team from the 1999/2000 Asia Pacific Championship, excluding the above-qualified teams.

E. Nations 10-12: The three highest-placing teams from the 1999 European Championships, excluding the above-qualified teams.

F. Nations 13-15: Additional highest-placing teams at the 1998 World Championships. In the case that the above criteria result in fewer than twelve teams qualifying via steps A through E, additional teams from the World Championships will qualify until the quota of fifteen teams is satisfied. Should this step fail to satisfy the quota, additional not-yet-qualified teams of at least four riders, all of whom have met the minimum requirements for Olympic Games participation, will qualify until the quota is reached.

The IOC has set a quota of thirty-six horse/rider combinations to compete in the individual three-day event at Sydney, with the stipulation that no more than three competitors per nation may take part. Riders may also participate in the team three-day event with a different horse. The FEI is using the World Eventing Rider Rankings as the criterion for selecting individual competitors, as follows:

A. Riders 1-6: The national federations (NFs) of the top-ranked riders from each of the World Ranking regions — the FEI's Olympic Qualification Group A (northwestern Europe), Group B (southwestern Europe), Group C (eastern and central Europe), Group D (North America), Group E (South America), and Group G (Asia/Oceania) — will qualify to send riders.

B. Riders 7-36: Additional NFs, selected according to the Global Ranking list, will qualify to send riders.

Show Jumping

Sixteen nations will qualify to send teams to the 2000 Games, as follows:

A. Nation 1: Host nation Australia.

B. Nations 2-7: The six highest-placing teams at the 1998 World Equestrian Games, excluding Australia.

C. Nations 8-11: The four highest-placing teams at the 1999 European Jumping Championship, excluding teams qualified above.

D. Nations 12-14: The three highest-placing teams at the 1999 Pan American Games, excluding teams qualified above.

E. Nation 15: The highest-placing team from Olympic Qualification Group F (Africa/the Middle East) at an FEI-approved event (in this case, the July 1999 CSIO-Falsterbo, Sweden).

F. Nation 16: The highest-placing team from Olympic Qualification Group G (Asia/Oceania) at an FEI-approved event (CSIO-Falsterbo).

Fifteen NFs not represented by teams will qualify to send individual show-jumping competitors

to Sydney; no more than two riders per nation may take part.

A. Riders 1-2: The NFs of the two highest-placing riders from Olympic Qualification Group A or B on the FEI-approved World Ranking List for jumper riders will qualify to send competitors.

B. Riders 3-5: The NFs of the three highest-placing riders from Group C on the World Ranking List will qualify.

C. Riders 6-8: The NFs of the three highest-placing riders from Group G at an FEI-approved event (CSIO-Falsterbo) will qualify.

D. Riders 9-10: The NFs of the two highest-placing riders from Group F at an FEI-approved event (CSIO-Falsterbo) will qualify.

E. Rider 11: The NF of the highest-placing rider from Group D at the 1999 Pan American Games will qualify.

F. Riders 12-15: The NFs of the four highest-placing riders from Group E at the 1999 Pan American Games will qualify.

If fewer than sixteen nations enter teams in the show-jumping competition, additional individual competitors may be added; NFs will be chosen according to an FEI-established rotational order and based on the World Rankings list.

Dressage

Under the IOC's quota system, ten nations will qualify to send teams to Sydney, to be selected as follows:

A. Nation 1: Australia, the host nation.

B. Nations 2-9: The highest-placing teams from the 1998 World Equestrian Games, excluding Australia.

C. Nation 10: The highest-placing team from the 1999 "Open" European Championship, excluding teams qualified above.

Ten slots are reserved for NFs not represented

by teams, with no more than two riders per nation taking part, as follows:

A. Riders 1-3: The highest-placing NF per region in FEI World Dressage Challenge Regions 1 through 3, that participated in the 1999 FEI World Dressage Challenge but did not qualify to send individuals to the 1998 World Equestrian Games or the 1999 "Open" European Championship, will qualify.

B. Riders 4-6: The NFs of the three highest-placing individuals at the 1998 World Equestrian Games in the team and the first individual qualifying competitions, will qualify.

C. Riders 7-8: The NFs of the two highest-placing individuals in the team and the first individual qualifying competitions at the 1999 European "Open" Championship will qualify; nations must not have already qualified through the 1998 World Equestrian Games.

D. Riders 9-10: The NFs of the two highest-placing riders from the FEI-approved World Ranking List for Dressage Riders will qualify.

Who's Going to Win?

We asked experts to gaze into their crystal balls and talk about the way the 2000 Olympic equestrian competition has shaped up — for themselves as well as for the top-ranked nations.

Three-Day Eventing

Roger Haller, U.S., 1996 Olympic three-day-event cross-country course designer: "The course designer for the Sydney Games, Michael Etherington-Smith, has designed the course for the Rolex Kentucky Three-Day Event since 1992, and he did the course for the 1999 Pan American Games in Winnipeg. He asks different questions of horses and riders. He incorporates elements such

SYDNEY 2000: EQUESTRIAN SCHEDULE

Friday, September 15
Horse inspection (three-day event, team)

Saturday, September 16
Dressage (three-day event, team)

Sunday, September 17
Dressage (three-day event, team)

Monday, September 18
Speed and endurance (cross-country, team)

Tuesday, September 19
Horse inspection/Stadium jumping/
Team medal ceremonies (three-day event, team)
Horse inspection (three-day event, individual)

Wednesday, September 20
Dressage (three-day event, individual)

Thursday, September 21
Speed and endurance (cross-country, individual)

Friday, September 22
Horse inspection (three-day event, individual)/
Stadium jumping/Individual medal ceremonies

Saturday, September 23
Training competition (show jumping)

Sunday, September 24
Horse inspection (show jumping)

Monday, September 25
Qualifying competition (show jumping)

Tuesday, September 26
Grand Prix (dressage)

Wednesday, September 27
Grand Prix/Team medal ceremonies (dressage)

Thursday, September 28
Team final/Team medal ceremonies
(show jumping)

Friday, September 29
Grand Prix Special (dressage)

Saturday, September 30
Grand Prix Freestyle (individual medal final,
dressage)/Medal ceremonies

Sunday, October 1
Individual final/Individual medal ceremonies
(show jumping)

(courtesy of Franz-Josef Venhaus, Sydney: SOCOG)

as lines involving corners, big oxers on curving lines, and sequences that incorporate the terrain.

"I think we'll have a strong team. We've been getting stronger and stronger every year. We have some young up-and-coming riders like Amy Tryon, Julie Black, and Kimberly Vinoski — plus, of course, our veteran star riders like Karen and David O'Connor and Bruce Davidson.

"But the country to beat is New Zealand, no question about it. They are on top of the world right now. They were first, second, fourth, and fifth individually and won the team competition going away at the '98 Worlds. Australia is tough, too: They have won two consecutive Olympic team gold medals, in 1992 and 1996, and this time they will be on their home territory."

Jack Le Goff, U.S., Olympic three-day-event veteran and former U.S. team coach: "The FEI Three-Day Event Committee, of which I am a member, had to report on how the three-day competition is coming along. They had the dry run (the test event) last September; that was all right. They worked a lot on the quality of the track, and it should be OK.

"As for the team and individual medalists, they'll be from the top countries: Australia, New Zealand, England, France, the U.S. Those are the top five."

J. Michael Plumb, U.S., Olympic three-day-eventing veteran: "I have a feeling that, although the New Zealanders are tough, the Americans might be contenders for a medal. Mark Phillips, our team coach, has worked very hard; he helps everybody the best he can.

"As for myself, you've got to have a wonderful horse to make an Olympic team these days. I've got a couple of possibilities, but I want to do it

right. You almost have to have something going right now, and I just don't. But we've got the two O'Connors, Kerry Millikin, and probably also Abigail Lufkin — all strong contenders."

Atlanta cross-country course designer Roger Haller (light blue shirt) thinks the American eventing team will be strong. Opposite: Veteran Olympian Bruce Davidson is an asset to every U.S. three-day team.

Show Jumping

Linda Allen, U.S., 1996 Olympic show-jumping course designer: "Germany has made a science of developing top horses; you can never count them out. The French tend to be very successful, but they are in a bit of a rebuilding process, so it depends on the horses. The Swiss have been extremely strong; they have a half-dozen horses and riders at the top of their game. In the individual competition, the Austrian rider Hugo Simon is very hungry for Olympic gold. He has primed his horse, ET, by giving him close to a year off to put him on a program. The horse will probably have a fairly strong campaign leading up to the Games. ET jumped four clear rounds in his first show back.

"The U.S. has incredible depth: Eighty or ninety combinations will probably compete in the

U.S. jumping co-chef d'équipe George Morris discusses strategy with rider Anne Kursinski.

first Olympic trials. We can be competitive on the right day, but we're not known for our consistency. The Olympic competition format suits us much better than the World Championships format, in which you go through five rounds of jumping just to get into the top four.

"The quarantine situation also may be a factor. There is a two-week quarantine period prior to leaving the U.S., and another two weeks after they arrive in Australia. The quarantine could affect those horses and riders who do best directly off another competition, but part of a trainer's job is to deal with that."

Ludger Beerbaum, Germany, Olympic show-jumping veteran: "Not much has changed in Olympic show jumping over the course of the Seoul, Barcelona, and Atlanta Games. I imagine that the course design in Sydney will be similar to that in Atlanta. Germany is favored to win

another gold medal; if we do badly we might end up fourth. But the top nations are closer together today. Our strongest competitors will probably be the Netherlands, the U.S., Brazil, Great Britain, and Switzerland. As for myself, I'm pinning my greatest hopes on the nine-year-old chestnut Hanoverian stallion, Goldfever."

George Morris, U.S., Olympic show-jumping veteran and U.S. co-*chef d'équipe*: "Everything changes, yet nothing changes. In the past, the Germans, the Italians, the French, and the English were the ones to beat. These days, the Italians are not as strong, but you can add the Swiss, the Dutch, and the Brazilians to that list. But as for our chances, we'll have to see how the trials shape up and how the horses go in the trials."

Paul Schockemöhle, Germany, Olympic show-jumping veteran: "Times have changed for the German team. We no longer have the outstanding horse/rider combinations we once had, but Germany is still favored to win an Olympic medal. We will have to wait and see whether Joli Coeur recovers from an injury in time for the Sydney Olympics with Franke Sloothaak. Ludger Beerbaum does not have Ratina Z any more, and we'll have to wait and see how Goldfever develops; the Sydney Olympics might be too early for him. The strongest contenders are Markus Ehning with For Pleasure, who won a team gold medal and were fifth individually at the 1999 European Championships. Meredith Michaels-Beerbaum is another rider who stands a good chance of making the team."

Opposite: The German show-jumping team, which won the gold medal in 1996, could be among the top contenders in 2000.

Klaus Balkenhol, part of the 1996 German gold-medal-winning team, expects the German dressage team to succeed again in 2000.

Dressage

Klaus Balkenhol, Germany, Olympic dressage veteran and current dressage-team coach: "Of course we will go for the gold. In my opinion, Germany will have the best team ever in Sydney.

"The Dutch and Danish riders have gotten better and better horses, and they have gotten very close to the Germans — especially with German trainers, such as Rudolf Zeilinger and Jürgen Koschel, helping them. As other countries move up to the top and the competition gets harder, it is good for the sport, and it spurs us to stay on a very high level. We always have to prove that we are still the best.

"The U.S. has a large field of good riders and horses, and the Americans are very open-minded. They like the animal-friendly way of working with horses, and with this attitude they are on the right track. I am sure they will have some impact in the Sydney Olympics. Lisa Wilcox and Rohdiamant appear to have a good chance of making the U.S. team."

Harry Boldt, Germany/Australia, Olympic dressage veteran and coach: "Since I now live in Australia and am married to an Australian dressage rider, I now care about the dressage sport in Australia. The Australian team does not have a chance at a medal, but I would be happy if we placed eighth. It would be great if one of the Australian riders makes it to the individual final."

Robert Dover, U.S., Olympic dressage veteran: "Our chances for a medal are much slimmer this year than they have been in past Olympic years because, at the moment, the Danes have two extremely high scorers. When a nation has one very high score, as we did with Michelle Gibson in Atlanta, that helps a great deal; but when you have two, it makes it close to impossible for us unless one of our horses goes well up into the seventies himself. My score is right at the seventy-percent mark. I think that my horse, Everest, can come up in the scoring; but, again, our difficulty in the U.S. is that our sport is played in Europe. Unless American riders can score better than the Europeans on their home turf — so everybody sees it and is reminded of it — it's very difficult to come up to that status come the Olympic Games."

Christine Stückelberger, Switzerland, Olympic dressage veteran: "With Daniel Ramseier we have great support for our dressage team. He is absolutely reliable. Another great plus is Francoise Cantamessa; she lost her horse Peron last year, but she is doing well with her new mount, Sir S. I am the third post of the team; now we have to find the fourth rider. Switzerland is a small country, so it is not easy: We have no team coach, everybody rides on his or her own, and we do not have the selection of horses that Germany and the Netherlands do."

Anky van Grunsven, the Netherlands, Olympic dressage veteran: "I want to participate as a rider; we will see if it will again be with Gestion Bonfire. I do have other up-and-coming horses, such as the Trakehner stallion Gestion Partout TCN; but the horse for which I have even bigger hopes is the eight-year-old Hanoverian Joker. Sydney might be a bit early for him, though.

"The favorites for the dressage team medals in Sydney are Germany, Holland, Denmark, and the U.S.A., in my opinion. For the individual medals, besides Isabell Werth and myself, the favorites are Dutch riders Arjen Teeuwissen (a student of Van Grunsven's and her coach and boyfriend, Sjef Janssen), Coby van Baalen, and Ellen Bontje;

and German riders Ulla Salzgeber and Nadine Capellmann. This is how it looks at the moment, but of course things might be different in a few months.

"Everybody dreams of gold, and I try to win it once."

Isabell Werth, Germany, reigning Olympic dressage champion: "In the dressage sport, the nations have come closer together. The Netherlands are very much on our heels; Germany's very dominant position does not exist any more. But we are still the strongest dressage nation in the world because the sport has immense depth here.

"It is my dream to give Gigolo FRH his farewell with a great performance at Sydney."

Bon Voyage!

A top class-facility, a beautiful and exciting destination, a temperate climate, a horse-minded country — with all these pluses, it's no secret that the equestrian events of the 2000 Sydney Olympic Games are shaping up to be among the best ever.

Said competition organizer Franz Venhaus, "The most frequent comment that has come back from visitors to the September 1999 test event has been how friendly and helpful the staffers were." He's also confident that spectators will be impressed with the natural beauty of the equestrian venue.

Professor Leo Jeffcott, who ran an FEI-sponsored course for veterinarians during the Sydney test event, summed up his impressions of the site: "SOCOG seems to have thought of everything. From what I saw (last) September, it looks as if the equestrian Olympic events will be even better than Atlanta — if that's possible." [3]

The 21st Century

The Sydney Olympic equestrian events are shaping up to be among the best ever in the history of the Games, but is horse sports' future in the Olympics really secure? Insiders have varying opinions as to whether the Olympic equestrian tradition will continue. Some dismiss concerns that the sports' status is shaky; others warn that horse sports are treading on thin footing, so to speak. Still others believe that the question is not whether equestrian sports will remain a part of the Olympics, but which ones.

Most equestrian experts, however, agree on one point: Horse sports, and the organizations that represent them, must do a better job of marketing themselves — in all disciplines and venues as well as at the Olympic Games. And equestrian-sport marketers must realize that the Olympic Games themselves are continually evolving. Baron de Coubertin's Olympic ideals may still exist, but at times it seems as if they are buried underneath layers of commercialism and slick packaging. Hosting the Games has become such big business that no sport can afford not to concern itself with how the International Olympic Committee (IOC) and the public perceives it — and with whether it pads or depletes organizers' pockets.

Horse Sports in the Games: Thriving or Threatened?

There are almost as many opinions on horse sports' Olympic future as there are experts to offer them. Here's what the people we polled had to say.

Catrin Norinder, manager, FEI Olympic department: "The feedback we've gotten from the IOC is very, very clear: If any one equestrian sport wants to get into the Olympics, it will be at the detriment of another sport. The Olympic program is so full it won't allow a fourth equestrian discipline. That's a given. It would be difficult to speculate more on anything because the IOC is in the middle of major reform. For the moment, I think the status quo is the most probable; but Juan Antonio Samaranch will not be president of the IOC for very much longer, and anything can happen when you get a new IOC president. You cannot foresee what that person likes or dislikes."

Joseph C. O'Dea, DVM, former U.S. Equestrian Team veterinarian and FEI Veterinary Committee member: "We'll always have to remember that the Olympic Games are for humans. We use horses in the Games to demonstrate the ability of the human — his ability to train and control that horse. The Olympics are not a competition for horses. I think that {equestrian events' future in the Games} will be up to the FEI and how well they handle the issue."

Catherine Kohn, DVM, president of the FEI Veterinary Commission for the 1996 Atlanta Olympics: "There's been considerable discussion about whether it's appropriate to have horse sports in the Olympics. Some people say that the horse is the athlete. But when you work closely with these

Some have questioned Olympic three-day eventing's future because of the expense.

competitors from all different countries, you very quickly figure out that the riders are serious athletes also. Yes, it's a partnership, but an amazing amount of energy and a lot of skill go into being

World Cup director and equine journalist Max Ammann thinks endurance could replace Olympic dressage or eventing.

able to pilot those horses, whether it's around a cross-country course, over jumps in a ring, or through a dressage test. When you're involved with the equestrian events in the Olympics, you really learn to appreciate what fine athletes the riders are."

Max Ammann, equestrian journalist and historian and World Cup director: "From the IOC's official standpoint, the inclusion of equestrian sports was never in question. I would think there is no question about horse sports' being included in the 2004 Athens Games. I don't see a future danger for show jumping. I do see a future danger for dressage because of the long-standing dominance of the Germans. When you award practically all the medals to one country, Games after Games, that's a liability. In addition, in dressage, you can buy your slot in a way — not if you are German or American — but if you're from Bermuda, say, and you buy a sixty-eight-percent-scoring Grand Prix horse, you can probably earn a sixty-four percent and qualify for the Olympics. The other sport that may be in danger is the three-day event," in part because of its expense, he said.

Robert Standish, executive director, USET: "I have been privy to some speculations that have been made — specifically, complaints from the Olympic organizing committees about the tremendous expense incurred in putting in a three-day-event cross-country course. Each time this issue comes up, there's always the question, Do we get rid of eventing? Equestrian is a very, very expensive sport to accommodate, such as with the costs of stabling. Usually there's some arena capability in whatever location hosts the Olympic Games, so the sports of dressage and show jumping don't really impact them from that expense perspective. But eventing does because of the costs of course-building."

Will the Horse-Sports Lineup Change?

As some experts have pointed out, dressage and eventing have been scrutinized in terms of their worthiness of remaining on the Olympic roster. It appears safe to say that, at the very least, the IOC is not going to allow the FEI to add sports to the existing three. ("If horse riding wants to introduce a new discipline, it will have to withdraw another," said the IOC's sports director, Gilbert Felli.) But are any other disciplines strong contenders for an Olympic slot? Not surprisingly, experts have differing opinions.

"We have another sport knocking on eventing's door, and that is endurance riding," said

Ammann. "I could see a scenario whereby endurance replaces eventing. Only about thirty countries currently take part in the Olympic equestrian events. If endurance were to replace eventing, we would immediately gain twenty countries. Suddenly we'd have fifty equestrian countries in the Olympics." And diversity of participation, he pointed out, is one of the IOC's chief objectives.

Nonsense, said O'Dea. "The Olympic Games are not a competition for horses; that's why we don't have trail riding in the Olympics. I realize that humans play an important role in that sport, but it's still the horses that are judged."

Another sport that's being mentioned a lot these days is reining, the Western discipline that's now USET-affiliated and that's up for adoption by the FEI this April. Ammann dismissed the idea that the IOC would ever approve reining's becoming an Olympic sport, stating that it lacks the level of international participation needed for a solid field of teams. Standish, however, pointed out that one of the FEI's conditions for having the reining issue placed on its 2000 voting agenda was involvement in the sport by at least thirty nations. "So it's my understanding that reining has met that requirement," he said.

"Reining is enjoying explosive international growth," Standish continued. "Perhaps the strongest reining competitors right now come out of Germany and Italy. The Italians have purchased millions of dollars' worth of horses and have established their own reining community. They have proven extremely competitive when

Reining is "enjoying explosive international growth" and could be adopted by the FEI.

Horse sports must become more media-friendly and endeavor to gain more TV time.

they send their horses back here to the U.S." Reining has other advantages, too, he pointed out: it's less expensive to stage than eventing ("all you need is an arena"), and it's popular with audiences, whose noisily appreciative enthusiasm attracts sponsor dollars and media attention.

Still, Standish said, reining fans probably won't see their favorite sport in the Olympic Games in the immediate future. "Some of my reining contemporaries have taken the position — which I consider almost premature — that reining is going to be a part of the 2004 Olympics. That's not going to happen. It would take at least a couple of quadrenniums."

Marketing and the Media

The Games themselves are changing — and not for the better, according to many. Said U.S.

Olympic show-jumping legend William Steinkraus, "I worry about the IOC's tendency to include ever more marginal sports in the Olympic program, as well as its preoccupation with power politics and big bucks. As an institution, the Olympics used to be virtually unique; now they're getting closer and closer in hype, glitz, and commercialism to the Super Bowl, and a lot of what used to be uniquely attractive about the Games seems to have become pretty much diluted."

For better or for worse, the forces that have turned the Olympic Games into the world's biggest media production also are affecting the sports that participate. The IOC's biggest single source of revenue is the sale of television rights, so it should come as no surprise that "the FEI, and all the Olympic sports, have to make a major effort to have their sports look good on television," according to the FEI's Catrin Norinder. "There is no way that they will televise a Nations Cup that goes on for ten hours — or the team dressage competition, or the eventing dressage. The message from the IOC has always been, 'Do whatever you can: We need the television; we need to make the sports attractive for television.' " The challenge to the FEI: "One shouldn't make it a Mickey Mouse sport, just to make it suitable for television. You have to keep your identity."

Some insiders also assert that the FEI must become more professional in its operation in order to remain in good standing with the IOC. "I have the positive feeling that the FEI is going to become more open toward the riders and the organizers," said Germany's Paul Schockemöhle. In the past, he said, "decisions have been made far away from reality." As an example, he said, "It cannot be the case that a country like Azerbaijan has the same vote via the FEI General Assembly as a country like Germany or the U.S." He favors adopting a system whereby regions, not individual countries, would vote. "In any case," he added, "a marketing manager should be a member of such a body, since no top sports in this world work without TV coverage any more."

So what kinds of changes will enhance horse sports' palatability to the networks yet preserve their equestrian ideals and objectives? Robert Dover and other dressage enthusiasts have said that the introduction of the Kür in Olympic dressage competition bodes well for that sport. As Dover points out, there's a lot to like about using the Kür as the individual dressage final: It's a crowd pleaser, and it's short enough in length to fit neatly into a conventional TV time slot — similar in advantages to show jumping's individual final.

Do Horse Sports Have An Image Problem?

Some say that the very traditions that most event, jumper, and dressage enthusiasts hold dear are actually hurting their sports' image in the eyes of the general public and the mainstream media — making their sports appear snooty, upper-crust, and financially beyond most people's means. "On a hot July day, to go do show jumping, you put on clothes you would normally wear to church — a tight necktie or stock tie and a coat. What other athletic sport do you get dressed up for in a coat and tails?" Denny Emerson, an international-level event rider and USET Vice President for Eventing, has asked. "What self-respecting boy wants to put on boots and breeches and a hunt cap and have all his friends roll on the ground laughing at him?" To make matters worse, he has said, the Olympic equestrian disciplines are "as lily-white a sport as there is. We don't have minority groups, and we are perceived as being incredibly unwelcoming of them."[1]

In the U.S., most people perceive English-riding attire as sissy (on men, anyway), while the popularity of line dancing, rodeo, and movies such as *Urban Cowboy* attests to the fact that Western riding and garb have an enduringly macho, rugged image. Traditionalists blanch at the thought of replacing their woolen coats and stock ties with polo shirts or other functional casual wear — and the mere suggestion provokes heated debate and outcry whenever the topic pops up in a horse magazine — but image is one aspect of equestrian competition that the FEI and other equestrian organizations may need to ponder in the years to come.

Media Coverage?
What Media Coverage?

Some equestrian enthusiasts will be quick to point out that all the image-tweaking in the world won't do any good if Olympic Games broadcasters continue to devote the same amount of time — that is to say, practically none — to horse sports. It's an undeniable fact that the most popular of the Olympic sports get the most airtime and the most ink. Each quadrennium, it seems, horsemen engage in a ritual of bemoaning the lack of coverage and roundly criticizing the TV network in question. In truth, they might be even more frustrated if they knew that the entire equestrian competition — along with every other competition at the Games — is painstakingly researched and taped.

The American Horse Shows Association's Kate Jackson should know: She accompanied the NBC crew to the 1992 Barcelona Games, serving as an equestrian-sports expert.

"What I learned is that, given the number of dedicated people and hours that are spent in creating a show, they could devote an entire day to any one of the sports at any time," said Jackson. "In the end, it is the final producer who makes the decision as to what gets on the air, but it's all there. Every minute is on tape, and every minute is commentated on, and it's all ready to go."

Unfortunately, there are just too many sports in the summer Games, vying for too few precious minutes of airtime. It does seem unfair, though, that some sports get hours of coverage while horse sports get about five minutes — or at least that's how brief the TV coverage from the 1996 Atlanta Games seemed to this viewer. So does any hope for change exist?

Yes, and the FEI's awareness of the need to make horse sports TV-friendly is a good start. "We have a lot of different strategic-planning, marketing, and television committees that are working on this whole aspect," said Norinder.

Marketing professionals offer plenty of ideas for boosting equestrian sports' popularity. Among them: promoting personalities and "heroes," both human and equine; launching exhibitions and personal-appearance tours by star riders and horses; becoming more proactive about inviting the mainstream media to equestrian competitions; dreaming up clever ways of incorporating mainstream interests into horse shows (for example, one marketing pro suggests staging a U.S. Marine Corps Reserve Toys for Tots benefit and presentation at a horse show, complete with uniformed recipients of the largesse), and, of course, doffing the dandy duds in favor of something more down-to-earth. [2]

Said Norinder: "We have to appeal to television; we have to appeal to spectators; we have to pull our socks up a little bit and stop thinking that we're the best sport in the world and that nothing can be done to improve it."

Except, of course, for that one aspect of Olympic equestrian competition that cannot be improved on: the splendor of horse and rider performing as one, in joy and harmony. Its magnificence cannot be sullied by commercialism, and its finest form is an enduring reminder of the power of horsemanship, of love, and of those Olympic ideals that, somehow, will continue to live on.

Olympic silver medalists Karen O'Connor and Biko illustrate the harmony and joy that exists between horse and rider — the equestrian ideals.

REFERENCES

Chapter 1: The Olympic Equestrian Disciplines

1. Schmit-Jensen, E. (1948). *Equestrian Olympic Games: Ancient and Modern.* London: Welbecson Press, pp. 7-15.

2. Ibid, pp. 22-23.

3. Ibid, pp. 23-27.

4. Ibid, p. 30.

5. Ibid, p. 29.

6. Ibid, p. 37.

7. Ibid, pp. 31-32.

8. "Polo and the Olympic Games." Equestrian International Productions (article on www.equestrianproductions.com/WPT/olympics.htm).

9. Wallechinsky, David. (1996). *The Complete Book of the Summer Olympics.* Boston: Little, Brown, p. 397.

10. Ammann, Max E. (1999). "A Century of International Equestrian Sport." In *L'Année Hippique 1999/2000.* Best, The Netherlands: Best Communications & Management, p. 285.

11. Wallechinsky, *The Complete Book,* p. 397.

Chapter 2: Behind the Scenes: The Organizations That Govern the Sports

1. Schaap, Richard. (1963). *An Illustrated History of the Olympics.* New York: Alfred A. Knopf, pp. 36-38.

2. "History of International Equestrian Sport." (1999). On Internet: www.worldsport.com/worldsport/sports/equestrian/history/history.html.

3. Steinkraus, William (Ed.). (1976). *The U.S. Equestrian Team Book of Riding.* New York: Simon and Schuster, pp. 9-10.

4. Cavanagh, Sara (2000, February). "USOC Letter Sets Up Showdown Over Control of American Horse Sports." *The Horse of Delaware Valley,* pp. 6, 52.

5. Bryant, Jennifer O. (1997, May). "Salute: The US Three-Day Event Selection Committee." *Dressage & CT,* p. 64.

Chapter 3: Are the Olympics Good For Horses?

1. O'Dea, Joseph C, DVM. (1996). *Olympic Vet.* Geneseo, NY: Castlerea Press, p. 36.

2. Ibid, pp. 36-37.

3. Ibid, pp. 113-114.

4. Ibid, pp. 131-132.

5. Ibid, pp. 146-147.

6. Ibid, pp. 152-156.

7. Ibid, p. 259-260.

8. Ibid, p. 260.

9. Ibid, pp. 261-262.

10. Ibid, pp. 81-83.

11. Ibid, p. 29.

12. Iliff, Elizabeth. (1998, March). "No More Weight!" *Dressage & CT,* pp. 27-29, 62-63.

13. Ibid, p. 28.

14. Jeffcott, Leo B. (1999, December). "Preview of the Olympic Equestrian Events for Sydney 2000." *The Horse: Your Guide to Equine Health Care,* p. 77.

Chapter 4: Those Who Went Before Us

1. DiMarco, Louis. (1997). "The Army Equestrian Olympic Team, Part 1." On Internet: www.geocities.com/Pentagon/Quarters/9517.

2. Scott, Charles L. (1935, May-June). "Tryout and Exhibition of Horses and Riders in Training for 1936 Olympic Equestrian Events." *The Cavalry Journal,* pp. 53-55.

3. Henry, Guy V., Jr. (1944). "A Brief Narrative of the Life of Guy V. Henry, Jr." Collection of the U.S. Army Military History Institute, Carlisle Barracks, PA.

4. Grimes, William M. (1931, November-December). "Army Equestrian Teams in Past Olympic Games." *The Cavalry Journal,* pp. 5-12.

5. Lear, Benjamin. As quoted in Grimes, William M. (1931,

November-December). "Army Equestrian Teams in Past Olympic Games." *The Cavalry Journal*, p. 6.

6. Ibid, p. 6.

7. Short, Walter S. As quoted in Grimes, William M. (1931, November-December). "Army Equestrian Teams in Past Olympic Games." *The Cavalry Journal*, p. 7.

8. Cootes, H. N. As quoted in Grimes, William M. (1931, November-December). "Army Equestrian Teams in Past Olympic Games." *The Cavalry Journal*, p. 9.

9. DiMarco, "The Army Equestrian Olympic Team, Part 1."

10. Good, Lara P. (1933, January-February). "The Horse in the 1932 Olympiad." *The Cavalry Journal*, p. 11.

11. Ibid, p. 12.

12. Mandell, Richard D. (1971). *The Nazi Olympics*. New York: Macmillan, p. 139.

13. Ibid, p. 291.

14. Ibid, p. 183.

15. DiMarco, Louis. (1997). "The Army Equestrian Olympic Team, Part 2." On Internet: www.geocities.com/Pentagon/Quarters/9517.

16. Ibid.

17. Henry, Guy V., Jr., p. 29.

18. Ibid, p. 32.

19. Ibid, p. 38.

20. "A Salute to a Distinguished Cavalryman: An Accolade to Major General Guy V. Henry, United States Army, Retired, on His 90th Birthday, January 28, 1965." (1965, January-February). *Armor*, p. 33.

21. Ibid, p. 33.

22. Henry, Guy V., Jr., p. 122.

23. "Army-Navy Recaps — 1900s." On U.S. Military Academy Web site: www.usma.army.mil/athletics/varsitysports/football.

24. Shambach, Barbara Wallace. (1996). *Equestrian Excellence: The Stories of Our Olympic Equestrian Medal Winners*. Boonsboro, MD: Half Halt Press, p. 28.

25. Ibid, p. 27.

26. Cole, John T. (1937, May-June). "Olympic Horseflesh." *The Cavalry Journal*, p. 201.

27. Chamberlin, Harry D. (1937, May-June). "The Conformation of Three-Day Horses." *The Cavalry Journal*, pp. 203-204.

28. Reusser, Stacey. (1999, December 24). "The 50 Most Influential Horses of the 20th Century." *The Chronicle of the Horse*, pp. 114, 116.

Chapter 5: Three-Day Eventing

1. Schmit-Jensen, *Equestrian Olympic Games*, pp. 29-30.

2. Ibid, pp. 40-41.

3. Ibid, pp. 49-52.

4. Ibid, p. 59.

5. Ibid, p. 71.

6. Ibid, pp. 71-74.

7. Ibid, pp. 83-86; Appendix, pp. 2-3.

8. Lechenperg, Harald (Ed.). (1964). *Olympic Games 1964: Innsbruck, Tokyo*. New York: A. S. Barnes, p. 369.

9. Wright, Lana du Pont. "Ice-Breaking in Japan." (1976). In *The U.S. Equestrian Team Book of Riding*, p. 157.

10. Steinkraus, Bill, and Savitt, Sam. (1977). *Great Horses of the United States Equestrian Team*. New York: Dodd, Mead, pp. 33-34.

11. Strassburger, John. (1999, December 24). "The 50 Most Influential Horsemen of the 20th Century." *The Chronicle of the Horse*, p. 78.

12. Wathen, Guy. (1991). *Great Horsemen of the World*. North Pomfret, VT: Trafalgar Square, pp. 238-245.

13. Ibid, p. 245.

14. *The U.S. Equestrian Team Book of Riding*, pp. 172-173.

15. Davidson, Bruce. (1990). "Making the Event Horse from Scratch." In Jaffer, Nancy (Ed.), *Riding for America: The United States Equestrian Team*. New York: Doubleday, p. 131.

16. O'Dea, Joseph C., DVM. (1996). *Olympic Vet*. Geneseo, NY: Castlerea Press, p. 234.

17. Mackay-Smith, Alexander. (1986). "History of Eventing in the United States." In O'Connor, Sally (Ed.), *The USCTA Book of Eventing*, 2nd ed. South Hamilton, MA: U.S. Combined Training Assn., pp. 37-38.

Chapter 6: Show Jumping

1. Schmit-Jensen, *Equestrian Olympic Games*.

2. Ibid, pp. 44-47.

3. Ibid, pp. 33-37.

4. Ibid, pp. 44-47.

5. Ibid, pp. 53-54.

6. Ibid, pp. 61-62.

7. Ibid, pp. 67-68.

8. Ibid, pp. 80-82.

9. Ibid, p. 5, Appendix.

10. "The Technical Aspects of Equestrian Sport." On Worldsport.com (www.worldsport.com/worldsport/sports/equestrian/rules/rules1.html).

11. "A Guide to Show Jumping." Gladstone, NJ: United States Equestrian Team. On USET's Web site: www.uset.org/sj/showjumpdis/htm.

12. Strassburger, "The 50 Most Influential Horsemen of the 20th Century," p. 46.

13. Wathen, *Great Horsemen of the World*, p. 134.

14. Rodenas, Paula. (1983). *The de Némethy Years: One Man's Influence on American Riding*. New York: Arco, pp. 29-47.

15. Strassburger, "The 50 Most Influential Horsemen of the 20th Century," p. 26.

16. Rodenas, *The de Némethy Years*, p. 85.

17. Ibid, p. 87.

18. Wathen, *Great Horsemen of the World*, p. 157.

19. Ibid.

20. Ibid.

21. Wathen, *Great Horsemen of the World*, p. 167.

22. Ibid, p. 174.

23. Jaffer, Nancy. (1998, November 4). "Rome Reunion for Morris and Chapot." *USET News*, p. 21.

24. Steinkraus and Savitt, *Great Horses of the United States Equestrian Team*, p. 78.

25. Shambach, *Equestrian Excellence*, p. 170.

26. Strassburger, "The 50 Most Influential Horsemen of the 20th Century," p. 26.

27. Ibid.

28. Quirk, John. (1989). "Seoul 1988." *Horses* magazine: Olympic Issue, p. 116.

Chapter 7: Dressage

1. Wallechinsky, *The Complete Book*, p. 389.

2. Schmit-Jensen, *Equestrian Olympic Games*.

3. Ibid, pp. 42-44.

4. Ibid, pp. 52-53.

5. Ibid, p. 60.

6. Ibid, p. 67.

7. Ibid, pp. 74-79.

8. Littauer, Vladimir S. (1962). *The Development of Modern Riding*. New York: Howell, p. 258.

9. Schmit-Jensen, *Equestrian Olympic Games*, pp. 86-88, Appendix p. 4.

10. Littauer, *The Development of Modern Riding*, p. 259.

11. Thackeray, D. W., Col. (1990). "The Trouble with Judging." In Jaffer, *Riding for America*, p. 187.

12. Furth, Elizabeth. (1998). *Visions of Dressage*. New York: Lyons Press, pp. 101-106.

13. Strickland, Charlene. (1992). *The Warmblood Guidebook*. Middletown, MD: Half Halt Press, pp. 15-19.

14. Bryant, Jennifer O. (1997, September). "The Great Dressage Debate." *Dressage & CT*, pp. 18-19.

15. U.S. Figure Skating Association Media Guide (www.usfsa.org).

16. Furth, *Visions of Dressage*, p. 104.

17. *Glory and the Games: Overcoming Adversity in Pursuit of Olympic Excellence.* (1998). Salt Lake City, UT: Commemorative Publications, pp. 64-65.

18. Ljungquist, Bengt. (1976). "The American Dressage

Outlook." In *The U.S. Equestrian Team Book of Riding*, pp. 237-239.

19. "Harry Boldt." On www.horsemagazine.com/clinic/boldt.htm.

20. Klimke, Reiner. (1987). *Ahlerich: The Making of a Dressage World Champion*. Gaithersburg, MD: Half Halt Press, pp. 155-156.

21. Furth, *Visions of Dressage*, p. 61.

22. Cooke, Sandra. (1997, April). "Gifted—He Kept on Giving." *Dressage & CT*, p. 72.

Chapter 8: The Millennium Games

1. Strachan, Laurie. (2000, January). "Sydney: Destination 2000." *The Retired Officer Magazine*, pp. 74-80.

2. Strickland, Charlene. (1999, December). "Countdown to Sydney." *The Horse: Your Guide to Equine Health Care*, pp. 75, 78-83.

3. "Countdown to Sydney," p. 77.

Chapter 9: The 21st Century

1. Iliff, Elizabeth. "Don't Change the Channel — Horses Are On!" (1998, May). *Dressage & CT*, p. 32.

2. Ibid, pp. 25-32.

INDEX

People:

Allen, Kent	50, 58, 62, 66, 114, 237
Allen, Linda	171, 175, 178, 245
Ammann, Max	252
Anderson, Charles	93, 144
Anne, HRH Princess	37
Argo, Edwin	86, 144
Ayer, Neil	117, 138
Balkenhol, Klaus	199-200, 202, 204, 229, 248
Barry, John	83-84
Beerbaum, Ludger	21, 167-169, 179, 185, 246
Boldt, Harry	201, 204, 209, 212, 227-228, 248
Bontje, Ellen	229, 249
Borg, Robert	92, 102, 226
Bradford, William	86, 91
Burr, Leslie	148, 157, 166, 185
	(see also Howard, Leslie Burr)
Burton, Jonathan	75
Caprilli, Federico	74
Carruthers, Pamela	174
Chamberlin, Harry D.	70, 81, 98-99
Chapot, Frank	45, 154, 156-157, 167, 183-184
Clark, Jane	62, 222
Clayton, Hilary	64
Coffin, Tad	126, 146
Cole, John Tupper	92, 102
Cortés, Humberto Mariles	144, 154-155, 182
Davidson, Bruce	28, 38, 117, 126, 129-130, 138, 146-147, 245
de Coubertin, Pierre	12, 14, 28, 30-31, 33, 250
de Mortanges, Charles Pahud	143-144
de Némethy, Bertalan	41, 57, 155-158, 160, 167, 174-175, 178
d'Inzeo, Piero	164-165, 183-184
d'Inzeo, Raimondo	164-165, 183-184
DiMarco, Louis	73-74, 91, 99-103

INDEX

Doak, Sloan 83-86, 143

Dover, Robert 36, 194, 206, 208, 213, 218, 220-221, 224, 229, 248, 255

du Pont, Helena (Lana) 110, 202

Emerson, Denny 255

Etherington-Smith, Michael 237, 243

Fargis, Joe 156-157, 185

Felli, Gilbert 31, 34, 252

Fleischmann, Torrance Watkins 28, 138, 147

Freeman, Kevin 117, 120, 125

Fritz, Jack 208

Gibson, Michelle 186, 222, 229, 248

Gurney, Hilda 199, 208, 228

Hafemeister, Dirk 167, 171, 185

Haller, Roger 113, 131, 134-137, 140, 243, 245

Hartel, Lis 202, 206-207, 227

Henry, Frank 75, 93, 144, 226

Henry, Guy V., Jr. 74-77, 79-80, 85, 91-92, 95-99, 192

Homfeld, Conrad 157, 166, 185

Howard, Leslie Burr 148, 157, 166, 185 (see also Burr, Leslie)

Ike, Sally 38, 240

Jackson, Kate 38-39, 67, 111, 180, 256

Jeffcott, Leo B. 49-50, 54-55, 58, 60-62, 65-67, 238, 249

Jeffery, Richard 175

Kitts, Isaac 86, 91, 226

Klimke, Reiner 123, 158, 211, 213-214, 227-229

Kohn, Catherine 50, 58-59, 62-64, 114, 250

Kursinski, Anne 45, 166-167, 180, 185, 246

Kusner, Kathy 156-157

Lavell, Carol 218, 229

Lavis, Neale 142, 145

Lear, Benjamin 77, 143

Le Goff, Jack 41-42, 45, 52, 114-121, 123-124, 127, 129, 131, 138-142, 145, 155, 208, 237, 245

Leng, Virginia 127

Lette, Eric 195, 206, 237

Linsenhoff, Liselott 202, 227-228

Ljungquist, Bengt 155, 207-209, 211

Master, Edith 208, 228

Matz, Michael 45, 156, 171, 180, 185

McCashin, Arthur 156, 162, 183

Michaels-Beerbaum, Meredith 171, 246

Millikin, Kerry 16, 147, 245

Moore, Alvin 86, 226

Morgan, Lawrence 104, 142, 145

Morkis, Dorothy 208, 228

Morris, George 45, 154-157, 161, 165-167, 172, 178, 183, 195, 246

Niggli, Wolfgang 206

Norinder, Catrin 34-35, 241, 250, 254, 256

O'Connor, David 138, 147, 245

O'Connor, Karen 38, 147, 256

O'Dea, Joseph C. 49, 52, 138, 250

Otto-Crepin, Margit 194, 202, 229

Page, Michael 111, 117, 122, 124, 142, 145-146

Peters, Steffen 222, 229

Petersen, Olaf 178

Philip, HRH Prince, Duke of Ediburgh 28, 37

Phillips, Capt. Mark 37, 43, 45, 121, 124, 245

Plumb, J. Michael 56, 117, 138, 145-147, 163, 245

Podhajsky, Alois 191, 226

Pollay, Heinz 190-191, 226-227

Raguse, Carl A. (Rags) 90-91, 102

Ramseier, Daniel 229, 249

Ransehousen, Jessica N. 44-45, 192-195, 200-201, 213-215, 240

Rothenberger, Sven 224, 229

Roycroft, J. William 142, 145-146

Russell, John 95, 162, 183

Saint Cyr, Henri 207, 226-227

Samaranch, Juan Antonio 31, 250

Schockemöhle, Paul 167, 169, 180

Schultheis, Willi 211

Sederholm, Lars 43, 124

Seidel, Guenter 222, 229

Shapiro, Neal 52, 157, 184

Simon, Hugo 185, 245

Sloothaak, Franke 169, 178, 185, 246

Smith, Melanie 157, 185

Standish, Robert 37-38, 252

Stecken, Fritz 156, 211

Steinkraus, William C. 42-43, 103, 126, 154, 156-158 160-163, 167, 183-184, 254

Stives, Karen 28, 43, 129, 137-138, 147

Stone, Whitney 36, 49, 103, 116, 123, 156

Christine Stückelberger 202, 204, 215, 217, 228-229, 249

Tait, Blyth 134, 142, 147

Thackeray, Donald W. 195

Theodorescu, Georg 220

Theodorescu, Monica 197, 229

Thiedemann, Fritz 163, 183, 227

Thomson, Earl (Tommy) 18, 75, 86, 91-93, 98-100, 102-103, 123, 144, 226

Todd, Mark 128, 138, 142, 147

Tuttle, Hiram 75, 86, 91, 100-101, 226

Uphoff, Nicole 26, 201- 202, 209

van Grunsven, Anky 22, 192, 195, 199-201, 204, 224, 229, 249

Venhaus, Franz-Josef 236-238, 240, 249

von Rosen, Clarence 12, 14, 33, 144, 182

Werth, Isabell 192, 200, 209, 213, 224, 229, 249

Wiley, Hugh 156

Willems, John 22, 91

Wing, Franklin F. (Fuddy) 93, 103

Winkler, Hans Günter 158-159, 183-184

Wofford, Jim 117

Wofford, John (Gyp) 86

Wolf, Jim 38, 240

Wright, Gordon 161

Zang, Linda 208

Horses:

Agent 118, 169, 184, 238

Ahlerich 211-213, 229

American Lady 86, 91, 226

Arete 155, 182

Ben Arthur 129, 137-138, 147

Better and Better 125, 146, 248

Biko 147, 256

Bold Minstrel 126, 145

Charisma 128-129, 138, 142, 147

Chiswell 76-77, 79-80, 95, 143

Christopher 138, 146, 194

Chronist 163, 227

Classic Touch 21, 167-168, 185

Corlandus 194, 229

Dahlwitz 208, 228

Deceive 77, 79, 143

Deister 169, 185

Democrat 95, 102-103, 183

Donald Rex 169, 184

Dr. Peaches 129-130

Dux 211, 227-228

Enigk 159, 184

ET 245-246

Everest 222, 249

Federleicht 194, 218, 221

Fidelitas 159, 183

For Pleasure	185, 246
Forstrat	214
Foster	34, 123, 146
Gauguin de Lully	217, 229
Gem Twist	172, 185
Gestion Olympic Bonfire	192
Gifted	100, 129, 218, 229
Gigolo	192, 229, 249
Goldfever	169, 171, 246
Good Mixture	125, 146
Graf George	222, 229
Granat	217, 228
Grande	171, 185, 213
Grasshopper	57, 122-123, 145
Grunox	197, 229
Halla	158-159, 183
Heyday	129-130, 147, 163, 165
Hollandia	160, 162, 183
Honolulu Tomboy	86, 103, 144
Irish Cap	129-130, 146
J.J. Babu	129-130
Jenny Camp	86, 91, 98, 100, 102-103, 144
Joli Coeur	171, 185, 246
Jubilee	207, 227
Jus de Pommes	153, 185
Keen	19, 40, 199, 208, 228
Klingsor	92, 226
Ksar d'Esprit	160, 162, 183
Landlord	167-168
Lectron	218, 220-221, 229
Main Spring	158, 160, 162, 184
Marcroix	142, 144
Markham	57, 126
Master Craftsman	127, 147
Mehmed	211, 228
Merano	165, 183
Metallic	218, 221-222, 229

Might Tango	129-130
Mirrabooka	142, 145
Monaco	208, 228
Meteor	143, 163-164, 183
Mr. Wister	110
Night Owl	162
Olympic	86, 101-102
Orpheus	194, 214-215
Our Solo	142, 145
Out and About	16, 147
Pagoro	165, 183
Pancraft	93, 100, 226
Peron	186, 222, 229, 249
Piaff	202, 228
Plain Sailing	129, 146
Pleasant Smiles	86, 103, 144
Posillipo	165
Priceless	127, 147
Ratina Z	167, 169, 185, 246
Ready Teddy	142, 147
Rembrandt	26, 194, 201-202, 209, 229
Remus	211, 227
Reno Overdo	93, 226
Reno Rhythm	18, 93, 100, 144
Rhum IV	171, 185
Riviera Wonder	162
Romantico	218, 220
Salad Days	104, 142, 145
Show Girl	86, 182
Si Murray	91, 101-102
Sinjon	160, 162, 166-167, 183
Slippery Slim	22, 91
Sloopy	52, 157, 184
Snowbound	157, 160, 162, 184
Swing Low	93, 144
Tansanit	217, 229
The Freak	167-168, 185

The Rock	165, 183
Torphy	159, 184
Trailolka	90-91
Udon	222-223, 229
Uruguay	165, 183
Vast	101-102, 239
Warwick Rex	169, 184
Water Pat	86, 226
Woyceck	211, 228

Olympic Games:

1912 (Stockholm)   12, 14-15, 21, 40, 72, 74, 77-81, 85, 95, 104, 143-144, 150-151, 171, 181, 188-189, 225

1920 (Antwerp)   12, 14, 24-25, 73, 81-82, 84-86, 99, 107, 143, 151, 181, 189-190, 225

1924 (Paris)   25, 30, 33, 70, 83, 85, 106-107, 142-143, 151, 181, 189-190, 225

1928 (Amsterdam)   26, 84-85, 100, 108, 142, 144, 148, 151, 153, 182, 189-190, 226

1932 (Los Angeles)   22, 85-86, 91, 96, 98-103, 108, 138, 142, 144, 153, 156, 165, 182, 190-191, 226

1936 (Berlin)   24-25, 75-77, 85, 89-91, 96, 100, 102-103, 108, 144, 150, 153, 182, 190-191, 200, 226

1948 (London)   16, 18, 42, 75, 92-93, 96-97, 100, 102-103, 108, 144, 153-155, 162, 165, 182, 191, 208, 226

1952 (Helsinki)   26, 37, 100, 102-103, 145, 156, 159-160, 162-165, 183, 201-202, 206-207, 227

1956 (Stockholm)   42, 49, 59, 102, 116, 122-123 142, 145, 158-160, 163, 165, 183, 202, 207, 227

1960 (Rome)   45, 96, 100, 104, 116, 118, 122-123, 125-126, 137, 142, 145, 156-158, 160, 163-167, 169, 172, 183, 212-213, 227

1964 (Tokyo)   37, 56, 110-111, 116, 122-123, 125-126, 145, 155, 159-160, 172, 183, 202, 207, 209, 211, 214, 227

1968 (Mexico City)   30, 37, 52, 116, 120, 122-123, 125, 131, 134, 142, 146, 157, 159-160, 162, 169, 184, 202, 211, 215, 228

1972 (Munich)   37, 52-53, 89, 115, 117-119, 125, 129, 134, 146, 157-160, 184, 202, 215, 228

1976 (Montreal)   37, 53, 115, 118-119, 122-123, 125-127, 129-130, 134, 142-143, 146, 159-160, 163, 167 169, 171-172, 184, 199, 202, 208-209, 211, 217, 228

1980 (Moscow)   14

1980 (Alternate Olympics) 125, 134, 172, 211, 217

1984 (Los Angeles)   28, 43, 111, 118, 120, 125, 127-130, 137-138, 142, 147, 157, 169, 174-175, 185, 202, 211, 217-218, 229

1988 (Seoul)   26, 34, 37, 54, 111, 122, 124, 128-129, 134, 142, 147, 163, 166-167, 169, 172, 175, 178-179, 185, 194, 200-202, 209, 211-215, 217-218, 221, 229

1992 (Barcelona)   21, 26, 34, 43, 45, 54, 60, 114, 120, 122, 124-125, 129, 134, 139, 141-142, 147, 160, 163, 167-168, 171-172, 180, 185, 199, 201, 209, 212, 218, 221-222, 229, 243, 245, 256

1996 (Atlanta)   16, 22, 31-32, 34, 38-39, 43, 46, 49-50, 54, 58, 61-63, 65-66, 104, 108, 111, 113-115, 125, 129-131, 134-135, 142, 147-148, 153, 163, 167, 169, 171-172, 175, 179-180, 185-186, 197, 199-200, 204, 208-209, 217-218, 221-222, 224,, 229, 235, 240, 243, 245-246, 248, 250, 256

2000 (Sydney)   16, 28, 31, 40, 43, 54, 58-59, 65, 110, 120, 171, 178, 180, 196, 217, 241, 249

Sydney International Equestrian Centre
                    232,234-235, 238-240

2004 (Athens)   252

Ancient Games   12

Olympic Committees   30

Future of Equestrian sports 250-252, 254

Modern Games   12, 15, 40, 163

    Revival of   12, 14-15

INDEX

Sports/Related Topics:

Army Olympic team   75, 80

Cavalry   15, 36, 40, 64, 70, 73-75, 78, 85-86, 92, 95-104, 115, 123, 155-156, 161-163, 165, 197, 199, 207

Chefs d'équipe   44-45

Combined driving   34

Dressage   12, 14-16, 18, 21-22, 24-26, 31-34, 36, 38-39, 44-45, 64, 66-67, 74-76, 80-81, 84-86, 89, 91-93, 100-102, 104, 106-108, 111, 113, 115, 117, 123, 127, 137, 155-156, 158, 163-164, 167, 186, 188-197, 199-202, 204, 206-209, 211-215, 217-218, 220-227, 229, 232, 235, 237, 241-243, 248-249, 252, 255

    Arenas   199, 224

    Attire   189

    Grand Prix   22, 25, 172, 174, 178, 191, 194, 199-200, 204, 206, 211-212, 214, 217-218, 220, 222-223, 243, 252

    Grand Prix Special   25, 191, 204, 212, 217-218, 223, 243

    Individual competition   189, 191-192, 194, 199-200, 202, 204, 206-207, 209, 211-212, 214, 217, 221

    Judges   64, 192-193, 196, 201

    Judging   192-195

    Kür   25, 202, 204, 206, 255

    Scoring   189, 194-195, 200, 204, 206

    Team competition   221

    Team selection for   242

Dressage tests   16, 186

Endurance riding   15, 34, 252

Polo   24-25, 73, 99, 102, 165, 255

Reining   15, 34, 38, 253-254

Image of equestrian sports   255

Marketing   250, 254-256

Media   21, 31, 49, 61, 63, 171, 220, 223, 232, 241, 254-256

2000 Sydney coverage   239-241

Prix des Nations (Nations Cup)   15, 75, 80, 84, 86, 106, 148

Show jumping   21, 24-26, 31-34, 38, 42-43, 99, 106, 111, 115-116, 148, 150-151, 153-157, 159, 161 163, 165, 167, 169, 171-172 174-175, 178-181, 183, 185 188, 202, 206, 217, 237, 242-243, 245-246, 252, 255

    Attire   151

    Course design   150-151, 155, 167, 171-172, 174-175, 178

    Course designers   171-172, 174-175, 178

    Individual competition   148, 150-151, 153, 155, 157-158, 160, 162-163, 165-169, 172, 175, 180

    Rules   150-151, 153, 171, 175

    Scoring   148, 150-151, 153, 167

    Team competition   148, 151, 172, 180

    Team selection for   153, 163, 242

Three-day eventing   18, 21, 31, 33-34, 37, 43, 62, 64, 86, 104, 107, 110-111, 113, 115, 117, 119, 121, 123, 125, 127, 129-131, 135, 137-139, 141-143, 145, 147, 171, 188, 206, 217, 241, 243, 250

Attire 106

Australians and 60

Course design 131, 139,

Course designers 131, 139

Cross-country 15-16, 18-19, 21, 37, 46, 49, 54, 60, 62-64, 79, 83, 85, 90, 104, 106-108, 110, 113-114, 120, 123, 127-128, 130-131, 134-140, 142, 171, 199, 236, 243, 245, 252

Dangers 111, 138

Individual competition 110-111, 113-114, 116, 118, 122-123, 125, 127-129, 142

Roads and tracks 15, 18-19, 107-108, 114, 142

Rules 104, 107, 108, 110, 113, 135, 139

Scoring 104, 106-108

Stadium jumping 15, 21, 107-108, 129, 137, 243

Steeplechase 15, 18-19, 49, 80, 107-108, 115-116, 123, 127, 142

Sydney International Three Day Event 236

Team competition 111, 113-114

Team selection for 118, 124, 241

Vaulting 15, 24-25, 34, 38

Veterinary issues 46, 48-50, 52-54, 60-64

Quarantine 59-60

Transportation 46, 55, 57-59

Transport study 58-59

Weight rule 64-65

Women, participation by
in dressage 199, 202, 207
in eventing 110
in show jumping 202

Organizations:

American Horse Shows Association 35, 39, 62, 67, 96, 111, 122, 214, 237, 256

Atlanta Organizing Committee for the Olympic Games (ACOG) 113, 134-135

Australian Quarantine and Inspection Service (AQIS) 60

Equestrian Federation of Australia 237, 240

Fédération Equestre Internationale (FEI) 14, 16, 22, 26, 28, 33-34, 38-39, 46, 49-50, 52-54, 58, 60, 62, 64-67, 96, 110-111, 113, 120, 134, 136, 139-141, 154, 160, 163, 175, 180, 192-193, 195-197, 202, 204, 206, 213, 238, 240-243, 249, 250, 252-255

International Olympic Committee 12, 28, 49, 74, 111, 114, 180, 206, 237, 240-241, 250

Sydney Organizing Committee for the Olympic Games (SOCOG) 28-29, 235, 237-238, 249

United States Equestrian Team 35-36, 41, 123

United States Olympic Committee 35-36

PHOTO CREDITS

Foreword

Tish Quirk: p. 7.

Chapter 1

Archive Max Ammann: p. 10-11, 12, 13, 14, 16, 26; *ARMOR (Cavalry Journal)*: 18, 22; CLiX/Shawn Hamilton: 27; horsesdaily.com/Phelps Photo(™): 17, 23; Tish Quirk: 20; *The Blood-Horse*: 24.

Chapter 2

Archive Max Ammann: 30, 41; Cheryl Bender: 38; Anne M. Eberhardt: 45; FEI: 35; Aaron Martin: 38; Tish Quirk: 29, 37, 43.

Chapter 3

Archive Max Ammann: 48; Anne M. Eberhardt: 47, 50-51, 61, 63, 66; Gemma Giannini: 56-57; Charles Mann: 58.

Chapter 4

Archive Max Ammann: 70, 72, 78, 81, 82-83, 84, 87, 90, 91, 92, 97; *ARMOR (Cavalry Journal)*: 71, 75, 77, 88, 93, 94, 98; Tish Quark: 68-69.

Chapter 5

Archive Max Ammann: 104, 106, 109, 110, 119, 121, 128, 134, 139, 141; CLiX/Shawn Hamilton: 105, 112, 115, 130; Anne M. Eberhardt: 116; Michael Page: 122; Tish Quirk: 124, 126, 132-133, 136; USCTA Archives: 127.

Chapter 6

Archive Max Ammann: 148, 150, 154, 156, 162, 164, 166, 192; CLiX/Shawn Hamilton: 149, 152, 170; Tish Quirk: 155, 167, 173, 175, 176-177, 179; William C. Steinkraus: 157, 161.

Chapter 7

Archive Max Ammann: 188, 190, 196, 201, 203, 206, 208, 210, 216; CLiX/Shawn Hamilton: 193, 219; horsesdaily.com/Phelps Photo(™): 187; Tish Quirk: 195, 197, 198, 205, 212, 215, 220, 221, 222-223, 224.

Chapter 8

CLiX/Shawn Hamilton: 230-231; McDaniel Woolf: 233; Anne M. Eberhardt: 244, 245; Leo B. Jeffcott: 234-235, 236, 239; Tish Quirk: 246, 247, 248.

Chapter 9

CLiX/Shawn Hamilton: 257; Charles Mann: 253; Tish Quirk: 251, 252, 254.

Cover images

CLiX/Shawn Hamilton, Charles Mann, Tish Quirk.

Note: all Cavalry Journal photos are reprinted with permission of ARMOR *magazine / The Cavalry Journal.*

Archive Max Ammann:
Jurastrasse 61, CH-3063 Ittigen, SWITZERLAND
Fax: 41-31-921-5683
editions.hippiques@bluewin.ch

ARMOR Magazine:
ATTN: ATZK-TDM, 4401 Vine Grove Road, Fort Knox, KY 40121-5210
Phone: (502) 624-2249/2610
www.knox-www.army.mil/dtdd/armormag/

CLiX/Shawn Hamilton:
5674 Gamsby Rd, Orono, Ontario, CANADA L0B 1M0
Phone: (905) 983-6430
www.clixphoto.com

Tish Quirk:
21 Greenview, Carlsbad, CA 92009
Phone: (760) 431-2772
HORSESUSA@aol.com

Charles Mann:
9236 Riggs Road, Adelphi, MD 20783
cmannphoto@msn.com

Phelps Photo:
Phelps/Hathaway Enterprises, Inc.
P.O. Box 868, DeLeon Springs, FL 32130
Phone: (904) 985.1429; Fax: (904) 985-4657
info@horsesdaily.com
www.horsesdaily.com or www.dressagedaily.com

ACKNOWLEDGMENTS

Many key players in Olympic equestrian history, past and present, gave generously of their time and perspectives to bring this book to life: Dr. Kent Allen, Linda Allen, Klaus Balkenhol, Ludger Beerbaum, Harry Boldt, Robert Dover, Gilbert Felli, Jack Fritz, Hilda Gurney, Roger Haller, Kate Jackson, Prof. Leo Jeffcott, Dr. Catherine Kohn, George Morris, Catrin Norinder, Dr. Joseph O'Dea, Michael Page, Mike Plumb, Paul Schockemöhle, Franke Sloothaak, Bob Standish, Christine Stückelberger, Anky van Grunsven, Franz Venhaus, Isabell Werth, and Hans Günter Winkler.

Thanks to the FEI's Muriel Faienza for providing me with valuable contacts and information; to the staff of the National Sporting Library in Middleburg, Virginia, for its hospitality and assistance; to Laura Rose for her generosity in sharing her knowledge of the NSL's collection and for her good company; to the U.S. Army Military History Institute in Carlisle, Pennsylvania, for providing access to its superb collection of historical documents; to Deb Lyons for her editorial assistance; to Barbara Berntsen and Kristin Lewis for their historical insights; and to *Armor* magazine for generously offering us access to photographs.

Birgit Popp, Liz Iliff, and Judy Marchman conducted several of the interviews with the people you'll read about in this book, and for their excellent work and additional assistance I am grateful.

The information I compiled in researching this book pales beside that collected over the years by equestrian Olympic Games historian extraordinaire Max Ammann. For his willingness to share information and leads, and for his allowing access to his collection of Olympic photographs, I am thankful.

Jack Le Goff, Jessica Ransehousen, and Bill Steinkraus went above and beyond the call of duty in sharing their Olympic experiences with me and offering valuable assistance. I am honored that they thought enough of this project and of me to give of themselves so unselfishly.

U.S. Army Lt. Col. Lou DiMarco brought the men of the Army Olympic teams to life with his tales and anecdotes and devoted countless hours to providing me with information, sources, and photographs. For his tireless efforts, support, and willingness to overlook my Naval Academy affiliation, I am grateful.

This book was the brainchild of Jackie Duke, my editor at Eclipse Press. I am honored that she entrusted it to me and thankful for her support. Thanks, too, to Jennifer Cummins, the artist whose imaginative design brought the book to life, and to Stacy Bearse, publisher of *The Blood-Horse*, without whose blessing this book would not have been produced.

Most important, thanks and love to my parents for their support and to my husband Michael, who read the manuscript and offered valuable suggestions, and who unselfishly and uncomplainingly supported my efforts on this project.

This book is dedicated with respect and admiration to the memory of Dr. Reiner Klimke.

ABOUT THE AUTHOR

Jennifer Olson Bryant is editor-at-large of the U.S. Dressage Federation's magazine, *USDF Connection*. She formerly served as editor of *Dressage & CT* magazine. An independent writer and editor, Bryant contributes to many equestrian publications, including *The Horse: Your Guide to Equine Health Care*, *The Whole Horse Journal*, *Horse & Rider*, *Horse Show*, and *Western & English Today*.

She also is the editor of numerous books on various subjects. This is her first book.

An avid dressage rider and competitor, Bryant also has competed in the hunter/jumper ranks and in combined training. Her current equestrian goals include preparing her Swedish Warmblood gelding, Entertainer, for FEI-level dressage competition. She and her husband, Michael, live in West Chester, Pennsylvania.

Editor — Jacqueline Duke
Assistant editor — Judy L. Marchman
Book design — Jennifer Cummins

ALSO AVAILABLE FROM ECLIPSE PRESS:

Baffert: Dirt Road to the Derby

Cigar: America's Horse (revised edition)

Country Life Diary (revised edition)

Crown Jewels of Thoroughbred Racing

Four Seasons of Racing

Kentucky Derby Glasses Price Guide

Man o' War: Thoroughbred Legends

Matriarchs: Great Mares of the 20th Century

Royal Blood

Thoroughbred Champions:
Top 100 Racehorses of the 20th Century

Whittingham

A Division of The Blood-Horse, Inc.
PUBLISHERS SINCE 1916